Encounter with GOD

Encounter with GOD

by Morton Kelsey

A Theology of Christian Experience

PAULIST PRESS
New York/Mahwah

Library of Congress Cataloging-in-Publication Data

Kelsey, Morton T.
    Encounter with God.

    Reprint. Originally published: Minneapolis: Bethany
Fellowship, c1972.
    Bibliography: p.
    Includes index.
    1. Experience (Religion)   2. Theology, Doctrinal—
History.   I. Title.
BR110.K4   1987   248.2'01   87-8869
ISBN 0-8091-2933-7 (pbk.)

Published by Paulist Press
997 Macarthur Boulevard
Mahwah, New Jersey 07430

Printed and bound in the
United States of America

Table of Contents

To my faithful wife
and co-worker,
Barbara

Preface

It is a real pleasure to have *Encounter with God* published by Paulist Press after a brief period out of print. This book presents in detail a world view and the reasons for it that is basic to each of the religious studies that I have published during the last twenty-five years. These books range from studies in Christian meditation, the Christian use of dreams, Christian healing, tongue speaking, Christian understanding of extrasensory perception, journal keeping, the practice of Christian love, discernment, spiritual direction or companionship, the Christian view of afterlife, Christian education and the transforming power of Jesus' resurrection to studies of the relation of Christianity to psychology and to the psychology of C. G. Jung in particular.

Encounter with God presents a theology of experience that, as far as I know, is nowhere else to be found in this form and lays a base for taking seriously our human religious experience—experience that has been life transforming in the lives of innumerable people throughout history. William James and Carl Jung give many examples of the effect of this human experience of the Divine. The idea that the loving God and the vast and complicated spiritual domain can still be encountered, experienced, is not held by many people today in the Western world, either on a popular level or among professional theologians.

In the pages that follow I will show that this lack of belief in our experience of the spiritual dimension of reality is a *mis*understanding of the nature of the God and the created universe, both physical and spiritual. Many popular theologians are still caught in the outmoded world view of the scientism (not science) of the nineteenth century or in the still more outmoded Scholastic tradition of the late Middle Ages. Much modern theology is still beating the dead horse of the last century's understanding of the universe or else is pinned under it.

Human beings do not have to be confined in the space-time box of the last century. I shall show that the latest thinking in physical science, mathematics, biology, medicine, anthropology, and even logic is less and less certain about setting limits on human experience. In each of these fields new views of the nature of reality and human interaction with reality are being provided that fit together like a Chinese lock to reopen doors that many theologians of the last four centuries have shut and locked. Together they offer a world view that can give an understanding of God in loving communion and interaction with ordinary human beings.

This book consists of two quite different parts. In the first part we look critically at the development of modern Western thought. As the story unfolds it becomes increasingly clear that the widespread idea that human beings are confined to experiences of the world of space and time can no longer be defended from a sophisticated and critical point of view. Indeed, we can support the idea that we live only in a meaningless material world by *faith*. All those who are interested in spiritual reality and our experience of it, no matter what their religious or philosophical background, will find evidence in the following pages to support and justify that interest. In addition, Christians who wish to affirm the religious experience of historical Christianity as well will find a congenial world view and, what is more, a framework within which to reach out to the doubting modern world.

In the second part of this book the presentation changes. We then step into the shoes of the believing Christian and look at some of the basic ideas and practices of traditional, orthodox Christianity. We will find that these central Christian convictions make perfectly good sense within the framework that we have provided. I make no attempt to provide either an historical or a critical study of these ideas, but rather to offer a suggestive and tentative description of Christian theology and practice.

Within the framework set forth in the first section of this book even the most careful and critical person can see that there is a place for the central foundations of the Christian faith: the incarnation, the resurrection of Jesus, the atonement, the coming of the Holy Spirit with its gifts, and the incredible potential of infinite growth with God in life after death. There is no need for Christians to be reticent or afraid to maintain the full Christian faith when it can be affirmed as a formulation of the deepest and most pivotal human experiences. In the list of my books preceding this preface will be found in-depth presentations of many of these central Christian practices and beliefs.

What I have to say there comes out of fifty years of questioning how we human beings can know the love of God, accept it for ourselves and share it with other human beings. This has not been an easy road. A brilliant agnostic father reacting against the fundamentalism of my devout grandfather laid deep within me the agnosticism of nineteenth century materialistic thinking. My mother's profound religious experience was belittled in our home. After the death of my mother I encountered the agnostic thinking of Immanuel Kant in a tutorial in Princeton Graduate School and this put the finishing touches on my painfully inadequate Christian education. Only those who have known the despair created by meaninglessness know its abysmal agony. In an effort to find some meaning I went to seminary. There I found a door out of this dead-end street in the writings of Baron Friedrick von Hügel and the great Platonist, A.E. Taylor. Later through the work of C.G. Jung I found an experiential way of relating to the spiritual domain of which all three of these thinkers spoke.

Jung, I discovered, had sketched out the philosophical and scientific implications of religious experience and had laid a philosophical foundation upon which modern religious thinkers could build. When Jung begins to theologize I part company with him, but his basic world view opened my mind to the world view of the New Testament and the Church Fathers. I am profoundly grateful to my friend, Dr. James Kirsch, a Jungian psychiatrist, for pointing out the philosophical implications of Jung's thought. Nearly ten years of analysis took place before I realized that Jung was speaking of a spiritual reality in much the same way as Jesus and the Church Fathers spoke of it and also the way Plato spoke of it.

Since this book was first published in 1972 a great deal of new data about religious experience has been published, in particular the work of Andrew Greeley in the 1972 book, *The Sociology of the Paranormal: A Reconnaissance* published by Sage Publications. In addition Paul Davies has presented the implications of modern physics in his 1984 book, *God and the New Physics* published by Simon and Schuster. At a 1986 conference held at Kanuga Conference Center over twenty-five percent of two hundred participants told of religious experiences of a transforming quality. Most of them had never shared these experiences before because of their fear of ridicule by the dominant materialism of our culture. How seldom have modern Christians been presented with an opportunity to speak of their deepest experience or given a way to explore a real communion with God. I have summarized much of the recent data about religious experience and the implications of modern science in my 1986 book, *Christianity as Psychology*.

When *Encounter with God* was first published it was criticized for presenting a dualistic view of reality. In the years that have passed I have developed a more comprehensive schema or diagram of reality. The diagrams on pages 111 and 154 need to be seen as partial aspects of the more inclusive picture of reality presented below and taken from *Christianity as Psychology*.

During the last fifteen years process theology has become an important part of the theological world. Most of the inadequacies I found in the theologies described in Chapters 2 and 3 also apply to process theology. Although this theology rightly emphasizes that we live in a world in process rather than a static world, this point of view is largely metaphysical and based upon rational thought rather than experience and has little or no place for the human experience of God or for a

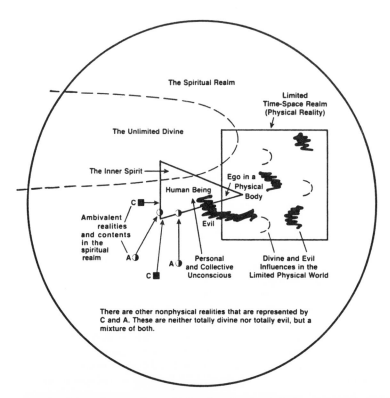

The Spiritual Realm

Limited
Time-Space Realm
(Physical Reality)

The Unlimited Divine

The Inner Spirit

Ego in a
Physical
Body

Human Being

C

Ambivalent
realities
and contents
in the
spiritual
realm

Evil

A

A

Personal
and Collective
Unconscious

Divine and Evil
Influences in the
Limited Physical World

C

There are other nonphysical realities that are represented by
C and A. These are neither totally divine nor totally evil, but a
mixture of both.

meaningful understanding of life after death. A.O. Lovejoy in *Revolt Against Dualism* reveals serious problems in Whitehead's thinking, the system upon which process theology is based.

I hope the reader will take in stride the sexist, non-inclusive language found in the pages that follow. The use of non-inclusive language has become offensive to me, a male, in the years since this book was first published but this was not the time for a total revision of this book.

This book was written in the very height of the charismatic movement in the Church, both Catholic and Protestant. Many references are made to this experience that is not as much in the center of the religious scene as it was fifteen years ago. The basic point of view of this book, however, applies as much to spiritual direction and companionship and to an understanding of religious experience as it did to the gifts of the Spirit so much emphasized in the charismatic movement.

During twenty years as rector of a large Episcopal parish the effectiveness of this theological formulation was tested again and again.

With the skilled help of Dr. Ollie Backus, who had come to the same framework independently, a unique program of religious education was developed for both adults and children. Time after time this world view proved invaluable for individuals wrestling with religious doubt and with the facts of our modern world.

In 1969 I was asked to teach at the University of Notre Dame. I became a tenured professor first in the Department of Graduate Studies in Education. Then, after that department was discontinued, I became tenured in the Department of Theology. I found that the point of view expressed in these pages was helpful to both the incredibly gifted undergraduate students who took my courses as well as to graduate students and seminarians. Since leaving the University my wife Barbara and I have lectured throughout the United States, Europe, Australia, New Zealand and Southeast Asia. We have found the same kind of response to this material from seeking people in each of these places. There is a real hunger for a framework in which people can take their religious experiences seriously.

I'm deeply grateful to my many colleagues at the University of Notre Dame with whom I discussed much of this material. However, my greatest helper in this and the books that followed it has been my wife, Barbara, who has served as midwife for each book.

John Sanford has been a friend with whom all of these ideas have been discussed for over thirty years. My friend, Leo Froke, a psychiatrist, also listened to and criticized much of this material. J. Andrew Canale has been a friend of seventeen years who has tested many of these ideas in his own life and in his psychological practice and has written several related books. John Vara, John Whalen, John Neary and Thomas Lischwe have also worked with me to provide a firmer base for the ideas presented here.

For the last five years I have been closely involved with San Francisco Theological Seminary in San Anselmo, California where a program in Christian Spiritual Disciplines has been inaugurated. The material presented here forms a part of that program. My friendship and discussions with Walter Davis, Roy Fairchild and Howard Rice of the seminary have added new evidence for the importance of the material and point of view of this book.

Mrs. F. Harold Roach, who has been helpful in the preparation of many of my other books, did much of the research for this book and put it in final form. Without her contribution this would be quite a different book.

Gualala, California
Lent 1987

PART 1

The Reality of Spirit

CHAPTER I

The Perplexing Religious Scene

Anyone trying to take in the total religious picture in this country today is likely to become perplexed. Among the most varied groups he finds an active new interest in things religious and spiritual. Young people in particular are searching in diverse ways—and many adults in very specific ways—for reality that could give religious orientation to their lives. But at the same time the religious institution in this country, the Christian church, is not doing very well. Outwardly, as the statistics show, the church has been losing ground steadily, and there is little evidence that its inner life, particularly at the higher levels, is touched at all by the present renewal of religious interest. One feels that he is looking at pieces of a puzzle that do not fit.

These are very much like parts of a jigsaw puzzle, and to find anything like an understanding of the whole picture, one must begin in much the same way—by examining the pieces first for shape and color, and then for signs of an integral pattern. Let us start by looking at some things that speak of religious renewal.

A Religious Revival

The ways in which young people are searching are almost too well known. After all, these are the youngsters we helped to raise, or who grew up next door. But the trouble is that this new generation is expressing in various ways its dissatisfaction with the way of life and values of our generation, and these are not always examined as carefully as one would the pieces of a puzzle.

Those who work closely with today's young people soon realize that, while they are essentially moved by anger and rebellion, what they are rejecting is the point of view of their parents, the values of twentieth century competitive materialism. The older generation has shown quite clearly that it accepted these values and, consciously or unconsciously, found them more significant than the values taught in the churches they attended. One set of values was taught, but when it came to making decisions, quite another attitude was involved. And consciously or unconsciously, many of their children have reacted to this contradiction. As one parent lamented to me recently, "But that boy takes the values I taught him seriously!"

In fact, the essence of the religious revival among this younger generation is their anger against the view of man which underlies the attitude of their parents. They have rebelled, with largely unconscious anger, at the idea of man as one more thing in a physically determined world, with no possibility of independent spiritual reality. This view, as B. F. Skinner expresses with utter clarity and honesty,[1] allows us to manipulate and condition men like any other thing, much like rats or pigeons. It is against this view of man, devoid of spiritual purpose, that the young have rebelled. With no particular philosophical base or well thought out reason for their reaction, they have none the less carried the rebellion even to the reasonableness that would seem to support this devaluation of man.

The very popularity of Charles Reich's *The Greening of America*, in spite of the many negative reviews, shows how many adults, as well, have reacted. Reich describes what he has observed in talking with college students at Yale. He shows youth groping for meaning and spirituality and reacting to both rugged individualism and the dogmatic materialism of the state, with its systematic power of enforcement. As my own experience confirms, his analysis can hardly be improved upon, although his solution leaves something to be desired.

Far more important confirmation of what Reich is describing comes from the work of Dr. Merton Strommen of the Youth Research Center in Minneapolis. His carefully developed surveys of religious beliefs and values, administered with equal care to a sampling of American Lutheran Church youth, have verified Reich's analysis at practically every point.[2] The same points are made by Theodore Roszak in *The Making of a Counter-Culture*, and in the sophisticated French study, *Without Marx or Jesus*, by Jean-Francois Revel. Those dealing directly with youth find the same dissatisfaction, the same growing undercurrent of search and striving. The articles reporting this are legion.

This ground swell of common reaction and thinking—for it

---

[1] For the notes, see pp. 246.

can hardly be called a movement—is characterized by interest in communal living, abolition of war, in the black culture, drugs, ecology, back to nature simplicity, sexual freedom, and the occult! Its hero is the American Indian, with his closeness to nature, his appreciation of the dream, his vivid rituals. Marijuana and the other "mind expanding" drugs are used by the large majority of these youths as a way of breaking out of ordinary perceptions of time and space and making contact with nonphysical reality, and for many this has a religious quality. At the same time there is a fascination with astrology, numerology, the tarot cards, the I Ching, transcendental meditation, yoga, witchcraft and demonology. On the Notre Dame campus a lecture on the I Ching, or one by Alan Watts, will generally bring out a capacity crowd.

One of the best discussions of this variety of experience was given before the American Sociological Association recently by Andrew Greeley, social and educational researcher at the University of Chicago. His paper, "Implications for the Sociology of Religion of Occult Behavior in the Youth Culture," [3] chided the profession for being so far out of things that they even lack categories to describe what is going on right under their noses. In it Dr. Greeley concluded that, from a sociological point of view, the present youth culture has all the characteristics of a religion.

There is a similar search by many adults for certain of these experiences, found in groups from Vedanta or the rapidly growing Spiritual Frontiers Fellowship to temples of the occult, and even in Scientology. And then there are other movements more specifically Christian and more obviously religious, which probably attract even more adults, as well as numbers of young people.

The More Obviously Religious Movement

The oldest of these reactions to purely conventional Christianity is Pentecostalism, which started some seventy years ago and has been gathering strength throughout this period. Developing out of the holiness movement of the last century, it broke forth as a separate religious movement in the first years of our century. In my book, *Tongue Speaking*, I have described in some detail the growth of these scattered bands of enthusiasts into the fastest growing segment of Christianity today. In time the spirit at work in these groups moved into the "old line churches," where the movement met with violent resistance, and then into the Catholic Church, where it has had

17

a special influence in the religious communities. At least one Episcopal monastery as well, a Benedictine order, reports that many within the house have found the experience of tongues a revitalizing experience. Thousands come from all over the country for the yearly gatherings of Catholic Pentecostals, and there are active local groups who meet regularly for prayer as at Notre Dame.

It would be difficult to assess accurately the influence of this movement. There is no doubt that many lives have been changed through this kind of religious expression, as David Wilkerson has described in *The Cross and the Switchblade*. Yet this movement, with its enthusiasm and its emphasis on a direct experience of God, remains one more reaction against the rationalistic churches which is largely peripheral to mainline American Christianity.

Another, similarly Christian reaction is the "Jesus Movement," which has been described with some sympathy by several religious authors.[4] These groups share many of the characteristics of the more pervasive youth culture. There is much the same emphasis on peace, on simple, communal living, accepting others without discrimination, along with a disdain for conventional, institutional Christianity. In addition, these young people, usually in markedly unconventional dress, show a passionate devotion to Jesus and the Bible.

Although this movement also shows a certain rigidity, both in interpreting the Bible and in patterns of action, it has unquestionably saved many young people from addiction to drugs and from the meaninglessness that can come to those who find only disillusion in the more general counter culture. Within their communes neither drugs nor sexual promiscuity are tolerated. Again, this is a movement that is difficult to assess, particularly in terms of size and relative importance, but it has touched many lives and is clearly growing in numbers and influence. All across the country, organizations of "Jesus people" dot the major college campuses, from Stanford to Dartmouth and Brown.[5]

On many campuses there is also a less extreme Christian renewal which varies widely from place to place. Increasing interest and participation are found wherever college churches provide services that are relevant to the needs of the student body. Here too, statistics are next to impossible to obtain, but talking with people on various campuses, one gets the impression that there is an openness to religious things today that would have been unheard of thirty-five years ago. When ministers are in tune with the students and speak their language, this interest is channeled into active Christian participation. These students, however, seldom find a congenial atmosphere when they return to their home parishes.

Still another instance of the rising respect for religion is found among many psychologists and psychiatrists, in a new attitude towards the value of religion in human life. Dr. Jerome Frank's *Persuasion and Healing* puts religious revivalism in the same healing category with psychotherapy, and finds faith as specific a remedy for some diseases as penicillin is for pneumonia.[6] Even twenty years ago one would have been hard put to find a psychiatrist from Johns Hopkins speaking like that. Carl Rogers, Abraham Maslow and the psychologists of the third force also see human values and peak experiences as central to psychology, therapy and education.

Then, there is the growing interest in the work of C. G. Jung who found religion essential for psychological maturity and wholeness. A friend at Pomona College tells me that, although no course on Jung is taught there, he often finds students pouring over the large black volumes of the collected works. Lectures on Jung draw crowds on nearly any campus; as many in my classes have found, Jung speaks to the perceptive student, helping one find answers about religion and its place in human life. Indeed, when the new professional journal, *Psychiatric Annals*, devoted a third of its second issue to "Religion and Psychiatry Today," [7] the article by a psychiatrist priest on the staff at Harvard took a passage from Jung for its conclusion.

Philosophically the current interest in existentialism has religious overtones. Although students are usually more convinced by the nihilism of Sartre and Camus than by the belief of Marcel and Jaspers, there is no doubt that one of the main thrusts of this amorphous development is an attempt somehow to retrieve man's values and uniqueness, of which he seems to have been robbed by scientism and rational materialism. Many who turn to Kierkegaard and his followers are trying to find meaning in what seems to be a meaningless universe. There are better methods of maintaining man's value than those of existentialism, as we shall try to show; yet one is impressed by the intention of these philosophers and the number of people who have turned to them to find meaning.

Among young and old there is certainly a rising interest in things religious, manifested in many ways, but this fervor has not caught on in the institutional church. Indeed as I talk with clergy in conferences all over the country, I hear the same sad story of decreasing attendance, dwindling financial support, and loss of interest and enthusiasm by church members. It is to this strange phenomenon that we now turn, first with some anecdotes, and then with the statistics.

The Decline of the Churches

Among students in religious education there is universal consternation at the failing ability of the church to communicate its faith. Catholic education is in crisis, with schools closing in every part of the country, and Protestant education is doing no better. The frankest statements about the problem have come out of Canada. When a minister of the Missionary Church in one of my classes at the University of Notre Dame brought the following article, it was gobbled up by the nuns and priests in the group. The story, from the October 1970 *Emphasis*, organ of the Missionary Church, expressed exactly their own problem, in these words:

Sunday Schools Doomed? Sunday school attendance in the United Church of Canada, the nation's largest Protestant church, "has plummetted to the lowest point in the history of the church, and willing teachers are harder and harder to find."

So said the September issue of the *Observer*, the church's official organ. "Children are less and less interested." Last year the church's total enrollment of teachers and pupils was 425,000—little more than half the 757,000 eight years ago.

The rate of decline is increasing. In 1966 Sunday schools lost 6%; in 1967 it was 7%; in 1968, 9%; and last year 12%. The *Observer* says that at the current rate of decline few Sunday schools will be able to stay open another five years.

The biggest losses are in the nursery and kindergarten departments rather than among the older children as was formerly the case. "We're losing them before they get started," says one official.

If such losses continue—and they show every sign of doing so—there will be no children left to move up into the junior and intermediate departments, with a corresponding decline in future church membership.

Two reasons are suggested for the decline. Lack of interest by parents is given as the prime cause. Few parents seem to care whether their children eventually join the church or not.

20

Also affecting attendance has been the church's "new" curriculum for Sunday schools, which was introduced in 1964. It regards the Bible as containing myths, contradictions, and errors of various types.[8]

The story concluded with the fact that in the same church the annual conference for evangelism had to be cancelled because only twenty-three signed up for the meeting which had drawn over a hundred workers only the year before.

A story of effort to find solutions also comes from Canada. In Alberta the Catholic schools are entirely supported by the province, including provision for religious instruction. A few years ago the enterprising superintendent of these schools surveyed his system to see how effective its teaching was. He was shocked to find that there were excellent educational results in all areas *except* religion. And so he tried something new. Every school principal who would take a year of advanced study in religious education was offered a sabbatical with all expenses paid. As a result, several of the most concerned students in my department at Notre Dame were those who had come to us from these Canadian schools.

For two years I have also held seminars for senior premedical students on suffering, dying and death, and from these classes I have learned quite a little myself. I have come to know well some forty of the most capable students in the University, most of them brought up in parochial schools, with full advantage of the church's teachings. Yet only ten percent believed in any form of life after death, and none knew any way to present the belief they did have to a dying person. None of them, in other words, saw any real possibility beyond the grave. Even more, most of these students were actively hostile to the church which had nurtured them. They felt that they had been trained and not educated in the church schools, and there was almost universal anger at the religious orders who had taught them.

There are some religious thinkers who consider that this attrition and shake-down of belief which the church is experiencing is healthy and good. But as we look now at the statistics, we may well wonder how much there is to shake down to.

Some Church Statistics

Hardly twenty years ago the churches in this country were crowded. There were years in the 1950s when nearly half the adults in the United States attended church regularly, and construction of churches kept increasing until a billion dollars a year came to be expected. Membership was growing until practically two out of every three Americans could, by one name or another, be called Christian.[9] Clearly things were going well for religion in America. One did not have to worry much about the future of the youngsters who gathered each week in well-appointed Sunday School rooms—or those in black ghettos. Naturally they would follow the way that was accomplishing so much good.

Not many statistics are needed, of course, to see that the picture has changed. One does not need figures to realize that there is room to sit back and keep a hymnal lying open in most pews today, or that the way no longer seems so certain for our young people. But there is more to the story of our religious dilemma than this, and some of it is told by the statistics gathered in recent years.

In the first place, surveys show that Americans over the age of 21 are great believers. Ninety-eight out of every 100 adults in this country say that they believe in God, and 73 out of 100 also express a belief in life after death. Of these, 65 say that they believe in hell, and 60 in 100 that they also believe in the devil. Except for Greece—and even there the percentage of believers is somewhat less—none of the other countries surveyed showed this kind of belief. Instead, a great many Western Europeans state out and out that they do not believe in these things.

The trouble is that Americans are saying this at a time when they not only find religion rapidly losing its influence in their lives, but 3 out of 4 of them are also convinced that life is deteriorating morally, and over half of them find that it is losing value religiously. And yet fewer and fewer of these believing Americans either attend church services or do anything else about it.

By 1970, 3 out of every 4 adults questioned, churchgoers and nonchurchgoers alike, found the effect of religion on American life declining. Dr. George Gallup, who made the surveys, has pointed out that this is one of the most dramatic reversals of opinion in the history of poll-taking. Between 1957 and 1970, in fact, the optimism of Americans about religion shifted, until today scarcely more than 10 percent of the people (instead of 69 percent in 1957) still believe that religion is gaining ground. And yet one of the most recent surveys by this group found clergymen in this country generally optimistic about the future of the church.[10]

At the same time church attendance has declined almost steadily. Between 1958 and 1971 congregations were reduced by nearly 20 percent or, at the least, by more than 10 million people. While Catholic congregations have had the larger loss, there were still 57 out of 100 Catholics who attended church regularly in 1971, compared with only 37 out of 100 Protestants.

But among younger people the loss has been even greater. By 1971, among the 21- to 29-year olds, 42 percent who would have been churchgoers have either quit or else never started going to church. Instead of 48 out of 100 younger adults in 1958—and these are now the 30- to 40-year olds who are keeping the churches going today—only 28 percent of the present young adults are coming to church at all. And the decline shows every sign of continuing, both here and in Europe, where in most countries attendance is even less than in the United States.

Religious leaders indeed seem to exert little influence. California churches had a taste of the growing disregard in 1964 when the referendum against fair housing legislation was passed in spite of the outspoken opposition of every major church in the state. Catholic leaders, in particular, have found opposition to their attempts to bring about better race relations, not to mention their more controversial efforts.

The church is also in financial difficulty; in 1969 the major Protestant bodies had to cut their national budgets for the first time since the Depression.[11] It is no wonder men in many denominations are leaving the ministry in disillusion and discouragement, and the idea of the parish ministry is rejected by many theological students. While Protestant seminaries are barely holding their own in number of students, the desperate situation is in the Catholic Church.

In 1968 alone, it is estimated, 2500 priests left their Catholic parishes and ministries, many of them to be married within a year.[12] Yet in 1970 Catholic institutions reported that 40 percent fewer men and women were preparing for religious vocations, including the priesthood.[13] Schools are closing for lack of religious personnel, who have left the orders in droves. There is a growing realization of inadequacy in communicating Catholicism, and new methods of teaching religion are being sought urgently. Indeed, in crisis over its approach to some of the most fundamental human problems, this great Communion no longer seems the rock of religious stability it once did.

Instead, the Catholic Church, overnight, is releasing into the ordinary, nonreligious world thousands upon thousands of people whose lives until now have been based on a closely held religious point of view which is no longer working for them. And this is a world that is already overburdened with "free" souls who no longer find any religious base for their choices between this and that. In other words, they are free to make choices on a basis of immediacy, regardless of what may be good or bad for them in the long run, and thus what may be good or bad for society and ultimately for you and me. There is good reason for every one of us in the church to do what we can to fill the gap—to help provide what will bring people's religion, Catholic or otherwise, to life again. But this is just what the church does not seem free to do. It is time to ask: What is its problem? and are there answers?

Are There Answers?

There is trouble in institutional religion today; this much is not hard to diagnose. At the same time, enthusiasm for religion is suddenly springing up from all sides; yet organized Christianity seems unable to tap or respond to it. Why? There are several reasons, each of them valid to a point.

For one thing, the church has not been consistent with its message. What it says, and what it has done, are two different things. Granted, the Christian church has a very difficult message to live up to. But today a more conscious and critical generation asks that the church meet itself in action; it demands social action towards the blacks and on other social issues. In realizing this may lie the first hint of an answer.

Again, instead of being a hospital for sinners, the church has found itself more a museum for saints. The picture of the Grand Inquisitor in *The Brothers Karamazov* strikes home when one remembers that the message of Christianity is given to us, not because we have learned to be good, or intelligent, but because we are hurt or miserable, and so that we can help pass it on to others who are sick and oppressed, to the deprived and even depraved. Granted, again, it is a difficult message. But this new generation asks to experience it, and an answer may well lie in this direction. An experiential religion acquires the conviction to risk trying to live up to its message.

Furthermore, the church has relied on authority and doctrine, on theological understanding about the experiences, instead of trusting the experiences themselves. But this new generation, both young and old, are not satisfied with authority; they want experiences of God and the Holy Spirit to verify the theology and the dogma. And this, as we shall see, is exactly what the modern church and modern theology are short on, even hostile to. Here may well be one of the most important answers to our question: why is the church declining in numbers and influence, and even in its power to deal with the social implications of the faith it confesses? Because of this lack of experience of the divine, a gulf has become fixed between the religious strivings of men and the church's ministry in the modern world. To bridge it, both practical actions and theoretical understanding are needed. Our intention is to attempt to provide in the following pages a simple world view which has a place for man's experience of God. Let us now consider the viewpoint of modern theology towards religious experience, towards the divine-human encounter, and then examine a possible alternative to that outlook.

CHAPTER II

The Theological Blind Alley
and a Door Out

It is difficult, if not impossible, for most people to keep a vital interest in religion without some conviction that a real religious reality exists. As a practical matter, once one has had experience of such a reality—that is not just a tail wagged by the physical world—he generally finds it just as difficult to avoid an interest in religion. He can then no longer close off the possibility that there *is* an independent and purposeful reality which men encounter beyond the physical world. Indeed it is just this experience of reality which is not physical, and gives meaning and purpose often counter to everything rational and sensible, that is convincing to say the least. But it is also just this kind of experience from which modern man is cut off by his beliefs.

The Problem of Experience

Man today has accepted as quite obvious that one obtains knowledge only through sense experience. It is hard for him to believe that anything is real which is not connected in some way to physical matter; "reality" means something that can be checked out objectively by the data of the physical senses. This attitude, which A. J. Ayer has outlined with superb clarity in *Language, Truth and Logic*, has become one of the most basic philosophic beliefs of our day. In fact, the entire outer life of Western man has been changed by the scientific and technological results of this devotion. It is difficult not to give wholehearted acceptance to an attitude which has changed life as much as this one.

Most men, given time, are quite consistent in their thinking; they live out the meaning of their basic beliefs. With reality clearly limited to that which can be tested by experiment men have come to look upon all their human experience in the same way. Their contacts that could be called personal or psychic, that might carry meaning and purpose, are strictly limited. A man can know his own purely subjective being (although this is even denied by behavioral psychologists like Skinner). He can, when he has the courage to enter such relationships, come to know other people like himself, strange combinations of body and mind. But this is the limit of a man's contact with reality that is not strictly physical.

Thus when modern man has experiences that seem to point to some being beyond the human, he either dismisses them as insignificant, or else tries to get rid of them as symptoms of a poorly oriented psyche. I am reminded of one very intelligent professor who remarked that if he had any place for religious experience, he would certainly have to be religious because he had so many amazing experiences. Another close friend of mine carefully avoided any display of hypnotism, knowing full well that if he found it credible, he would have to change his materialistic world view.

Whatever name we use for the object of religious seeking, "the divine," "God," "the numinous, " or "the Holy" certainly refers to just such a reality as we have tried to suggest. The divine is that which has power and autonomy, gives meaning and purpose, and at least contains the qualities of our inner and personal nature. If man has no experience of such a reality, then, as far as men are concerned, God is dead. Involved logical explanations do not impress many modern men without some verification. If there is no experience behind the logic, it may be scholastic or existential, based on deductive reasoning or ontological analysis; it still does not carry much conviction.

How does modern theology treat the possibility of such experience? Probably the most impartial and comprehensive study of the religious thinking of our time has been done by John Macquarrie, of Union Theological Seminary. His recent survey, *Twentieth Century Religious Thought*, carefully analyzes the work of more than a hundred men who represent the leading schools of religious thought between 1900 and 1960. Out of all these thinkers there are only two who clearly suggest that theological understanding requires a basis of some direct encounter with a more than human reality and purpose. One of these is Baron Friedrich von Hügel, and the other Carl G. Jung; but in neither case is much attention given to this aspect of their thinking. While Macquarrie remarks on the impressive scope and depth of von Hügel's work, there is some question as to whether he has understood the contribution of Jung, whom he classifies as a naturalist. There the matter is dropped.

In fact, the rest of these thinkers so consistently reject the idea of ordinary men having contact with the "supernatural" or numinous (that which is real and independent of the physical world), that Macquarrie does not even mention it as an option still open for theological discussion. Since this possibility has no place in any currently accepted theory of religious knowledge, it is simply considered a dead issue. Macquarrie concludes that the best that modern theology can do is to go along with the demythologizing of Rudolf Bultmann.

With this background, which certainly offers a student protection from easy or superstitious belief in a divine encounter, let us take a look at some of the major schools of Christian thought to see just what they do have to say about the divine breaking into human life or into the physical world.

Liberal Theology and Experience of God

Once the Enlightenment was under way in Europe, a liberal and critical tradition began to develop among Christian thinkers. These men have done Christianity a great service. They have brought the spotlight of man's rational thinking to play into every corner of the Christian tradition. Not since the church was fighting for acceptance in the ancient Graeco-Roman world had so much intellectual controversy surrounded Christian ideas. The liberation of men's minds from the domination of authority and the development of a freer use of reason and knowledge allowed all elements of Christian life, theology and literature to be subjected to the most critical scrutiny.

At the same time, under Schleiermacher's inspiration, this thinking was imprinted with his idealistic philosophy and his critical analysis of man's religious feeling. It also accepted as final the findings of the naturalistic science of that day, without turning its criticism upon the presuppositions of that science. Most of the "miraculous" elements of the Bible and of later tradition were either doubted or found to be false, because they seemed to contradict the tacitly accepted ideas of reason and natural law. God was understood as living within his creation, which he had made as a self-contained and rationally explainable unit. Thus the way men could come to know God was to know themselves and the world around them, particularly through history.

Liberal Christian thought succeeded in bringing the intellectual attitudes of the nineteenth century into confrontation with the Christian religion, but its solution to the problem eliminated the possibility of a direct experiential encounter with divine reality. It left no way for the divine to break through into natural processes. We shall look at this more fully in a later chapter.

On the Continent we find this point of view expressed in a sophisticated and highly developed way in the writings of Harnack, Herrmann, and Troeltsch. Christianity was being recast by these men to fit the tenor of criticism; as Otto Pfleiderer, who followed them, wrote just before 1900 with uncompromising frankness:

> The appearing of a heavenly being for an episodic stay upon our earth breaks the connection of events in space and time upon which all our experience rests, and therefore it undoes the conception of history from the bottom.[1]

The same ideas were expressed in England with great intellectual force by F. R. Tennant, Francis Bradley and McTaggart, and a little later in the United States by Fosdick, Wieman, and *The Interpreter's Bible*. Tennant has put the matter as clearly as anyone in his statement that religious knowledge, apart from psychology (which he has already dismissed), depends entirely on sense experience and reason. He concludes:

> Such immediate *rapport* between God and the human soul as theism asserts, cannot be discerned with (psi) immediacy . . . nor can any transcendent faculty, mediating such contact, be empirically traced.[2]

According to this school the men who wrote the New Testament were informed by an incorrect world view that clouded their judgment. The job of the modern theologian is to separate the wheat from the chaff in the Biblical narrative, and so reveal the gradual development of man's moral conscience and religious understanding. Once the chaff is eliminated, the true grandeur of the Gospel is manifest. It is man's task, as the final product of the evolutionary process, to carry this understanding and civilization to new and greater dimensions. Man was in the upward swing of progress. This was the outline of practically all liberal Christianity by the first part of this century.

Dispensationalism and Karl Barth

The natural reaction to this critical and liberal theology was to hang on to the very letter of the Bible and maintain the literal truth of the text against all comers. To do this fundamentalism or literal theology needed to explain how there could be such radical differences between the experiences described in the Bible and those of men today. The theory of dispensationalism provided the answer.

The Biblical experiences, it held, particularly the encounters of God with men, were not natural happenings. On the contrary, divine contact with man in visions, healings and through angels, runs counter to the essential nature of the world as God made it. In New Testament times, and to an extent in the Old Testament period, God allowed these things to happen by a special dispensation. He set aside the ordinary structure of the universe long enough to break through man's resistance and establish the people of Israel and, through them, the church of Christ. Then he withdrew this dispensation and the normal order was restored. While men can no longer expect such divine encounters, they can have the faith that God did break through in this way, and will do so again at the end of time. Living by faith is considered superior to living in continued expectation of experiencing God and God's action through the church's life.

This was essentially the point of view of both Luther and Calvin, who simply continued the Thomistic distinction between the natural and the supernatural. In fact Luther and Calvin were even more skeptical than Aquinas about setting aside the natural order in our time. One wonders what direction Protestantism might have taken if these men had seen the Bible as a guide to present experience, rather than preparing their followers in this way to take Biblical authority on faith.

There is a direct kinship between the theology of Karl Barth and that of dispensationalism,[3] although Barth expresses it with infinitely greater dialectical subtlety. His thinking takes off from the point that God broke through once in history, to underscore the idea of the transcendent God whose action was like a tangent touching a circle, and then speeding on into outer space. God had to overcome his ontological aversion to dealing concretely with broken, sinful men, and the only way he could do this was to provide just one, total, physical revelation in Jesus Christ. Naturally at that time strange and wonderful evidences of God's presence were seen in visions and dreams, healings and angels. But because of men's brokenness and sin, God does not enter into ordinary human life. He gives them no direct contact, no direct religious experience, naturally or otherwise.

Not only is no natural religion available to men, but the fact that they erect assorted systems of religion is one evidence of how separated they are from God. Barth sees these "religions" as man's prideful creation, rather than imperfectly understood revelation. But as men turn in faith to the one emergence of God in history, they are then within the fellowship of the Word and are informed by it. Their minds are then grasped by an understanding which they cannot get in any observable natural way.

Barth's theology is a theology of the Word of God, which is known intellectually (as if it spoke cognitively to men) through those who are united by faith in this central revealing event in history. Although he is careful not to deny that revelations could continue in dreams, visions, healings, and tongues, the whole weight of his basic point of view is against it, and Barthians certainly do not look for this to happen. Careful study of the references in various volumes of *Church Dogmatics* reveals the view that the Holy Spirit is not intended to be the giver of these experiences to men, but is only sent to give the conviction that they did happen when God once set aside natural law to enter the world as Christ. The important thing is to have faith in the one great revelation.

One's relation to God, then, is not a matter of a divine-human encounter, of two realities coming into confrontation, but rather a one-way street of the Word of God slipping into man's mind and instructing this part of him, regardless of any action on man's part. Barth's theological value in emphasizing the transcendence and otherness of God can hardly be overstated. His work rescued Christian theology from the complacent optimistic liberalism of his predecessors, but his handling of how we know this transcendent God leaves something to be desired.

Bultmann and Demythologizing

Barth had company from the beginning in his revolt against the ruling liberal theology in Germany. And in Rudolf Bultmann's early association with Barth another idea was being quietly impregnated. Bultmann started by accepting man's helplessness up against the transcendence of God, and gradually became convinced that theology needed a philosophical base to maintain such a position. This he found in the existentialism of Heidegger. Straightforwardly and with utter honesty he has worked out the implications of this point of view for Christian theology and Biblical criticism. His position is more streamlined and radical than Heidegger, who leaves a possibility open, at least in theory, that man could experience an encounter with God.

Bultmann, on the other hand, considers that every description of a nonphysical reality influencing man is *myth*, whose "real purpose . . . is not to present an objective picture of the world as it is . . ." Instead, as he defines it,

> Myth is an expression of man's conviction that the origin and purpose of the world in which he lives are to be sought not within it but beyond it—that is, beyond the realm of known and tangible reality—and that this realm is perpetually dominated and menaced by those mysterious powers which are its source and limit.[4]

He sees myth, then, as an effort "to speak of a transcendent power which controls the world and man," [5] but it is an "obscure" effort which uses a language of images that only *appear* to have a connection with reality.

All ideas of direct contact with God are, according to Bultmann, mythological (in this sense)—everything in dreams and visions, all healings, angels, demons, and prophecy. These experiences did not happen in New Testament times. The writers only described them as a way of speaking *about* the truth. If men are to accept the *kerygma*—the essential message of Christ and the early church—the Bible must be stripped of this humanly fabricated language of myth, which was simply an unsophisticated, pre-modern way of looking at things. This fanciful coating merely serves to conceal the truths laid down by Christ.

By stressing the value of Heidegger's philosophy as a secular revelation of these truths, Bultmann has helped bring home to modern theology the fact that it cannot ignore its philosophical foundations. But in the end the religious solution is not very different from the philosophical one. For both Heidegger and Bultmann, man discovers meaning through ontological analysis (a conscious rational process), and then finds God at the other side of the crisis of meaning through the blind jump of faith. There is no natural, continuing human-divine encounter.

Many of Bultmann's followers go even further than he has. Some of them believe that even Christ's crucifixion and resurrection were also myth. Schubert Ogden maintains this position in *Christ Without Myth: A Study Based on the Theology of Rudolf Bultmann*, as does Fritz Buri in his writings. In America the radical theology of Hamilton, Altizer and Van Buren carries the ideas of Barth and Bultmann jointly to the conclusion that

God is dead. They say that since God broke into history only once, and since none of the ways a man could reach out or be touched by Him are anything but "myth," then for men in their utter sinfulness and separation, God no longer lives. He may have lived once, and He may live again, but for modern man Nietzsche spoke the truth. There is no out but to wait and hope that God will return to life. In the meantime one takes the human Jesus for an example and gets involved in social action. These writers portray very clearly the attitude of large numbers of today's "secular Christians."

In most of our Protestant seminaries one of these points of view is taught today, and it is interesting how little they differ in their ideas about the actual action of God in the world today. From the most liberal demythologizers to the most conservative fundamentalists, they are equally convinced that God has no contact with living individuals. One of the leading Catholic writers on existential phenomenology, W. A. Luijpen, fares little better in his recent effort to find a base for Catholic theology within the existential framework. He does his best in a sincere and reverent little book, *What Can You Say About God?* *(Except "God")*, but I am not sure that it will be very convincing, even for existentialists. It shows with remarkable clarity the difficulties of presenting the traditional Christian faith within this framework.

In fact, as Andrew Greeley suggests so clearly, one reason for the present difficulties of the Catholic priesthood today is the fact that "the American Church was simply not prepared to deal with process philosophy and psychology. Caught as it was before the (Second Vatican) council in an ossified Aristotelianism, it was swept off its feet by a simplified existentialism." [6] Priests have been left, thus, with nothing to fill the gap between statements of faith and the world as it actually is.

For anyone who is preparing to minister to people in our modern world, it is hard to see how the ideas of Karl Barth or Rudolf Bultmann, or any of the radical theologians can effectively replace belief in a personal relation to God—unless the minister plans just to hold people's hands and hope for something to resolve the crisis favorably.

Neo-Thomism

In Neo-Thomism we find a change from this theological sameness, and instead an actual attempt to deal with ways of knowing God. It is made in terms of the best of medieval thinking, from the time when the human mind was making its bid for recognition, and yet was sure of the reality of God. The Neo-Thomists like Maritain, Gilson, and Copleston are first-rate thinkers, who try to show that man can still know God apart from pure revelation, that all men have glimpses of the reality of God. Because they see the possibility of a natural theology, here the question is still being discussed.

But there are two basic problems that are not dealt with by the Neo-Thomists. First, the thinking of Aquinas is essentially deductive, being based upon Aristotle's thought; and as modern logic shows, deductive systems give no new information. They can offer hypotheses, but man is informed by experience, either through the physical senses, or by nonphysical means (which Thomism does not encourage, although admitting that they can sometimes be used by God supernaturally). Once man has reasoned, his deductions need to be checked by experience. Knowing God through an exercise in logical reasoning does not always produce the same knowledge as overwhelming experience.

Second, there is the problem of men's resistance to the idea that divine intrusion in the world can produce effects upon physical matter. This was as difficult for Aristotle and Aquinas as it was for the naturalistic philosophers who followed after them. According to Aquinas it is possible for God to break through into this world only as he sets aside his own natural laws (thus the word supernatural), and this was an idea that became increasingly repugnant to men in the Enlightenment. Aquinas, like so many whose faith is solid, could not comprehend how difficult it would be to look back again once the human mind had taken a new direction.

In three places in my books, *Dreams: The Dark Speech of the Spirit, Healing and Christianity,* and *Tongue Speaking: An Experiment in Spiritual Experience,* I have made careful studies of St. Thomas' views on the particular subjects of dreams, healing, and tongues. Thomas was in a difficult position. He could not deny that these things had happened. It was written in the New Testament that men had had direct contact with God and other nonphysical realities in these ways. But he did not see these things happening around him very much, or else he did not notice them, just as there are so many things we do not see from behind our own philosophic blinders.

In addition, the Aristotelian thinking which the church felt Christianity was forced to adopt, has no place for a separable realm of nonphysical reality, and so there was no place from which such direct contacts could come in a natural way. Therefore, Aquinas avoided these subjects as much as possible, and maintained that such happenings occur only (by inference so rarely as to be almost never) when God intervenes directly to set aside his natural law.

Aquinas' treatment of angels and demons has much the same confusion about it. He could not deny their existence, and so he accorded them reality as *intelligentia intelligibilia*, or "thinking thoughts." They could have no *direct* influence on the human psyche, since that might infringe upon human freedom. It had to be understood that deviltry in particular was communicated by afflicting the liver and so causing humors to rise before the mind and leave their impression as apparitions. Even the most agile of Neo-Thomists finds it difficult to maintain any encounter between God and man that is both natural and direct, and still remain faithful to St. Thomas as the master-thinker. Maritain, however, has attempted this in "The 'Natural' Knowledge of Moral Values," found among the selections from his works included in *Challenges and Renewals*.[7]

Karl Rahner has pointed out in his excellent work, *Visions and Prophecies*, that

> . . . orthodox theology has never paid any serious attention to the question whether there are prophets even in post-apostolic times, how their spirit can be recognized and discerned, what their role is in the church, what their relationship is to the hierarchy, what import of their mission for the exterior and interior life of the Church.[8]

He also speaks of the gulf between mystical and orthodox theology, taking note by inference that mystical theology does have a place for prophecy and for the direct encounter of God with men. As one Catholic friend has put it, the Roman Church is blessed with a Platonic heart beneath its Aristotelian head, and it is just beginning to find the way to get them together.

In fact, the only large group of Christians who take the idea of the a direct divine encounter seriously, aside from certain conservatives, are the Pentecostals, and they have come in for derision from every side since they emerged as a modern movement about 1900. Yet they are still the fastest growing group of Christians today. The Pentecostal leaders have realized that they cannot stand against the powerful rationalistic and naturalistic thinking of modern society, and so they have withdrawn into their own structured sub-culture. They have their own religious, social and educational life, and have discouraged contact with the secular world or non-Pentecostal groups. They have even adopted their own forms of religious language. After *The Cross and the Switchblade* was published, John Sherrill told me that when he was working with David Wilkerson on the book, one of his big jobs was to translate the language of the original manuscript into words that would have meaning for the general public.

The basic tenet of Pentecostal faith is that the supernatural experiences described in the New Testament can also happen in the same way in our time. They believe men today can have direct contact with the Spirit of God just as the apostles experienced it, and they find this happening in visions, healing, prophecy, tongues, and in dealing with the demonic. One almost has to experience the tongue speaking in a Pentecostal assembly to appreciate the reality of their faith. While the telling of it sometimes seems naive, there is also a wisdom of the spirit often expressed. The Bible is read with a diligence and interest that is hard to believe if one has been around only orthodox Barthians, Thomists, Bultmannites, or liberal Protestants. This book is their constant companion in daily life, as well as the guide for their direct encounter with divine reality.

Is There An Alternative?

For most people there is not much to choose in the church today. There is the sophisticated theology of our time that practically eliminates a natural and direct experience of divine reality from men's lives. And there is a naive approach to God that turns its back on most of the secular and scientific world. But there is not much to suggest to most people today, with their very real problems, that anything divine, anything more than human might be within reach.

Is there any real alternative to these two ways of thinking? Our suggestion in the pages that follow is to propose that there is, and to describe a world view in which the idea of divine-human encounter, far from being naive, is considered a reality which is essential to the world today. The survival of human personality as well as Christian civilization and culture may well depend upon our ability to understand the more than human breaking in and touching men's minds and lives, not as a romantic notion, but as a needed reality.

Why is it necessary to use words like these to talk about the religious ideas with which theology deals? The truth is that the great scientific minds of today are far more open to this view than most of modern theology. Science itself has changed from within; its own discoveries, both within the atom and beyond our galaxy, have destroyed the mechanistic naturalism that had so little place for free men or their contact with more than human reality. Such a change has not occurred in man's religious ideas.

Theology is accused of being too critical; in reality much of it is not critical enough. It has not questioned its Aristotelian-Thomistic base, and much of it is still a reaction to the determinism and naturalism which are no longer as certain as they once were. But this philosophy, fathered by Descartes, was fed by the Enlightenment until it took over almost the whole establishment. The liberals, who saw God working immanently within a causally determined framework, were putting up the best defense they could imagine against this idea of the natural order in a closed and mechanistic universe. Our thanks are due to Hegel, Harnack, Troeltsch, the British and American liberals, for this effort.

We also owe it to them to question their ideas and find our own creativity in the situation we face. Instead, one pole of religious thinking today is still trying to modify the concessions of the liberals to the secular world, while the other pole continues to accommodate to the same naturalism in a new way. Modern theology has not grasped in depth the radical intellectual climate of the twentieth century, nor made use of its own critical tools to start the search that could bring encounter with divine reality and some assured understanding of religious realities.

My own introduction to the idea that man can relate directly to the divine did not come to me through the work of any theologian. I first realized that this was not a dead issue through the work of a psychiatrist who was well versed in philosophical matters and deeply concerned with vital religion, Dr. Carl Jung. In fairness I should add that I had read two theologians, Baron Friedrich von Hügel and A. E. Taylor, who both discussed the divine encounter in a sophisticated intellectual manner. They supported this idea as a live option, but gave few workable suggestions as to how it could be put into action.

I had been brought up in an environment that was predominantly rationalistic and materialistic. I doubted from early childhood that man had contact with anything beyond his own reason and the space-time world. The religious convictions of my mother, held without much intellectual depth, were the object of good humored scorn from my scientific father. I found very little in college, graduate school or seminary to contradict this secular background. Although the skepticism in seminary forced a quick adjustment onto many students who had been given little chance to look at what they believed, it hardly caused a ripple in my thinking.

Some years later I needed help to solve some real problems in finding meaning, and was directed to a man who had studied under Dr. Jung, and then to the writings of this eminently successful psychiatrist. I found that Jung had dealt with the religious experiences of his patients, with their numinous dreams, with religious healing, the phenomena of tongues and extrasensory perception, and prophecy—in short, with the divine-human encounter. He had also made careful and empirical scientific studies of some of these areas of experience. In addition, I found that what Jung said was verified in my own dreams and other experiences.

Then I began to speak of this in my parish, and soon my parishioners started to come to me, tentatively and half afraid, to tell me of similar experiences in their own lives. Almost every time the person thanked me for trying to understand, and wanted me to know that they had been afraid to speak to anyone of these experiences, particularly around the church, for fear of being considered unstable. In recent years I have spoken to both clergy and lay groups in many parts of the country, and invariably the same thing has happened.

C. G. Jung as Theologian

In order to help people make some sense of these experiences, Dr. Jung turned theologian. He proposed a working hypothesis, essentially theological, by which the actual situation of modern man could be understood in his worst, as well as his most desirable, experiences—particularly in depression and neurosis, in religious vacuum, anxiety, meaninglessness, in the grip of compulsion, and also in war and racial hatred.

Jung sees modern man torn between a physical world of which he is almost too aware, and a nonphysical world of which he is almost entirely unconscious. Nineteenth century materialism deprived man of the ability to consider the nonphysical, and so what goes on in this world is often negative to him. It still touches his consciousness, unknown except as revealed suddenly in moods or depressions, by loss of interest and energy, in hatred and fighting and spiteful little actions, or sometimes in a new romance that wrecks a home. There are endless ways in which the nonphysical realm turns negative for modern man. Yet it also contains positive aspects, and out of it can come man's highest intuitions, his deepest and most enduring love, his most complete religious commitment—but only on one condition, that consciousness cooperate in such experience.

Most of the time, however, consciousness is focussed on the outer world that comes to us in sense experience, and these psychic contents, both negative and positive, are unknown to us. Therefore Jung calls them "the unconscious," and this is confusing, because there are personal contents in the unconscious which can merge with consciousness. But by far the most of these psychic contents are separate from consciousness, and only impinge upon it so as to affect one's reactions without his knowing why. These realities of the nonphysical or psychic world become known only when experienced with awareness, as the separate realities which they are, which play upon consciousness but do not merge with it.

These contents can be experienced and come to consciousness in images in dreams and visions, and sometimes in imaginative fantasy. There are realities among them as real as those of the physical world, and there are both good and evil powers among them that come from beyond the individual's own personality (as is sometimes evident where extrasensory perception is involved).

Philosophically it can be supported that man has real, though not final or logically certain, knowledge of both a physical and a nonphysical realm of reality. Over the past fifty years this has been verified in a vast number of individual experiences, of both psychiatric patients and normal people, experiences that had meaning and effect upon both the person and his world. Thus the New Testament idea of spiritual reality and divine encounter is far from outmoded. On the contrary it is a good deal more relevant to the modern world than either nineteenth century naturalism, or the thinking of those who are still reacting to that view.

Logic, in fact, has no way to prove, once and for all, that man's psyche has direct contact with even a physical world outside his own body. This men have to prove as best they can by experience. For this reason they go into laboratories or out into the field to get the fullest experience they can, which can then be considered logically, demonstrating with increasing subtlety that their encounter with the physical is real. Men give themselves very thoroughly to test this by one method after another.

But meanwhile, if men think at all about their experiences

of encountering divine reality (or any other reality than the physical), they think of it as something else again, something rather dubious. On the surface, of course, there is good reason for thinking this way. Encounters with divine reality are *not* common. Neither is it easy to pin them down experimentally. But the same thing is true of demonstrating radioactivity, or of space travel to the moon. Man simply believes in the possibility of these things and does them. When men arrive at an equal conviction about the possibility of encountering God in their experience, they will find ways of discovering this reality waiting to be tried.

The odds against our doing this are astronomical, however, unless we make a radical change in our world view, and take the primary step of realizing that it is not silly to consider the possibility that there is a nonphysical or spiritual reality which can be experienced by men. And this involves something that is very difficult for us today. It means stopping dead in our tracks and examining what lies behind our present thinking—stopping even though the things that face us in the next hour look like life and death problems. Lacking the reality of God in facing them, we have not been doing a very good job up to this minute, and our approach is not likely to change without His help. This, in reality, is the life and death problem of our time.

For Western Christian people there is probably no better way to effect this change than to take the New Testament itself, in its entirety, very seriously. The necessary insight can be found in several ways. But to put a new view to work in today's world again involves difficulty. Communicating with other men requires that we understand the assumptions on which our own beliefs are based, as well as the bias which makes others understand the world as they do. If we remain caught up in conventional Christianity, in the Christian collective today, we probably will not even see the need to communicate anything more than externals. Or if we simply find satisfaction in Christian piety, it will be difficult to see the need for anything but the traditional Biblical language and ways of communicating.

Those who are seeking, both within the church and outside of it, have lost these traditional ways of finding meaning in their lives. They are the ones who are open to the Christian message right now, and they need to be found where they are right now, intellectually, emotionally, and spiritually. To do this we must have an approach which bridges the gap—an approach to reality, rather than to what we think we believe. And this is our task in the chapters that follow, to seek an intellectual and practical approach to religious reality, which is the only possible foundation for vital religion in our sophisticated modern world. There can be no lasting effect upon our present world unless we can speak to this world with conviction and understanding.

To lay the necessary groundwork as soundly and still as rapidly as possible, we propose to trace historically the various ways in which man has understood the reality in which he lives and his own relationship to it; in other words, the various ideas of the philosophy of religion. We shall first of all describe the view of man that has been almost universal outside of modern Western culture, which was stated with literary and philosophical brilliance by Plato. We shall then trace the development of nineteenth century deterministic materialism and its effects upon religious thought.

With this background we shall look at the newer hypotheses of physical science, evolutionary biology, psychosomatic medicine, symbolic logic, and depth psychology, which have all cast grave doubts upon the adequacy of the more rigid and certain science of the last century. We shall point out how these newer disciplines prepare the way intellectually for critical study of our own view of man, and for a return to a view of man as a being with a field of experience larger than that of sense experience, in fact the only being known to us that can reach consciously into another, crucially important dimension of experience. It is this dimension which is manifest in religious experiences, and in many other ways such as scientific intuition, visionary experience, extrasensory perception, and dreams. The question of how words and language can be more adequately used will then be discussed. We shall then go on to discuss the implications of this view of man and his experience in several ways: first, for theology and the study of religious experience; second, for the practical development of one's inner devotional life and his outer expression of it in ethics and social action; and finally, for religious education and the communication of Christianity. Let us turn now to a view of man and reality very different from the popular one today.

CHAPTER III

Man in Touch with a Spiritual World

People laughed a few years ago when some chemists announced very simply that the value of the human body, trace elements and all, was about 98¢. The trouble is that few of us were quite sure why we were laughing. The idea of man as just another piece of matter in a totally physical universe has become almost too commonplace to talk about. Perhaps we laughed in relief at being able to deadpan it.

The fact is that this idea grew up so gradually, accepted bit by bit into the culture we have inherited from Western Europe, that most of us no longer ask whether man's soul, his spirit or mind or reason, have any substance apart from his material body. We simply accept that we have been washed ashore by a mechanistic process of evolution, and left on our own to live for a time—and then die. There is no reality that touches us except the physical, and nothing that gives us basic value or sets us apart from any other animal or thing. As B. F. Skinner has shown so obligingly in *Beyond Freedom and Dignity*, freedom and dignity are no longer the right of men who regard themselves in this way. Yet most of us are quite unaware that there is any other point of view that is not totally unrealistic.

There is another view of man, however, found wherever the influence of Aristotle and nineteenth century Western thought have not been felt. In most cultures from primitive ones to the developed cultures of China, India, Islam, and of Byzantine Christianity, nonphysical realities have been seen as a more powerful influence on man's destiny than the physical world. In this view, man is seen as having contact with two essentially different kinds of reality, as having the capacity for two kinds of experience—one of the physical world and the other of a nonphysical world, both exerting tremendous influence over the individual.

The experience of these cultures shows that the nonphysical realm is considered both the more powerful and the more dangerous; realities of spirit which are a part of this realm can be either benificent or hostile to man. Special groups of leaders have developed, whose task it is to deal with this reality and mediate between it and ordinary human beings. These are called shamans, prophets, seers, and priests of the major religions of man. The essential role is most clearly defined in the shaman.

Mircea Eliade, in his book *Shamanism*, has described the nature of the shaman's role and its function as the basis for a definitive study of primitive man's religious ecstasy and experience. He shows quite conclusively that a profession for dealing with spiritual reality is found among practically all primitive peoples, and that, even where there appears to be no possible contact of any kind, the same elements and themes appear in the widely separated shamanistic practices. It would seem that they reflect ways of dealing with a reality which is objective, although not physical. This view of reality has been called mythical.

The Meaning of Myth

To the people who believe in this realm of reality, myth and legend, story and saga are important. It appears that the stories and the images of familiar material objects are used by these people to describe in symbolic ways the encounters they have had with a nonmaterial reality. To discuss this, however, opens up the problem of the meaning of the word *myth*. For most modern Western men, "myth" carries so much the meaning of the untrue that I have looked for another word to describe these stories and the meanings they express. But I have found no good substitute, and so I suggest stretching our minds and imaginations to revalue this word and see that it expresses an important and essential truth.

First of all, just as there are two basically different views about man and his world, so there are two essentially different meanings to the word myth. If one holds that man is only a material being, whose reason has developed only recently, then the myths of peoples, whether ancient or modern, are nothing but fanciful elaborations of something that was not true to begin with. At best, they are called pre-scientific cosmology, because they are seen as man's prerational attempt to explain how the world works and give reasons for the way the cosmos moves. Otherwise, the myth is only interesting because it helps modern men understand the irrational layer of the human mind which has to be put in order on the way to becoming rational.

If, however, one finds that the spiritual world is real and

that man is in contact with it, then myth is the symbolic description of men's encounter with this reality, represented with color and drama, often poetically. The encounter itself may come in visions or phantasies, through poetic inspiration, in dreams, religious experiences or ecstasy, or through observation of meaningful coincidences in the physical and historical world. Once the experience is given in some such way, it is then repeated in the story of the myth, and carried into outer action.

It must be noted carefully that intuitive understanding of the historical world gives just as valid an encounter with the spiritual as a personally lived out experience of this reality. The essence of myth is in the pattern expressed, whether springing from dream or vision, poured out in saga, or lived out in the historical process. If one believes that there is a spiritual world, then history and myth are not opposed. Thus myth rises or falls in meaning and value with the possibility of a real spiritual world and the possibility of man's interacting with it. Let us withhold judgment about the meaning of myth, then, until we have asked whether man could have experiences that give him knowledge of a realm of reality different from the physical world.

The idea of denying that any reality can be known except through sense experience was fathered by men's certainty about the world. By the end of the last century nearly all educated Western men, as we shall trace later, were convinced that man had reached final knowledge of the world, and that man's experiences all originate from the immediate, physical world. Although the twentieth century scientists have left this dead certainty far behind, it had already put a limit on man's possible experiences which altered men's understanding of themselves, their religion and their myths.

In theology the shape of this change was largely due to the influence of one man who was looking for a philosophy of man that would give the same certainty to its conclusions about human beings that physical science seemed to have given to chemistry and physics. Edmund Husserl, whose life bridged the old and new centuries, picked up the ideas of Comte and James Frazer and passed them on through Heidegger, Bultmann and others, tailored to fill the growing gap in theological thought. In Auguste Comte he found the enthusiasm of the Enlightenment, its confidence in man standing alone. Comte had seen man developing through three stages—first a theological and then a metaphysical stage, which men had to pass through and go beyond to reach the ultimate, or positive stage. He believed that by giving up his reliance on any divine being or meta-physical principle to explain things, man could come to rely totally on observable and measurable experiences, and thus reach his highest development.

Frazer supplied a similar classification of religious phenom-ena in his monumental and classic study of primitive myth and religion, *The Golden Bough.* He found that man first tries to manipulate nature by his own occult powers, and so becomes involved in magic; then he turns to higher powers for aid and goes through a religious phase. But he believed that neither of these lead to any objective truth about the world and that finally man finds this truth through science, by returning to the self-reliance expressed in magic, but using it to apply himself to rational methods of exact observation.

In much the same way, Husserl considered that the myths and most religious activities and experiences of man belonged to a primitive and pre-scientific attitude, which he called the "mythico-religious attitude." In his view all such activities that might suggest contact with a realm of the spirit—anything from myth to magic, including theological and metaphysical descrip-tions—were lumped together as a preparatory stage of develop-ment which leads man finally to the pure pursuit of knowledge.

Since it did not occur to any of these thinkers that there might be some reality other than the physical, none of them considered that the religious attitude and the development of man's religions had given real experience of the world or brought men any satisfactory knowledge. Thus religious activities and religious attitudes as a whole were considered as outgrown stages of man's development, suited only for primitive—that is, unsophisticated and simple—people. They thought that mod-ern thinking and modern life required that the mythico-reli-gious attitude be discarded.

This point of view sees no particular difference between the myths and religious activity of less civilized peoples and those of more developed cultures. Thus it sweeps away the highly developed religious attitudes of ancient China, India, Babylon, Egypt, Rome, and the Greek thinkers through Plato, along with the Hebrew ideas found in the Bible and Islamic thought of the last thirteen centuries. No matter how sophisticated, they have no more to offer man in his present advanced state than, for instance, the recently discovered primitive culture of New Guinea.[1]

Yet modern thinkers about religion, who would raise their eyebrows at basing work in other fields on such assumptions, see no need to check the facts behind this view to see if it is true or not. They simply assume that there is no world of spirit, and that only modern men understand and accept the truth. And so we find such a statement as the editor of *The Dream and Human Societies*—a study put together at the University of California at Los Angeles in 1966—wrote in his preface:

> For our purpose, we designate Descartes as the first fully self-conscious spokesman of the recent West, and we term all civilizations before his time, Eastern or Western, "medieval" or, more blandly, "premodern."[2]

Still, there are critical thinkers today who question whether one can prejudge in this way and still consider a subject objectively, and who find that such conclusions are a bit premature. Jung dealt with many of the neurotic products of the society that is based on these scientific presuppositions, and he came to the conclusion that these ideas represent a one-sided view of the world which actually leads to neurosis. He wrote early in his career:

> Failure to adapt to this inner world is a negligence entailing just as serious consequences as ignorance and ineptitude in the outer world. It is after all only a tiny fraction of humanity, living mainly on that thickly populated peninsula of Asia which juts out into the Atlantic Ocean, and calling themselves "cultured," who, because they lack all contact with nature, have hit upon the idea that religion is a peculiar kind of mental disturbance of undiscoverable purport. Viewed from a safe distance, say from central Africa or Tibet, it would certainly look as if this fraction had projected its own unconscious mental derangements upon nations still possessed of healthy instincts.[3]

Let us look at what some other students have to say about man's basic experiences of religion.

Primitive Man and Religion

Recent studies of primitive man have revealed quite a different picture of human development than that assumed by so many naturalistic thinkers. It appears that man does not fit neatly into the simple categories of Comte and Frazer. And so students here and there have suggested that more needs to be known about his myths and religion, and even his relation to magic. In philosophy Ernst Cassirer, who left Germany because of Hitler and wrote his *Essay on Man* at Yale in 1944,

46

reviewed the attempts to relegate most aspects of religion to an early stage of man's development. He came to several conclusions, among them that:

> Theoretically speaking, . . . (magic and religion) cannot mean the same thing and we are loath to trace them to a common origin. We think of religion as the symbolic expression of our highest moral ideals; we think of magic as a crude aggregate of superstitions. Religious belief seems to become mere superstitious credulity if we admit any relationship with magic. On the other hand the character of our anthropological and ethnographical material makes it extremely difficult to separate the two fields. The attempts made in this direction have become more and more questionable.[4]

The British anthropologist R. R. Marett had already reached the same conclusion, following the descriptions of South Pacific beliefs by the remarkable missionary R. H. Codrington. Religion and magic, he held in *The Threshold of Religion,* arise out of the same religious matrix, which is characterized by "awe" and filled with wonder, admiration, respect, even love, as well as fear. Even Max Scheler, Husserl's follower in phenomenology, found much the same thing true in his study of religious phenomena, *On the Eternal in Man.* Writing of religious values as the highest values, he held that the eternal both embraces the whole of time and penetrates every moment in timeless fashion, and that its presence in man gives him the ever-present possibility of religious experience.

It is Mircea Eliade who has picked up these suggestions and gives exhaustive evidence for a more objective view of primitive man and his religion. The research materials used for his work, *Shamanism*, make up fifty pages of bibliography. This is the most important work done thus far for those who would talk fact, rather than fancy, about primitive religious experience.

In this book, and certain of his other works, Eliade shows that all of the leading aspects of religion are found in shamanism. The shaman is the one who knows the world of spirit, who reveals the knowledge of its power. He heals by bringing beneficent powers into action against malevolent ones. He also brings knowledge of life after death, and does this through poetic and artistic means and through ritual. The parallels between the finest of shamanism and what is encountered in the best of classical Christian experience are striking to say the least. One crucial difference, however, is that in the classical Christian community the ordinary Christian could have an encounter with the divine, while in shamanistic religions this was only for the specially elect, and such an experience led to the vocation of shaman. But Eliade specifically suggests that coherent experiences, similar at least in quality, "are possible at any and every degree of civilization and of religious situation." [5]

Still, it is often argued that this attitude towards another world of experience is actually suited only to very primitive peoples, because concentration on the "other world" prevents individuals from paying attention to this one. Thus they fail to develop the ability to handle the physical and material environment that more advanced and scientific cultures require. The facts, however, do not bear out this contention; as Cassirer has pointed out in regard to primitive men:

> We can scarcely explain the instability of the mythical world by the incapacity of primitive man to grasp the empirical differences of things. In this regard the savage very often proves his superiority to the civilized man. He is susceptible to many distinctive features that escape our attention. The animal drawings and paintings that we find in the lowest stages of human culture, in paleolithic art, have often been admired for their naturalistic character. They show an astounding knowledge of all sorts of animal forms. The whole existence of primitive man depends in great part upon his gifts of observation and discrimination. If he is a hunter he must be familiar with the smallest details of animal life; he must be able to distinguish the traces of various animals. All this is scarcely in keeping with the assumption that the primitive mind, by its very nature and essence, is undifferentiated or confused, a prelogical or mystical mind. [6]

The studies by anthropologists, in fact, which suggest that modern cultures have much to learn from so-called primitive peoples are almost too numerous to mention.

In addition, there is a handful of important religious thinkers—plus at least one student of psychology—whose findings also suggest that theology should take a second look at its assumtions about the possible effect of a realm of spirit upon the lives of men. Among this group the most recent work is the book, *God and the Ways of Knowing*, by Cardinal Jean Danielou, a study of how man can know God. In it Danielou accepts the findings of modern anthropology and relates them to Catholic doctrine. He points to the reality of what he calls Cosmic religion, the genuine expression of the divine in symbolic form, and demonstrates that many of the symbols used by man have a common and objective value; they are not something that can be outgrown or completely rejected. Rather he sees Biblical religion building on this base and infusing it with new meaning and concreteness.

He also points to the work of Eliade and Georges (Gerardus) van der Leeuw, whose studies confirm the thesis that pagan religion brings men into an actual relationship with the divine, though not a complete one, a position quite contrary to that of Barth and Bultmann. The other three in this group of religious thinkers also maintained an attitude close to that of Danielou. This was presented by Rudolf Otto in *The Idea of the Holy*, where he studied man's religious encounter in depth, and in more strictly theological terms by John Oman in his chief work, *The Natural and the Supernatural*. Much the same point of view was also maintained by Baron von Hügel throughout all of his writings.

Yet most modern theologians are still caught, without really knowing it, by a thesis that no longer appears to hold water. Academic theology is still struggling with the idea that anything in our religion which claims to be a direct contact with reality other than the physical—i.e. symbols, myths, experiences, and all—comes only from the childhood of man, and represents only his effort to explain something that he was not rational or mature enough to understand.

At the same time some of the most perceptive thinkers of our time, from physical scientists to students of man, are fast coming to look upon these myths and symbols and descriptions of experience as valuable expressions of man's continuing contact with a powerful reality that is not physical, a reality of the spiritual. This spiritual view is affirmed from far beyond the studies we have been discussing. Jung, in particular maintained that this view is in accord with the facts of experience. And even Jung's critics, like Antonio Moreno, acknowledge that the twenty volumes of his collected works contain some of the most significant studies of religious data that can be found. Physicists like Werner Heisenberg, students of modern thought like L. L. Whyte, and many others have spoken for this view. It is expressed by the very attraction the supernatural has for people, particularly young people today. Nearly all great literature has portrayed this view—for instance, Faust, MacBeth, or today the novels of Hermann Hesse, who presents much the same material that Jung has described more formally. Is it any wonder that Hesse is the most popular novelist on the college campus today?

This view, which has been described as an understanding that man is in touch with "a plastic power pervading nature and providing the basis for conscious thought," [7] is found both among primitive peoples and among many who make their way quite well in the modern world. It has been held naively, and put forward by some of the most sophisticated thinkers of all times. This point of view is clearly expressed both in the prophetic passages of the Old Testament and in place after place in the New Testament. Before we turn to the philosophic understanding which so many of us need for any kind of belief in today's world, it is well to anticipate our conclusions and ask how this is possible. What is the difference between primitive and more advanced religion?

The basic difference does not lie in whether or not a religion seeks direct relationship with God, the "holy," or the numinous. It is even questionable whether a living religion is possible unless someone within the community is in touch with the divine, unless God does break through to someone in the space-time world in some observable way. Rather, the essential difference between primitive and more mature religion lies in *the individual's relationship* to that supra-personal reality. If one's religious attitude is conventional, or "collective," and is simply accepted as part of the cultural heritage and not reflected upon, then it is mainly an archaic and primitive attitude.

When man's relationship to God is therefore governed largely by social rules or invariable laws (what primitive societies call *tabus*), then men are given a way to relate to the nonphysical world, but at the same time they are imprisoned within the collective structure of the law which becomes oppressive and destructive. Few things are more confining to the individual and more resistant to change than a structure of law and ritual which is accepted as final and inevitable.

Mature religion, on the other hand, comes as the relation to God is seen as personal, involving individual and personal response and reaction. God is then seen as interested in individuals, each unique in qualities and destiny, rather than in conforming members of the group. The importance of the individual is one of the most significant teachings of Jesus of Nazareth. In Christianity one's value is not measured alone by what he can offer to others; it exists mainly within himself.

In the past it was understood that each Christian received the Holy Spirit, and thus was endowed with a relationship reserved for the shaman alone in various primitive religions, or for the prophet in Old Testament religion. Indeed in these religions, one who was given a direct relation with God was usually obliged to become a prophet or a shaman.

While mature Christianity is individual and looks for a relationship between God and the individual, it is easy for collective forces (or group patterns) to reassert themselves and create again a religion of law, rules and *tabus.* One of the great achievements of the Second Vatican Council was to reaffirm the necessity for an individual response to God and to the Christian Gospel.[8] In Christianity following authority is not enough.

The difference between collective (or conventional) and personal religion has been described with great force by Henri Bergson in *The Two Sources of Morality and Religion.* Indeed Bergson found them so different that he considered them utterly opposed to one another. There seemed to be no bridge between them. The same contrast between the collective and the personal is also found throughout Jung's writings, but Jung saw the collective as having within it the germs of the personal. When encouraged and allowed to develop, these are the seeds which lead to consciousness or to personality as a conscious reality. And as the ego emerges from the unconscious, so personal religion grows out of the collective. The religion of Jesus, in this way, grows out of the collective attitudes which so much of the Old Testament legalism represented. Jesus makes central the personal encounter of God with man of which the prophet spoke.

Let us consider now the philosophical understanding which can help to bring this encounter closer to home for us and others who have learned well enough to live with legalism and this modern world of externals and collective ideas.

Plato and Religion

The belief that man is in touch with spiritual reality can be held naively, and also by people who think about it with great care. Some people have held this belief who found, as in Hinduism and Buddhism, that the spiritual alone has reality, while the physical world is only illusive appearances or "maya." And some have discarded it, equally convinced, as in the nineteenth century, that only the physical is real and the spiritual is illusion. Once men have begun to think about the problem, it is very difficult for them to bear the tension of relating to two such different realms of experience. But bearing the tension is just what men had to do before they thought about it and that is also what the early Christians did by conviction, with the help of some of the most sophisticated thinking the world has known.

One reason the Christian world was able to maintain this belief as long as it did was because Christian conviction had the thought of Plato for a foundation. On this basis, Christian thinkers were able to go out and explain their position to the pagan world, and later they could explain it to each other and stay aware of why they believed as they did. And the reason that thought was important was that Plato had a unique understanding of the existence of the two realms of reality, and a theory of knowledge to back it up.

It is this theory of how men know both the physical world and the spiritual world which we shall sketch in some detail. Plato's dialogues are generally known both as great literature and as great thinking, and there is no need to go into a systematic presentation of his thought. Many writers have done this, and to anyone intrigued enough to study further, we heartily recommend Paul Friedländer's *Plato* for its depth of understanding.[9] But for the most part Plato's theory of knowledge has not been dealt with fully; the important aspects of it for present Christian thinking are unfamiliar to most people educated in the Western European tradition. The prejudice has been so strong against admitting contact with two different kinds of reality that, for instance, in a graduate school course on Plato at Princeton in 1938 I found the scholars did not even see the reality of these aspects in the very thinker they were investigating.[10] Let us look at them carefully.

On one hand, Plato believed that man was in touch with physical reality, which he knew through sense experience and reason; but this was a shifting, often unpleasant reality. Plato was born into a difficult age, a time when the old ideas and values were crumbling. He could not enter political activity because the chaos that followed the Peloponnesian war alienated him from all the current political groups. Philosophically his world was also in flux. He was much influenced by the doctrine of perpetual change as stated by Heraclitus; yet he was also drawn by the ideal of Parmenides which pointed to the essential unity of all things.

Plato's solution was to see man's knowledge of the world as coming to him through sense experience, and at the same time to search for the spiritual realities which shaped present reality out of the original and chaotic matter. He believed that man could find—in the midst of all the changing—some permanence that gave form to this principal, original stuff. He never denied the value and essential reality of sense experience, but his philosophy was an attempt to find these unchanging elements of reality. These he believed were separable from the material stuff. By his rational powers man could also come to know and deal with an intermediate realm of mathematical reality.

But the realm of the Ideas, the spiritual forms, did not come to man in any large measure through sense experience or reason, as Aristotle later maintained; it was reached through a direct contact and participation in the realm of the eternal. Reason and dialectic pointed the way, but they did not give participation in this realm, which consisted of the Ideas, and also of the gods and other nonphysical realities. Instead, there were four ways of finding this participation.

It is interesting how little concern is shown today with these four ways of knowing, even in the most sophisticated discussion of Plato's theory of knowledge. W. G. Runciman, for instance, in *Plato's Later Epistemology*, published at Cambridge University in 1962, makes no mention of this theory of knowing. These were ways of knowing in addition to sense experience, and most of the current world rejects any possible belief in objective experience other than sense experience and so does not even consider Plato's thinking.

Yet these four methods of knowing are essential to an understanding of Platonic thought and of man's direct contact with non-material reality. "There is also a madness which is a divine gift, and the source of the chiefest blessings granted to men," Plato wrote in the *Phaedrus* (244),[11] and he carefully outlined how this is true.

The casual reader may be turned off by the word "madness," particularly if he feels that it certainly is mad to think that man has contact with anything but a physical world. But for the Greeks and various other peoples, the word madness did not have the entirely negative connotation that it has for us. These were experiences of madness because they possessed the mind, and could not be changed by the mind. In the same way sense experience was viewed as irrational and akin to madness also.

The first of these ways, which Socrates was represented as describing, was prophecy, and he began by stating that the words in Greek for madness and prophecy are related.

These are *maniké* (μανικη) meaning madness and *mantiké* (μαντικη) meaning prophecy. In the divine madness of prophecy man is possessed by the god and often given a glimpse of the future or the meaning of the present.

> ..and in proportion as prophecy (μαντικη) is more perfect and august than augury, both in name and fact, in the same proportion, as the ancients testify, is madness superior to a sane mind . . .[11]

were Socrates' words. It never occurred to Plato to doubt that man can be possessed by the divine and so have touch with the non-space-time world in a prophetic way. He believed that man could encounter this world of spirit and learn from the encounter.

The second of these ways of experiencing divine madness he then described as cathartic or healing madness in these words:

> Again, where plagues and mightiest woes have bred in certain families, owing to some ancient blood-guiltiness, there madness, inspiring and taking possession of those whom destiny has appointed, has found deliverance, having recourse to prayers and religious rites. And learning thence the use of purifications and mysteries, it has sheltered from evil, future as well as present, the man who has some part in this gift, and has afforded a release from his present calamity to one who is truly possessed, and duly out of his mind.

In other places it is quite clear that Plato believed that healing of the body can only take place as the soul or psyche is healed, and that this can only be accomplished through divine catharsis.[12]

The third kind was described as what is known to us as artistic inspiration or

> the madness of those who are possessed by the Muses; which taking hold of a delicate and virgin soul, and there inspiring frenzy, awakens lyrical and all other numbers; with these adorning the myriad actions of ancient heroes for the instruction of posterity. But he who, having no touch of the Muses' madness in his soul, comes to the door and thinks that he will get into the temple by the help of art—he, I say, and his poetry are not admitted; the sane man disappears and is nowhere when he enters into rivalry with the madman.

Real art, Plato saw, with its apprehension of the form, comes only through divine inspiration. In Plato's appreciation of the source and the effect of great art, one is reminded of the value which Christianity places on beautiful churches, as well as the place of the icon in Eastern religion.

The fourth kind of divine madness is love. The passage goes on: "And we, on our part, must prove . . . that the madness of love is the greatest of heaven's blessings, and the proof shall be one which the wise will receive, and the witling disbelieve." Plato then proceeded to describe the myth of the soul which explains love as the coming together of the fractured soul so that in its wholeness the soul can see reality as it is. He then concluded that

> . . . the soul which has seen most of truth shall be placed in the seed from which a philosopher, or artist, or some musical and loving nature will spring; that which has seen truth in the second degree shall be some righteous king or warrior chief; the soul which is of the third class shall be a politician, or economist, or trader; the fourth shall be a lover of gymnastic toils, or a physician; the fifth shall lead the life of a prophet or hierophant; to the sixth the character of a poet or some other imitative artist will be assigned; to the seventh the life of an artisan or husbandman; to the eighth that of a sophist or demagogue; to the ninth that of a tyrant . . .

The importance of love as a knowing process is so important to the thinking of Plato and Socrates that it can hardly be overestimated. Chapter II and Chapter III of Friedländer's *Plato* make this point with great clarity and force. They describe the relation of the divine* and love in the thinking of Plato, and how as a man's spirit is empowered by love, as one is actually allowed to see and feel and love the beauty of another, one can be led on to the very idea of beauty and the good, to the mystical contemplation of God.

For Socrates and Plato men's psyches have a spiritual or a divine element, and as this is activated they are able to love and so to be led upwards on the journey to meaning and life. In this way men are led beyond Being to the mystical encounter, but not one in which the ego merges with the "All" as in Eastern mysticism, or in Plotinus, but in which the ego remains distinct and separate. Love implies some object to love, and since the journey starts with the foundation

---

*The word actually used by Plato is "demon" (daimónion), which means a spiritual reality of a lower order than the gods. I have avoided this word because it has such a different meaning for most Christians.

of love there must remain an object, and the individual psyche with its spiritual core also remains a separate unit. Friedländer writes: "What ordinary people experience only in the relaxation of sleep is given to human beings with a pure, serene soul—whom we then call holy or demonic—in their waking lives." [13]

Such a "demonic" or spiritual person is touched and motivated (even possessed) by the greatest of the spirits, Eros, the one who alone can control the other gods. Not only is this basic Socratic idea found in Plato's writing; Xenophon in *The Memorabilia* gives the same understanding of Socrates. And this essential Platonic belief and experience is found throughout Plato's writings, particularly in the *Phaedrus*, the *Lysis*, and the *Symposium*. Josef Pieper has clearly delineated the relationship between love and inspiration in *Enthusiasm and Divine Madness*.[14] The connection between this essential idea of the great Greeks and the heart of the teaching of Jesus of Nazareth hardly needs to be mentioned.[15]

Thus Plato saw man as having four methods of direct access to the realm of nonphysical reality, the realm of Ideas and gods, of spirits and spirit. In summary, these represent one of man's three basic ways of knowing:

1. He comes to know the physical world through sense experience.
2. Through reason he examines and comes to understand this experience and also comes to know mathematical reality.
3. Through divine inspiration, possession, or madness, man is given access directly to the realm of the nonphysical in: a) *prophecy;* b) *healing* actions; c) *artistic inspiration;* and d) most particularly, *love.* Through all of these man comes *to know.* These are all ways of knowing *in addition* to sense experience.

One very important implication must be recognized at this point. Since man's most important knowledge comes, not through his sense experience and reason, but through these direct methods, man's knowledge is never certain or final. Men cannot find unchangeable truth through the capacity of their reason working on sense experience or developing the first principles of reason, as Aristotle later taught. Each man has direct access to reality. Thus this theory never gives a firm basis for authority and never gives finality, since the latest developments of human reason may be overthrown by some new divine revelation or inspiration. Platonic thought can never be wholly systematized; his conclusions are always tentative and subject to new revelation. This is one reason Plato used the dialogue form and seldom wrote a systematic presentation. Truth was not final but alive and growing as men grew.

Plato and the Early Christian Church

Let us skip over the thinking of Plato's great disciple and follower, Aristotle, for the moment. Aristotle's thought was not too popular in the ancient world, and it did not acquire a culture in which it could develop and become the central force until the Moslem Arabs discovered his point of view in the seventh century and made Aristotle the basis of their cultural renaissance. From there his point of view penetrated Western Europe and had an impact which we shall trace later. But meanwhile the influence of Plato was felt in nearly all Christian theology.

Christian theology in the modern sense began when Justin Martyr (c. 150 A.D.) realized that the philosophical ideas of Platonism gave an intellectual expression to what had been lived out and taught by Jesus of Nazareth. They also made sense of the Christian experience of the incarnation and the atonement, particularly as Justin found them being lived in the Christian fellowship. Plato's theory of how the two realms of reality interact, and how men come to know these two realms of reality, was clearly consistent with the experiences of both the Old and the New Testaments. Since Plato gave the clearest and most systematic account of this theory of man in contact with both spiritual and physical worlds, it also expressed the thinking of the Bible, both religious and secular.

With Justin a great theological tradition began that consisted in joining the essential categories of Platonic thinking to Christian experience. Thus the attempt was made to understand the basic Christian experiences, as well as to continue encountering them. And this was done by considering these experiences within the most adequate world view available to man; for this is the basic task assigned to theology in this tradition.

It was not a matter of fitting Christian experience into a strait jacket of Platonic thought, but rather of using Platonic thought to explain and systematize the experiences in order to take a defensible stand before the hostile pagan world. Much of the Old Testament could be understood in these terms, as Philo Judaeus had shown in the first century. For example, the dreams and visions, God's speaking in the human heart, the healings, the prophetic messages all speak of a spiritual world in touch with a physical one. The Hebrew prophets were possessed by something outside the space-time world and spoke of God trying to get through into that space-time box.

But the understanding of Plato was far more important when it came to the New Testament. Here the spiritual world had broken through into the lives of ordinary men, and any Christian could now look for essentially the same relationship to that realm which had been only for the prophets in the Old Testament. The early Christians knew the effects of the spirit tangibly, in the nine ways which Paul listed in I Corinthians 12, and mentioned in other places. These were the gifts of the spirit—gifts of wisdom and knowledge, faith, healing, the power to perform miracles, prophecy, the discerning of spirits, tongues and the ability to interpret them—which individuals were to expect to receive. And these gifts continued to be received in the church.

It is hard for us today to realize the enthusiasm that resulted, which carried the Christian message out into the world. But the record is clear. In the first place, these specific promises of Christianity, which brought with them a change in quality of life, are referred to in nearly half the verses of the New Testament. In the appendix, I have included the results of a study of the New Testament in which I looked for these passages, instead of trying to avoid them as most liberals and followers of Barth and Bultmann do. Practically every book of the New Testament, I found, is thoroughly 'contaminated' with these influences of the spirit!

As the tables show, the nine gifts fall into five categories or types of experience: First, the direct action of God upon the individual, bypassing his consciousness as in healing and miracles; second, the indirect revelations as in dreams, visions and inward hearing; third, the intuitive discernment as to whether an influence comes from the angelic or the demonic, and as between the points of origin or locus of each, heaven and hell; fourth, is the direct knowledge that comes out of the blue without sense experience, akin to the parapsychological experience of ESP or extrasensory perception; and fifth, is the direct possession of a human agent in which spiritual powers speak through him as in prophecy, tongue-speaking and in the interpretation of tongues. Out of the 7,957 verses of the New Testament, 3,874 of them have something to say about one or more of these various experiences of the spirit.

In order to dramatize what happens when Christian philosophy has no place for the spiritual, I have used a large New Testament from which all of these verses have been carefully snipped out—a very "holey" Bible, one listener remarked. This has an impact on groups from every church and religious background. One finds that people are rather embarrassed to realize how important such experiences were for Christianity, when the church no longer sees grounds for believing in a continuing relationship with God or the spiritual. But for centuries the church did hold such a belief.

The record is equally clear that the attitude of the New Testament continued with no real break so long as the ideas formed by theology were influenced by Plato. I have made extensive studies of these five kinds of experience for my books on *Tongue Speaking, Dreams: The Dark Speech of the Spirit*, and *Healing and Christianity*, and also for an unpublished paper on "Spiritual Beings." In each case the evidence is overwhelming. Every one of the major church fathers discussed the occurrence of these things, and the conclusions they drew about Christian experience were stated in basically Platonic terms.

These experiences of spirit are easily understood in the light of Plato's thought which we have sketched. Even the categories are similar; nothing has to be cut out. And the basic Platonic understanding of the nature of reality and how man obtains his important knowledge also offers something else. It gives an intellectual approach to these experiences which helps ordinary men accept them and still keep their grasp on the reality of the immediate world and the other, equally important side of Christian life and experience.

This Platonic point of view was expressed by all of the major church fathers. Most of them had received the best education in philosophy offered by the pagan schools before they went into the church. These men knew why they were choosing Christianity. They had the conviction of a vital Christian experience empowered from beyond the human world, and they also had the understanding to express that conviction. With it they went out to conquer the ancient world on its own terms. And they very nearly accomplished the job before authority gradually began to take over following the reign of Constantine.

In the West there were Irenaeus, Tertullian and Cyprian, who followed the ideas of Justin Martyr, while in Alexandria Clement, Origen and Athanasius were bringing the tradition to great fruition. Origen was one of the greatest minds of the ancient world, and brought an originality to his Christian speculation which later involved him in ecclesiastical censure. Yet it was on the same Platonic base, handed on by Origen, that Athanasius withstood the attacks of the Arians, the only Christians in the ancient world who turned to Aristotle as their intellectual guide.

This tradition was followed and expanded by the great doctors of the church in the Eastern and Greek side of the empire. Basil the Great, Gregory of Nyssa, Gregory of Nazianzen, and Chrysostom, basing their works on Platonic thinking, shaped the foundation of the Eastern Church, which continued as a world force until the Turkish conquest of Constantinople in 1451. The Greek church is to this day based upon the same view of man and the world. This Orthodox tradition, so little known in the West, still looks to Plato for its philosophic formulations.[16]

The four Western doctors of the church—Ambrose, Augustine, Jerome and Gregory the Great—used this same base of Platonic thought. On it they laid the foundation for thinking in the West for nearly a thousand years. It was Augustine who developed the implications of this point of view in a sophisticated theory of man as both spirit and body.

Augustine saw man's essential nature as spiritual, made of the same reality as the other realities of the spiritual world, angels and demons. This spiritual being dwelled in a body. The physical world touched this physical body and as it did it left impressions on the spirit or psyche which dwelled within it. These impressions are stored up in memory. In addition to the knowledge which comes through the senses and the body, which are sorted and catalogued by reason, the psyche is touched by spiritual realities directly. Thus angels and demons as well as God touch the psyche leaving impressions in images, which can be stored in memory and sorted by reason just as sense experience. The dream and the vision are examples of this second kind of experience, and it is in this way that the demonic and the angelic can touch man.[17] Like Freud 1400 years later, Augustine believed in causes working through the psyche independently.

Augustine's psychological theory was as advanced as any we find until the late nineteenth century. Since man came to know spiritual reality through the soul or psyche, it was essential for the cultivated Christian to know the psyche, and this Augustine and the other church fathers did well. Unfortunately the Christian framework in which Augustine wrote has kept most secular thinkers from even looking at his contribution to purely psychological thought, and the groundwork he laid has had to be discovered all over again in our time.

But then a change took place. The world that Augustine knew disintegrated. Another point of view became current in Western Christianity, and the thinking of Plato was displaced. Men came to believe that they had no experience of anything real but the physical world, and the foundations were laid for the problems of the modern church. Let us look at the medieval church and the influence that Aristotle had upon it and upon Western thought in general.

CHAPTER IV

Out of the Medieval Church—
A Revolution and a Quest

Western Christianity did not have an easy start in life. By Augustine's time the civilization of the past was already giving way. While technically the Roman Empire was still one, the division by Constantine had weakened the wealth of Rome—the synthesis of cultures it represented. Frontier tribes were beginning to migrate into Western Europe, leaving a trail of ruin and devastation. Byzantium remained the cultural and political hub of the empire, but there were problems on its borders, and as the invasions continued, the separation between East and West grew wider. Cut off from the center of life in Byzantium, men in the West learned to live with the ruins and fear of attack, alongside half-literate strangers, and they came to look back on the earlier time as a golden age that was lost.

Gradually a new culture emerged, but one that was very different from the old. The new peoples adopted Roman law—and adapted it to their own customs. Under Charlemagne they began to appreciate learning, and the church became the center of study and literacy, with Latin accepted at least as the language of scholarship. But the knowledge of Greek was lost, and with it the Greek spirit, and also Plato's careful understanding of human experience which had given Christians some handle on the kind of superstition that now came to pervade the entire culture.

By spurts, Catholic Christianity won acceptance. But pagan ideas remained, and even worse, many of the new peoples had already been converted to heretical Arian Christianity.[1] They had brought its Aristotelian ideas with them, and at first they even persecuted the Catholic Christians who believed otherwise. It is no wonder that in the end the thinking of Aristotle completely replaced that of Plato as the basic approach to Christian ideas and experience. Arianism, with its Aristotelian acceptance of an unknowable God and its worldly stress, was easy for pagans to accept. They were at home with its ideas, and simply accepting the Catholic creed did not do much to change these ideas.

Except for Augustine, there was little left in Western thinking that could change or even oppose these ideas. By the fifth century few men in the West could read the basic Greek works of philosophy and science, or the Greek fathers; it had not been necessary to translate them into Latin so long as educated men read Greek. Now it became almost a point of honor to be separated from things Greek, and when the final break with Byzantium came in 1054, the Latin world went on its way, convinced that its thinking was equal to any that had gone before.

Most of the understanding from former times that survived into the Middle Ages was found in a few summaries written by men who wanted to keep some of the ancient civilization alive. One of the most influential was Boethius, a Roman official under the Arian king Theodoric. Boethius' writings were comprehensive; medieval education was modeled on the seven part curriculum he laid down, and for a long time it was thought that his mixture of Neoplatonism and other ideas expressed the essence of all knowledge. By translating Aristotle's logical works in the "Organon" he made one sector of Greek thought available to become the keystone of medieval thinking.

As for Plato, however, practically nothing was known at first hand. Even Aquinas, superb scholar that he was, had never read the basic Platonic dialogues. The mystical ideas of Neoplatonism were a far cry from the practical teachings of the dialogues. Otherwise, the Middle Ages saw Plato through the eyes of popularizers, particularly Macrobius, whose *Commentary on the Dream of Scipio* [2] presented a simplified, far from accurate account which made people *think* they understood Plato. It, too, gave them the picture of a mystical, otherworldly teacher, who talked about an ethereal ideal world and looked down on the everyday world of physically concrete experience.

This so-called Platonic philosophy was fine with people so long as their world was in such trouble that they were really looking for release into another world. But once civilization was stirring again and people saw that something could be done about their destiny, this otherworldliness was no longer so alluring. Macrobius' *Commentary* was still widely circulated, long after the invention of printing, since some understanding was apparently needed of man's contact with two realms of experience. But Plato's sophisticated understanding of Eros and the connection to another world were so completely forgotten [3] that even today Platonism carries a popular meaning of devaluing the immediate world. No wonder there was dissatisfaction with "Platonic thinking" as men sought to win back their power over the world.

Scholasticism, Aquinas and Medieval Thought

Meanwhile the thinking of Aristotle was revived by the Arabs, and the brilliance of his physical and biological studies were truly appreciated for the first time. This thought was undoubtedly one of the things that sparked the new Islamic civilization, and from there it swept into Europe soon after 1200. Almost overnight the universities were faced with groups of students demanding courses on Aristotle. Thomas Aquinas, at the University of Paris, saw the handwriting on the wall. He also saw some dangerous ideas being spread among students through the use of the Arabic texts on Aristotle, ideas that denied the value of the individual, and so he began to study Aristotle for himself.

Aquinas became convinced of the truth of Aristotle's world view—particularly his view that man receives direct knowledge *only* through sense experience and reason—and he came to the conclusion that this was a basic truth which Christians could and must accept. Consequently, he set out to show that this world view was consonant with the Christian tradition. His first step was to write the *Summa Contra Gentiles,* to persuade the Moorish intelligentsia in Spain that Christian convictions need not interfere with the Aristotelian understanding in which they were brought up. He then began the *Summa Theologica* for Christian students.

Aquinas was not the only thinker to make this connection, but his thinking was undoubtedly the best of his time. His integration of Christian and Aristotelian thought was one of the most impressive pieces of constructive thinking ever produced by the human mind. If anyone could have fitted Christianity into the thought patterns of Aristotle, Aquinas could have done it. He was not a slavish follower of Aristotle, but an original thinker of the first caliber who used Aristotle as a base. This was made easier because in the Middle Ages certain works of a Neoplatonic cast were included among Aristotle's writings, and so the great Greek thinker could be understood as having a soft Platonic underbelly.[4]

The important thing for Western society and for the church, however, is that Aquinas did not question Aristotle's basic idea of how we get knowledge, and so he handed down to our culture and our theology this understanding that knowledge comes to man in *only* two ways. According to Aristotle, man first obtains knowledge of the external world through sense experience; indeed his humanness develops directly through sense experience. But once man has come to maturity, he can learn to use his reason, first to understand and classify his sense experience, and then to provide direct access to logically certain knowledge. Thus knowledge is provided by reason as well as by sense experience.

Aristotle had realized that all information given by sense experience is subject to change, always uncertain, and he was looking for some access to certain knowledge. For this reason he favored the logical certainty of deductive reason over the tentative character of inductive thought; in this way one could find absolute knowledge about certain things. This certainty of knowledge is sketched in his *Metaphysics,* which might be subtitled "Theology," for in it he deduces the ultimate nature of reality, or God, from first principles which are intuitively known to everyone. Thus the system he sketches here is seen as the logically necessary, utterly certain result of human thought—a more ambitious system than Plato's. There is no questioning it. One obtains this knowledge, not by divine inspiration, but by human rational activity.

Indeed there is no place for experiences like divine madness in Aristotle's system, since then any simple person might have as direct access to truth as the learned metaphysician. He clearly states this in his little treatise on dreams;[5] this is why God does not use dreams to reveal himself to men. It would be unthinkable for him to reveal to simple men in dreams what the intelligent man must use effort to discover by his highly developed reason. God becomes known to men for certain through deduction from the principle of efficient causality, therefore rationally, and in no other way.

In harmony with Aristotle, Aquinas also produced his certainty about God logically, at the same time bypassing serious consideration of dreams and visions, of healing, tongues and prophecy in present experience. He did discuss the influence of demons and particularly angels, but only in a most involved way as influences on the body, stirring up humors in the liver which present phantasms to the mind. He feared, as Aristotle did, that direct influence of such realities upon the mind would infringe on man's freedom, and so he carefully detoured the idea of man's direct contact with these realities.

In its place, he developed one of Aristotle's basic beliefs, that the form is known only in conjunction with the object, and only through sense experience. The idea of any separate ontological realm (outside of the physical) that could come into contact with man's psyche was ruled out, and so man has two ways of knowing. He comes to know physical reality through sense experience and reason, but this knowledge, being based on inductive logic, gives only hints of what the forms are like; it is never logically certain or final. Man comes to know the essences of things in another way, through reason working by deductive logic from first principles; and thus through reason working on itself, man has access to final and secure knowledge of reality as it is.

The possibility of supernatural knowledge was not denied—there were New Testament passages about another realm of being that had to be quoted—but the way it could be received was not discussed much. This was *revelation*, which was confined largely to the past and was not really to be expected any longer. Revelation was a deliberate act of God, principally his voluntary self-manifestation in Jesus; and this was beyond the mind's comprehension. *How* God could get his revelation into the human mind was less interesting to Aquinas than the possibility, for instance, that astrology might explain a direct, physical influence of God on men that could be understood rationally. Direct supernatural knowledge, without some physical intervention, was indeed supernatural and not a matter for human reason.

In these sections Aquinas stood close to Barth, who sees God breaking through once in the historical process to reveal in Jesus Christ all that men need to know supernaturally; they cannot expect further revelation because there is no natural process by which God relates to man. Aquinas, however, left the door open to continuing experiences of the supernatural in a way that Barth does not. Like Aristotle, he was a sophisticated and subtle logician, whose thinking cannot be pinned down to a simple formulation. Aristotle has at least a limited place for the demonic, and as Victor White shows in his excellent study, *God and the Unconscious*, Aquinas dealt at length with imagination. Neither of them denied that experiences from beyond the physical world were theoretically possible.

Then, in the end, Aquinas himself had a tremendous, direct experience of God.[6] Just before this experience, he had been considering whether penance could be related in form to the healings that happened when Jesus laid his hands on the sick. And after it, while he continued to work for the church in other ways, he wrote no more; all his writing, he said, had become as straw compared with what had been revealed to him. Yet after his death the close reasoning of the *Summa Theologica* caught men's minds, and his ultimate importance came from the way his ideas were understood by ordinary thinkers in the church.

The Position of the Church

The official doctrines of the church became shaped by the writings of Aquinas, rather than holding to his experience, and so the ideal of certainty based on logic rather than experience became the chief cornerstone of theology and the church. Since this certainty could not be given by sense experience, or any other kind, churchmen turned more and more to deductive reasoning and the subtle logic and dialectic that flowed from it. Even today the understanding is found in the church—as Karl Rahner shows in *On Heresy*, published in 1964—that the heretic is essentially one who attacks the certainty of man's knowledge, and thus the dogmatic structure of the church. This is quite a different certainty from that of a direct religious confrontation or encounter.

But the ideas of Aquinas did not immediately win out. Until after he was canonized there was even opposition in his own Dominican order. For years Franciscans—under the influence of Bonaventure who was trying to integrate the thinking of Aristotle into the framework of Plato and Augustine—were forbidden to read Aquinas. And even as his thought became dominant, it remained one philosophy among several not recognized officially. His point of view had to compete for its place, and one reason it swept the field was unquestionably the personal sanctity the man himself had shown. His ideas stood for Christian devotion and love, and for the value of the individual. In many ways it was the influence of Aquinas, his ability to handle Aristotle's thought that prepared the ground for the emerging culture of Western Europe.

On the basis of his monumental work, the lesser scholastic thinkers created a simplified dogmatic scheme, which left none of the loopholes, either in thought or for personal experience, that can be found in the two original thinkers. The new product was quite different from the careful and sensitive fusion Aquinas had produced, with real appreciation for the human intellect and spirit. In the period after the Council of Trent, this dogmatic and "emasculated Scholastic Aristotelianism" was taught in most Catholic seminaries and schools. In fact one reason for the recognition finally given to Aquinas by Pope Leo XIII in 1879 [7] was to bring Catholic thinking back to his sensitivity and philosophical stature, and this has been achieved in the brilliant work of the Neo-Thomists, Cardinal Mercier, Gilson and Maritain.

It is not easy for most of us to realize how much influence Aquinas and scholastic thought have had outside of Catholic circles, particularly if we have studied only Protestant views of the Reformation. This was the world view in which the reformers lived. Luther broke out of it in his experience, but without developing a system of thought in which to integrate his experience. Calvin's view remained just as scholastic as that of Aquinas. The reformers broke up the game and organized new teams; but when they started out to look for a new ballpark, there was only one road in sight, and they took it—towards modern Christianity.[8]

The systematic fusion of Aristotelian thought and Biblical revelation (at least in idea) was still regarded as unquestionable up to their time. For princes, scholars and ordinary people, it was a description of the way things were. There was little distinction between what was taken from the Bible, or what came from Aristotle's logic and metaphysics, or from his more questionable physical world view. The total system was all a part of the same ball of wax, beld by the church to be beyond doubt. Aristotle's physics took on the same sanctity as the sermon on the mount, and this view could be enforced since the church had secular power in its own right, as well as in its influence over secular governments.

Specifically, the earth was seen as the center of a universe divided between the sublunary—the place of transitoriness, change and motion—and above and beyond this, the region of the heavenly bodies. There in the heavenly region lived the angelic powers, and there the spirits moved the heavenly bodies upon their way in ceaseless, eternal, circular motion. The heavenly bodies were understood to revolve in the epicycles of Ptolemaic astronomy, which was added to Aristotle's cosmology and considered an equally certain truth. Space was naively seen as sensuous space extending outwardly indefinitely. And all this was known partly through sense experience, and more completely through man's supreme reason. Medieval man was the center of things; he lived in a world which he understood, one in which the physical, religious and moral were integrated about the one, specific Christian revelation.

And then came the revolution ... It began with Nicolaus Cusanus, a priest-philosopher and his questioning of the categories of Aristotle. It grew with the strange investigations of Paracelsus, the theorizing of Telesio that led others to investigate, the insistence of Vesalius on learning about the human body. But the earthquake that leveled the world of medieval man came with the findings of Nicolaus Copernicus, who did not even have a decent view of the heavens he observed, far north in Warsaw.

Copernicus realized the radical nature of his work and refrained from publishing for fear of an accusation of heresy. But it could not remain hidden. Others brought out the discoveries which removed man from the center of the universe and called the entire Aristotelian world-view into question. For the church, committed to that view, such questioning was heretical since it cast doubts upon the church's religious authority as well. The split between the questioning scientific spirit and the official church came to a head with the burning of Giordano Bruno for heresy in Rome on February 17, 1600. Essentially Bruno's sin was that he stood for the spirit of free inquiry over and against the authority of the establishment.

In the 1970's when we can laugh at the somewhat overdone parody of the film "Planet of the Apes," [9] it is sometimes hard to remember what was involved in Galileo's retraction, or the flight of Descartes to Holland. For several generations thinkers had to cloak their beliefs, often to escape a rather painful death. And liberal Protestants tend to forget that their ancestors could become involved in the same enforcement of authority. The story of Michael Servetus, for instance, and the part Calvin played in securing his conviction is one that has not so often been told. Although Calvin wanted him beheaded, Servetus died at the stake; his sin was trying to spread an understanding of the Trinity which he felt would restore Christianity to its original purity. But for Calvin reform was one thing; radical ideas quite another.

From the church's point of view the conservatism was understandable. With belief in the direct experience of the divine ruled out by its philosophic base, the reformers attacking from another quarter, and the intellectual structure of its authority crumbling, the church retreated. Behind walls of static infallibility, it made war upon the entire scientific spirit. As L. L. Whyte has pointed out, here and there a man suggested that science was revealing the actual, natural base of religion which should be studied. But tragically the church stayed put. It allowed individuals to take daring exploits into the new intellectual current that was overwhelming the age, and then return to safety within the same dogmatic walls. Churchmen could "become" scientific, even liberal, on the outside, without changing anything within. The church, already out of touch with its own roots, saw no real reason to test itself in the modern ferment.

Equally tragic, the gulf widened from the other side. The new science saw in religion nothing more than legal and intellectual restrictions. Religion as it had been known had to be discarded if science was to advance. And so the realities for which the church stood were rejected, along with its outmoded formalism; and a new one-sided world was shaped by science, alienated from the religion out of which it had sprung. The scientists were left alone to expand their naturalistic and mechanical world, until there seemed to be no other place for men or church to exist. Only after centuries has a rapprochement begun—coming through physical discoveries like those of Werner Heisenberg, and more important, as we shall see, in the work of Teilhard de Chardin from the church's side, and of Jung from the secular world. Yet both of these men are viewed with suspicion, equally from within their own professions and by the other side.

Meanwhile naturalistic science germinated and spawned. After Kepler had perfected the theories of Copernicus, showing that the heavenly bodies act as any physical thing and need no heavenly beings to account for their movements, scientists gradually became interested more and more in what could be measured. Qualitative distinctions among things were ignored and their quantitative aspects alone considered. Then Newton produced the brilliant mathematical and physical theories that showed the whole universe as one vast machine working according to precise mechanical laws. Finally Darwin was convinced by his discoveries about evolution that man was the product of natural selection—merely a present terminal stage of matter evolving by a mechanical principle from simple forms to highly complex ones.

Man—who had once stood in the center of the universe as a unique and favored product of the Divine—now found himself one more outgrowth of a tiny and far from central bit of planetary matter. Even his life itself was explained as the result of purely mechanical and natural causes. Where was God and man's spirit in all of this?

Darwin had not meant to hurt anyone's religious beliefs, but his followers were not always so kind or cautious; they were also joined by Marx and Engels who saw the implications for their materialism. For the church, the theory of evolution was another denial of the authority of the Bible. Since the idea of seeing God working through the evolutionary process (or breaking through in other ways) never occurred to the leaders, a pitched battle was under way once more between the church and the scientific world. But by this time there were no more burnings; with little power of enforcement, the church simply began to look foolish in the eyes of intelligent men as it clung to the Bible as a text in paleontology. Men began to wonder if it actually had anything to offer man whose mind had been opened by the spirit of free inquiry.

The mechanistic point of view had been popularized by Auguste Comte in France and Herbert Spencer in England. By the end of the nineteenth century it had emerged, as universally accepted as the Aristotelian-medieval view had been in the fourteenth century. It was believed that man, by the exercise of his reason, had seized upon truth. He had discovered and now had in his possession the immutable natural laws which undergirded the physical universe—the laws that controlled physical motion, regulated the heavenly bodies, and applied to atomic particles, as well as to man himself. This popular thinking had grown far from that of Newton, who saw his discoveries as part of God's universe. Instead, the view prevailed that man had come of age in the midst of a purely mechanical universe, in which there was no place left for God.

Hippolyte Taine expressed this thinking with disarming honesty and clarity in the opening pages of his history of English literature, published in an English edition in 1872:

> Here as elsewhere (speaking of literary criticism) we have but a mechanical problem; the total effect is a result, depending entirely on magnitude and direction of the producing causes ... Though the means of notation are not the same in the moral and physical sciences, yet as in both the matter is the same, equally made up of forces, magnitudes, and directions, we may say that in both the final result is produced after the same method.[10]

Modern living and thinking are far more immersed in essentially this point of view than we like to realize. It runs through our culture, fed and absorbed with our first nourishment, and so generally accepted, so obvious that few people ever question it. Granted, it is difficult to question what one does not know he believes. But usually it is the obvious things that most need questioning. They lie in the bedrock of a culture where nothing can get at them until you and I are faced with a need to question them.

The idea that mind might act directly upon matter, or that a spiritual (a *non*physical) reality might break through and change something seems unthinkable. We do not even have words in modern English to convey clearly the understanding that man is in contact with a realm of experience separate and different from sense experience. In contrast, as is shown in my book, *Dreams: The Dark Speech of the Spirit*, the Greek contains some twelve words which can carry this meaning clearly.[11] Thus our very language betrays how thoroughly we accept the idea that only the physical and physical laws have substance and reality.

None of the attempts to budge this idea have been successful. The best efforts of modern philosophy have hit a stone wall, including Hegel's attempt to deny the physical world and the latest shift of positivistic thinkers into existentialism. Since modern theology—as seems to be par for the course—is caught in the main thinking of the time, religious thinkers are left without much alternative but to break with the record of the Bible, or deny the sweeping claims of physical science and look the other way. Thus, there are modern attitudes (largely unconscious ones), and there is modern reasoning, but there is little cohesive modern thought about man, his place in the universe, and the meaning of his life.

The Quest for Certainty

If one is to understand the plight of modern theology, he must understand, at least in outline, the development of modern thought. The possibility of a God who can be experienced is worth this much stretching of the mind. And as we shall see, the final dogma of yesterday has become far less than certain today. Let us take some giant leaps through the last three and a half centuries.

Modern thinking takes off from the Aristotelian scholastic base in a quest for certainty—but now certainty about external reality as well as about logical ideas. It was inaugurated by Descartes when he attempted to apply the model of analytical geometry to all experience in order to find solid ground for what we know. What better subject to start with than this? In analytical geometry, which Descartes himself had discovered, mathematical concepts and algebraic formulae were found to apply to space; each algebraic formula could be pictured as a curve or line on the graphs which Descartes had also developed. Thus it would seem logical to believe that spacial and extended things could be known and understood with the same logical certainty that is found in algebra. In other words, all of life could be reduced to a mathematical formula.

His first premise was that of universal doubt. All unclear or shadowy ideas or beliefs were eliminated,[12] and all else was to be doubted until proven true. But Descartes did not prove many things very satisfactorily, and besides a scheme which few accepted, he bequeathed to modern thinking mainly his proof of the reality of his thinking mind, and a large-scale problem of how we know. In the famous *cogito ergo sum* (I think therefore I am), he demonstrated to *his* satisfaction the reality of his own subjective being, and he also derived the idea of viewing the subject as pure consciousness, or rational intellect.

This was an entirely new idea. Indeed the word "unconscious" came into use as a noun only as men realized that something had been left out in such an understanding of the nature of the psyche and man. But Descartes himself did not seem to notice that he was leaving no room for the experience that had suggested his whole method to him; this was a triple dream experience on the night of November 10, 1619, which led him "from chaos to clarity." As L. L. Whyte has remarked, he made one of the great intellectual blunders of all time in so limiting the scope of human knowing that he excluded the source of his own inspiration, and the problem he left has remained for our time. A study of this dream by a Jungian analyst can be read in *Timeless Documents of the Human Soul.*[13]

Descartes' work was soon followed in England by the great deductive system of Thomas Hobbes. In it most of the rationalistic conclusions of modern thinking were offered, along with disbelief in the miracles of the New Testament, since they did not fit into a rationalistic system. In turn, Hobbes was succeeded by the empiricists, who stressed the place of empirical or sense experience. The first of them was John Locke, who held that the only sure knowledge was mathematical and all else must be derived empirically, from sense experience. The dangers of this position were sensed by the brilliant and graceful Bishop Berkeley, who proposed the first modern Western idealism. Technically idealism holds, as in Hindu thought, that only the idea is real, and physical reality is only an appearance. Berkeley's proposal, however, was to rescue the material world as ideas held in the mind of God, and so bridge the Cartesian split between mind and matter.

With David Hume the ideas of empiricism were carried to their logical conclusion in ultimate skepticism. Here man was seen as knowing only the stream of sensory impressions which come before him, and their associations, nothing more. Hume questioned the whole idea of efficient causality because he found that man has no empirical experience of cause and effect. Thus he brought into question the entire basis upon which scholastic Aristotelianism had proved God. For Hume believed that only tangible personal experience provides knowledge.

At the same time the monumental thinker, Emmanuel Kant, was at work in Germany. Kant came to believe, not only that we have no certain knowledge of the external, physical world, but that we have no certain knowledge of the subjective mind either. Logic does not unlock the secrets of either the intellect or the outer world. In *The Critique of Pure Reason,* which is one of the most important books of all times, he found man's reason to be the result and product of the interaction of two unknown realities, a subjective thing-in-itself, and an objective thing-in-itself. Meshing together, they produce a field of phenomenal experience which gives us all the knowledge we have of ourselves and the world.

Kant spent hundreds of pages describing the phenomenal subject, both as experienced, and also its structure and nature in experiencing. But his interest was only in understanding man's rationality and consciousness, and he never presented any other aspect of the subject. He still followed the idea of Descartes that thinking had to be clear and conscious. Nor did it occur to him that any reality except things of the senses could influence man. Men's speculations about another realm were simply amusing to him; in "The Dreams of a Ghost-Seer" he made fun of such systems, and showed how absurd it was to believe that a vision could give access to any reality.

At the same time, by denying the possibility that man's mind could come to any final knowledge, even about the human subject, Kant also cast doubts upon man's ability to know God through any logical process. He carefully pointed out where the deductive logic of the scholastic arguments had broken down, and how inadequate they were to prove the existence of God. His own effort was to show that there were completely different grounds for believing in God, and he tried to base men's belief on an understanding of man's moral sense.

The impact of Kant's thinking was and is tremendous. There have been few greater minds in the history of human thought. It was his task to open up the completely new understanding which leaves man with real phenomenal knowledge, but with the final doubt as to whether man will ever know reality in itself. There are thinkers in some number who believe that many of his critical conclusions still stand unequaled, and that he defined the limits of human experience. Yet Kant, like most men of genius, did not get off the scent he was tracking. Thus he left for our time to carry out the implications of his thinking for more than just consciousness and intellect, as C. G. Jung has done, bringing the insight of Kant to fruition for the whole man who is open to another level of experience.

The uncertainty left by Kant was what stimulated Hegel, however, to develop his own dialectic, by which he believed he could obtain true and certain knowledge of reality. Through his dialectical analysis of experience, idea and mind, Hegel came to believe that all reality was spiritual in content, and that everything was a manifestation of the absolute mind. Hegel's thought was voted into style in the middle of the nineteenth century in a landslide reaction to the agnosticism of Kant, and to the even more powerful agnosticism of the naturalistic thinking that was sweeping Europe. Those who followed Hegel and the other idealists like him, heaved a great sigh of relief. Man was not mere matter after all.

But what so many failed to see was that in Hegel's system the individual was as lost, as meaningless, as in the most deterministic naturalism. For Hegel only the essence was of value; the concrete, the individual, had none, and so man in his concrete meaning was little better off in this system than in naturalism. The theology based on this system hardly spoke to man's final, concrete need, his religious need. The loss of the individual was reflected in Hegel's political writings as well as his philosophical ones. He used the same dialectical logic to establish that the nineteenth century German monarchy, under which he lived, was the ultimate, logical development for human life, culture and religion.

Just preceding Kant and Hegel were two others who looked at the universe in a different way and who had glimmerings of meaning in the historical process. But neither of these men had a major influence on the thinking that was developing then. They are rather suggestive of things to come. Each of them struggled with the problem of finding meaning in a mechanical universe. Spinoza, who developed his ethics as logically as Euclidian theorems, came to the view that the universe itself was God, or a force streaming from him. This pantheistic view, which is common in Eastern religions, was anathema to the church and Spinoza, who was a Jew, was severely censured for trying to break the deadlock.

Leibniz has been called the last universal scholar. His contributions to the thought of his time touched every field from law to calculus (which he discovered simultaneously with Newton). His metaphysical speculations were way ahead of his time. Like Einstein—but without Einstein's equations or Mme. Curie's findings to back up his intuition—he saw force and substance as identical. His view of mechanical causes and effects, as a graduated series of means and ends, also offered a teleological or purposeful meaning in the material world. To him existence consists of individual substances or monads. "In each one of these the world is expressed on one of the infinitely many possible sides from which it may be viewed in the divine thought; every individual is an idea of God, actualised by means of a continual 'emanation.' " [14] Since such speculation was out of context with the time, its significance was not realized until the new discoveries of modern science.

And so thinking about God came to a series of roadblocks in recent Western thought. The conservative tradition based upon Aristotle and deductive thinking was being undermined by pressure from empiricists and mechanists, from Kantians and Hegelians. In none of the accepted points of view was there a suggestion, like Plato's, that man might find another level of experience. The thinking of the Cambridge Platonists came and ended without affecting the spirit of the time. The very idea of a divine-human encounter became ridiculous, and this we shall return to later on.

Even Schleiermacher, who tried to bridge the chasm, never suggested that man's experience of religious feeling could be objectively understood, or that it might give understanding of an objective and independent realm of existence. He saw miracles merely as natural events that happen to occur when religious feeling is in high gear, and revelation as ordinary knowledge similarly received. Since it never occurred to him that anything could break in to influence the natural order, he considered religious experience a phenomenon that cannot be looked at critically.

Thus man's critical ability and his religious *feeling* were on different planes, and could not be brought into relationship. Man was in a space-time box, programmed by the laws of natural science. There was no natural experience that came to him from outside the box, which he could try to understand, and there was no one until Jung to suggest such a thing.

Two Violent Reactions

Even though man doesn't always feel boxed in, there seemed no way of avoiding that conclusion. The materialistic philosophers seemed to know that nature works on invariable mechanical laws, which completely determine natural reactions. And since man is part of nature and of course analogous to it, man must be determined by natural law too, and individuals can be only a result of this mechanism. The trouble is that in the nineteenth century two men came to feel that something was wrong with this, and reacted violently without quite knowing what they were reacting to. Kierkegaard and Nietzsche were both victims of this naturalism, and also of Hegel's spiritual mechanism, which seemed to make some people more comfortable. And both of these tragic, half-conscious men have come to have more influence on our time than they did in their own.

The first was Kierkegaard,[15] who knew at least his conflict with Hegel, and who presented so much of his own sensitive and deeply troubled life in his brilliant, moving analyses. His dialectic was as facile as Hegel's, and he demonstrated quite clearly, by Hegel's own method, that reason by itself could bring no knowledge of religious significance. Kierkegaard put the concrete, individual experience above any Hegelian essence in value. But he never became aware of how much more there is to man's personality than just consciousness and rationality. As his *Concept of Dread* in particular reveals, he had no understanding of dealing with unconscious forces; he did so unconsciously.

His investigation was also restricted to immediate and physical phenomena, since he had no place in his system for direct experience of the nonphysical. He doubted the value of history and showed no belief that spirit could reveal itself in human history. He never seriously questioned the scientific naturalism that was becoming so popular, but only avoided it. Unfortunately, when one reacts, particularly as he did, without a great deal of awareness of unconscious forces, one often incorporates that against which he reacts. Kierkegaard's method was that of the rationalism that he attacked, and yet incorporated along with naturalism. He let them lead him into the existential crisis, into the despair from which he made the leap of faith, and died of a stroke at the age of 42.

Søren Kierkegaard never had a satisfactory human relationship. He knew little of the human, existential meaning of love. The existence of which he spoke was an intellectual analysis of his own lonely agony. In his pages one looks in vain for some understanding of love such as that which gave Plato his experience of another realm of reality meeting this one. No wonder it did not occur to Kierkegaard that the power of spirit could or would break through and touch man in the concrete here and now of physical existence.

At this point I wish to make it very clear that, in my criticisms of Kierkegaard and other religious thinkers, I am speaking only of their attempts to present a valid theory of religious knowledge to oppose the all-engulfing naturalism and rationalism of their time. Men need a firm intellectual base for their religious life so that it does not give way when there is stress or time of darkness. Each of us needs the best over-all, *valid* understanding that can be found.

Kierkegaard and those who follow him offer much of rich religious meaning. They offer insights into man's agony and dread and pain as no other philosophers before them. But they do not provide understanding that can offer a way out of the dilemma. In the last few years, I have known too many theological students who met a dead end from reading Kierkegaard to believe that he is helpful in bringing a person to a real relation with God.

There is much of great value to be found in each of the thinkers we shall discuss, but much the same is true of each of them. They do not attack the basic problem of religious knowledge. Thus they find it necessary to play down the direct action of God or the Holy Spirit in the world today, and we are left in the same naturalistic box with no way to find a meaningful, direct encounter with God in our own lives. Too often the result is a religious life that is barren, emasculated.

The opposite extreme is found in Nietzsche, who was caught between intellectual naturalism and his own sensitive spirit which was close to the unconscious and its deepest meanings. He was a prophet who could not believe his own prophecy. Nietzsche's last writings show the insupportable conflict between his naturalistic mind and his deeply religious spirit. He, again, never had a close, enduring human relationship and so was not anchored in reality. He was torn psychically in two by the conflict and lived the last years of his life a hopeless psychotic in an asylum.

Ironically, shortly after his breakdown, his prophetic spirit was recognized throughout Europe and the royalties came pouring in to support him regally in the asylum.

What Nietzsche saw, of course, was the death of God presented by the naturalistic attitude of his time, and the necessity for the new man (the superman) to step into the gap and affirm the reality of Spirit and value. But the task was more than he could bear, and he disintegrated as a person. His utter honesty, which he pursued straight to his destruction, portrayed the situation of Western man as few have done before or after him.

It never occurred to Nietzsche that there could be any way in which his prophetic insight could be integrated into the naturalism of the time, or understood by it. The naturalism was fixed as truth, and could not be questioned. And yet he pursued his spiritual intuitions to their very limit. The attraction he holds for so many of the modern theologians is strange. If his way is the only solution to man's place in the world, then man is in a bad way. I wonder if the death-of-God theologians grasp anything of the agony of tension which drove Nietzsche mad. He knew the spiritual world and, having no place in his life for it, it drove him mad.

A Third Development

A third reaction has grown in this century from the work of Edmund Husserl, whose roots were essentially Hegelian. I feel like apologizing to the reader in describing the thinking of Husserl. It is complicated and abstruse and there is no way to simplify it. It is, however, essential if one is to understand how modern theology got into its present dead-end street. In developing the method of phenomenology, he proposed to find absolute certainty and to make philosophy a science with as solid a base as he believed the physical sciences of his time possessed. He even defined philosophy as just such certain knowledge, and sought rather fancifully to find antecedents among early Greek thinkers for his point of view. This philosophical ideal was clearly defined in *Philosophy as a Rigorous Science*, written early in his career, and in *Philosophy and the Crisis of European Man*, written at the end of his life;[16] it remained constant.

Husserl's phenomenology must be clearly distinguished from the ordinary use of that word, which implies a satisfaction with mere phenomenal description as opposed to seeking for inner reality. To the contrary of this, Husserl was trying to find sure and final ground for all knowledge by deriving it from an analysis of the conscious intentional act. What philosophy must do was analyze pure phenomena logically and, by logical intuitions and by bracketing experience that does not fit, so arrive at knowledge of the eternal essences which underlie reality. This is the method of ontological analysis, which seeks knowledge of reality by a process of discovering the logically necessary conditions for the most immediate experience of a thing.

Since the philosopher's task, as he saw it, is to obtain certainty, one must avoid the dualism between subject and object which, thanks to Descartes, has gotten man into the present split between immediate experience and the objective physical world. One must not take too seriously the idea of experiential contact with any realm of reality not known directly to consciousness or discovered through logical inference. Thus any idea of the spiritual or the unconscious, either one, as an independent reality offering valuable experience is automatically ruled out.

Husserl also believed, as we have already indicated, that the earlier attitude of religion, what he called the mythico-religious attitude towards life is opposed to the scientific search for absolute knowledge. Since he accepted without question the ideas of nineteenth century anthropology about myth, he made no effort to investigate its significance to religion, but went on the assumption that the mythico-religious attitude was an inferior step on the road to a scientific understanding of life. Religion of that kind, he considered, had been superseded and needed to be eliminated from the lives of mature men.[17]

Husserl was an enthusiastic student and teacher who devoted his life to his idea. He made a real effort to rescue the integrity of man's consciousness and keep it from being reduced to mere mechanism by Newtonian-Darwinian naturalism. The impact he had on his students has made him one of the most important influences underlying European thought today, except in the scientific world. But his effort to base knowledge of reality entirely on man's conscious, intentional act is uncomfortably close to Hegel's one-sidedness, without the label of idealism. One finds himself out on a limb without noticing it, unless he is forced to ask where man's consciousness and intention come from. As a friend asked me, half joking, one day when we were discussing Husserl, "Have you ever seen a purely conscious, intentional act on the part of anyone?" And I replied, more than half seriously, "I doubt if I ever have."

Jung made the point that the followers of such thinking are

pushed towards a dangerous isolation from the roots of the reality they seek. In his words:

> The victory of Hegel over Kant dealt the gravest blow to reason and to the further spiritual development of the German and then of the European mind, all the more dangerous as Hegel was a psychologist in disguise who projected great truths out of the sphere of the subject into a cosmos he himself had created . . .(And,)
>
> The peculiar high-flown language Hegel uses bears out this view: it is reminiscent of the megalomaniac language of schizophrenics, who use terrific spellbinding words to reduce the transcendent to subjective form, to give banalities the charm of novelty, or pass off commonplaces as searching wisdom. So bombastic a terminology is a symptom of weakness, ineptitude, and lack of substance. But that does not prevent the latest German philosophy from using the same crackpot power words and pretending that it is not unintentional psychology.[18]

This applies to a good many later thinkers, so many of whom have followed the lead of Husserl.

In various combinations, Kierkegaard, Nietzsche, and Husserl were responsible for shaping much of modern European philosophical and theological thought. The principal spokesman linking these men to modern thought has been Martin Heidegger, the foremost figure of modern existentialism who dedicated two of his works to Husserl and succeeded him as professor of philosophy at the University of Freiburg. Heidegger took his method from Husserl, and also his conviction that ontological analysis is a means of obtaining truth. His understanding of experience comes from Kierkegaard. He has made brilliant and acute analyses of anxiety, death, nothingness, and other concepts of modern man, although in the most difficult and involved language.

One can learn from his insights, but they are built on a base in which there is no realm of reality or experience with which man can deal other than the rational and physically empirical. Having dealt with some anxiety, both in myself and others, I am very dubious of the value of intellectual analysis of anxiety by itself. Without some system—such as Jung provides in his understanding of the unconscious—to bring the realities underlying an anxiety out into the open, analysis cannot come to grips with them, and the anxiety and its causes remain untouched. Yet continental psychology takes what Kierkegaard, Nietzsche and Husserl had to say at face value in a way that makes me doubt whether the experience of these men is fully understood.

The insights of these three can also be seen, combined in various ways, in the other leading thinkers of existentialism on the continent—Karl Jaspers, Gabriel Marcel, Sartre, and Merleau-Ponty. Interestingly enough, the same frame of reference is used by Sartre to maintain a nihilistic agnosticism in which he sees nothing for man but striving authentically into nothingness, and also by Marcel to maintain a profound and quite orthodox catholicism, as well as by Rudolf Otto to produce his understanding of religious experience.

It is only in Merleau-Ponty, one of the youngest, most brilliant and consistent existential thinkers, that questions arise about the validity of the whole method of phenomenological analysis and existentialism. He realized that the existential movement had avoided the question of the unconscious ever since the original encounter with Freud's understanding when Husserl, early in his career, considered and, in true Cartesian form, rejected it as a logically inconsistent idea. In his introduction to Hesnard's standard French work on Freud, Merleau-Ponty took pains to show that philosophical existentialism has left out something of great importance. Where this thinking might have gone, no one knows, since Merleau-Ponty was in a stage of transition at that time and he died shortly after writing this introduction.

The Husserl-Heidegger philosophy seems to have won the day in liberal Christian circles, as Hegel's thought did a century or so ago. The place so carefully made for man and religion in the midst of a mechanistic, naturalistic world seems to be accepted today as simply one more fact of the world as it is. In place of the primitive ideas expressed by myths, man must now strive to find God and meaning by coming to know his own authenticity. According to this thinking, the task of theology is to fit man's experience of a religious nature into this framework, even though the understanding it offers of Christian experience is much less adequate than the Platonic understanding offered by the fathers of the church.

Existentialism in Religion—Bultmann, Bonhoeffer and Tillich

Several of the theologians whose influence is most felt today were deeply influenced themselves by this thinking. It seemed the only way out of the modern dilemma. But at the same time it involved quite a few alterations in Christian understanding.

Rudolf Bultmann, whose thinking we have touched on, knew both Husserl and Heidegger and felt almost awe for their thinking. He accepted as axiomatic Husserl's view that a scientific search for certainty must replace the "mythico-religious attitude." He also assumed that man is unable to change his world view and must adjust to the one in which he finds himself, particularly if he is to communicate with others in his culture and era. In the same way, if the Bible and Christian history are to say anything to modern existential man, they must be made understandable and palatable to him by a process of demythologizing.

This means explaining away every idea of something spiritual, other than physical, acting upon the physical world. For Bultmann these descriptions—from healings or angels and demons to prophecy and extrasensory experiences—were not things that had happened, but "myths" that spoke indirectly to people of God's power coming into their lives. If the same message is to get through today, to deliver us from our "inauthentic existence," the stories must be reinterpreted to eliminate all suggestion that anything concrete happened. As we have shown, very nearly fifty percent of the New Testament is 'contaminated' with these concrete elements, and would have to be recast to say something else.

The trouble is that this theological Bultmann is quite different from the Bultmann of Biblical criticism, who developed hermeneutics as a method of interpreting and getting at the meaning of the original Biblical expressions. His contributions in this area are of incomparable value for understanding the New Testament. But the same man could also remark to a questioner that in his whole life he had never begun to understand the Holy Spirit. In his theological works like *Jesus Christ and Mythology* and *Kerygma and Myth* Bultmann ignores the possibility that Jesus actually came because men needed healing and comfort, as well as to learn how to live authentically. Yet these books have the biggest circulation among theological students today, and we can only be grateful that he showed as honestly as he did the effects of trying to fit the Christian gospel into an existential framework.

Bonhoeffer was caught up in essentially the same process. His book *Act and Being* was a frank attempt to see Christianity in terms of existentialism, and his thought was carried a step further in his posthumously published *Letters and Papers from Prison*. Here he openly rejected the idea of religion as action rising out of man's need. He saw no "use" for God and the

Spirit in the modern, scientifically-determined world. Man is come of age and requires some new relationship to God. He did not even recognize a need to consider the unconscious, or any spiritual or mythological realm with which man could be in direct contact, or with which men might need to relate for their own wholeness. His disillusion with pietism closed his mind to this possibility.

Dietrich Bonhoeffer was a magnificent man, courageous and heroic. His suggestions about how Christians can and ought to live together are superb. His stress on man's life in the world and on living an authentic morality are needed by the church, but when it came to ways in which men could tap the power of God in order to accomplish these suggestions, he had nothing to offer. Obviously, he had such experience and was empowered himself, but he did not understand it in a way that could be communicated to others. Yet it is doubtful if man can follow his suggestions, either in or out of the church, without God's power.

Paul Tillich, who has probably done more than anyone else to awaken intellectuals to an interest in Christianity, has also carried many of the ideas of existentialism into systematic theology in his great work of that name. Another Tillich, however, of deep religious experience and great depth and understanding, is revealed in the last volume of the systematic theology, and also in his sermons and certain conferences. But this mystical Tillich is separated from the theological one, and he makes little bridge between them.

In *Theology of Culture*, where he summarized his late thinking and dealt with many of the problems we are discussing, he spoke of two philosophical routes to knowledge of God, suggesting that:

> In the first way man discovers *himself* when he discovers God; he discovers something that is identical with himself although it transcends him infinitely, something from which he is estranged, but from which he never has been and never can be separated. In the second way man meets a *stranger* when he meets God. The meeting is accidental ... there is no certainty about the stranger man has met. He may disappear, and only *probable* statements can be made about his nature.[19]

It did not seem to occur to Tillich that there was any experience in which God could be met in both ways at the same time—or that *either* way gives only probable knowledge. Theology, in fact, had become uncomfortable with probability and, as most of us are aware, it is hard to search around, even for a new doctor, when something hurts inside.

Here again was a great Christian who offered the most profound insights. His realization of man's estrangement from God, and his effort to bridge it outwardly, produced suggestions of the greatest value for the culture and for education. But in the basic matter we are considering—how one can find a transforming experience of God—he had little to say about concrete immediate experiences. Even in his remarkable *The Courage to Be*, he did not give a philosophic base for his own deepest religious experience. For Tillich as for Bonhoeffer, his own personal faith bridged the gap, but he did not try to show how this came about.

The views of Bultmann, Bonhoeffer and Tillich spread rapidly among students. After all, they wrote in the first place for other theologians, who were expected to understand and be able to shape people's belief. But it was the English bishop, John A. T. Robinson, who saw the struggle people were having with Christianity in today's thinking. He felt that the ideas of these men might speak to them, and so he presented their thinking in a clear and readable form in his popular book, *Honest to God*. It was a best-seller among religious books. Men were deeply troubled by religious doubts and they hoped that this thinking offered some answer.

Another popular work, that tries to show what the new thinking can do for faith, is William Luijpen's recent book, *What Can You Say About God?* * (*Except "God"*). As we have said, Luijpen is a leading writer on phenomenology, who makes a real effort to support Christianity on this basis, but it is not convincing. The experiences that once provided a base for Christian faith have been sheered away in order to fit the Christian religion into a naturalistic framework. This philosophy does not consider that they were even important to begin with.

None of this basic theology gives consideration to the unconscious, the value of dreams and visions, or the healing effect of the divine on the total man, let alone extrasensory perception, the angelic and demonic, or the direct prophetic encounter with the divine. These things are rejected, most of them as part of the superseded mythical attitude. There is no relation to God, or any nonphysical reality, *as object*. These men fear that knowing something as object turns the object into a cold datum of analysis and robs it of life, and so God should not and cannot be known as object.

The fear that God may become the dissected object of my

(or your) experience would be humorous if it were not so tragic. As anyone who has had profound religious experience knows, one need not worry about God dissolving under our icy, rational scrutiny. It is we who dissolve in the encounter, as men who make that encounter have learned. Nietzsche, for one, knew it all too well. What dissolves is the *idea* of God, giving way before the reality itself. And the two are quite different, although this has scarcely worried theology since the nineteenth century. Instead, even before the collision of Kierkegaard with philosophy and the growth of this existential understanding, theology was already occupied with its own reaction and counter-reaction to the ideas of Kant and Hegel.

Liberalism and the Thinking of Karl Barth

This movement began in Germany with Albrecht Ritschl, who was still a student when his conservative beliefs were shaken by a professor's enthusiastic teaching of Hegel. Ritschl turned to the idea of the Christian revelation as a purely human and historical process that would not require any belief in miracles. He put the thinking of Kant to work so effectively that the German schools became dominated by his followers, and by the idea that God must be found immanently in history and in the world. Therefore, man's business was to be rational about his Christian faith and fit it into the understanding provided by the secular world.

Liberal thinkers in England and America followed the same lead, and these ideas became incorporated in their sophisticated studies of religious knowledge. John Baillie in *The Sense of the Presence of God*, Douglas MacIntosh in *The Problem of Religious Knowledge*, and F. R. Tennant in *Philosophical Theology*, all maintain that man is tied to his reason and to sense experience, and that there is no direct knowledge of any realm of spirit or of God. The same idea permeates *The Interpreter's Bible*, as well as most popular Christianity. This religious thinking is still contained within Aristotelian categories, and the result is inescapable: Jesus, the church fathers, the Eastern church, Plato, all were wrong (and Dr. C. G. Jung as well where he is known), and it is up to modern Christianity to correct their errors. It is also no wonder that many such thinkers welcomed existentialism as a new escape.

Meanwhile in Germany the similar conclusions of Adolf Harnack, Ernst Troeltsch, and especially Wilhelm Herrmann, Ritschl's closest follower, guided what could be accepted in the gospel, and expected in the church today. Whatever the individual framework, whether that of Kant or Hegel, Schleiermacher or a man's own brand of rationalism, this attitude and these ideas were accepted as the final Christian position. It was this rationality which Karl Barth found practically useless in society or in a pastoral ministry.

Barth's revolt is understandable. His Swiss eyes were opened when the leaders of German liberal theology signed a declaration in November 1914 supporting the Kaiser's war as a holy cause. Under these conditions he doubted their much touted objectivity and rationalism. He became convinced that, since these rational men were not very objective, no man could be capable of finding God or religious truth by his own reason. And so Barth rejected the use of reason or philosophy as an aid to finding God.

Instead he turned to the Bible as the source of his inspiration. Backed by a small group of friends, he began to point out the failings of the liberal tradition, and then to awaken continental theology to serious consideration of the Word of God, the Bible. In this his influence was successful, and he cannot be thanked enough for turning the attention of both Protestants and Catholics to the Bible as their prime source of inspiration. But like most innovators and preachers, Barth in his enthusiasm went a good deal further in making his point. He maintained that God can be described only in dialectical opposites, and also that the *only* genuine understanding of God is that found in the Bible.

He believed that all other religions are erroneous and idolatrous, and he taught that the Word of God communicates in a self-authenticating manner which can be understood and discussed only within the fellowship of faith. The idea he turned to most often in the Bible is the idea of salvation through Jesus Christ. In the first twelve chapters of Romans he found a magnifying glass through which he could look at the whole Bible, but without focusing much attention on either the elements of divine power revealed in the ministry of Jesus, or the gifts of the Spirit that continued in the apostles' ministry and after.

In his famous commentary on *The Epistle to the Romans*, Barth made no comment whatever on Paul's statement in Romans 15 that he had spread the word "by the power of signs and wonders, by the power of the Holy Spirit...." The similar passages in Galatians 3:5 and II Corinthians 12:12—where Paul stressed again that God's power continued to break through—were scarcely mentioned in other works. While there are hints in his last writing, as J. Rodman Williams points out in *The Era of the Spirit*, that Barth wanted to find a place for the Spirit, he did not alter his conclusion. In *Church Dogmatics*, as we have seen,[20] he held that the function of the Holy Spirit is to convince Christians that God entered the world once with His revelation in Jesus Christ. In one section the healing ministry of Pastor Blumhardt was even discussed, and then dropped without connecting it with the present work of the Holy Spirit.[21]

Barth was so caught up in his idea—he refused to call it a philosophy—that man is separated from God by his brokenness and sin that very likely he could not comment on these passages. Feeling as he did that God had done in Jesus Christ all that man could expect, and that God could not tolerate another contact with human beings, Barth had to come to a kind of dispensationalism. But this makes of God a God of theology, and not the loving person revealed in Jesus of Nazareth. Instead, in this most central revelation one finds a God with loving concern for men, so much love that He died in Jesus Christ upon a cross to save men, so much that He sent His Spirit to continue the same kind of loving action.

The history of the New Testament church and the church that followed is one of God the Spirit breaking into men's lives in healing, visions, prophecy, and the other gifts of the Spirit because He cares. Barth's failure to emphasize this aspect of the New Testament is a strange rejection of the Word of God, a rejection of the way it was actually communicated in power, in order to adhere to a *theological idea* of man's utter separation from God. In fact, this is enough off key that it appears to be an unconscious accommodation to the rationalistic world view, which had also rejected the gifts of the Spirit. Barth wished to break with this tradition, and yet in certain areas it was still much with him. He did not look carefully at his own unconscious assumptions, and so they dictated to him.

Thus, our criticism of Barth is not that he was too Biblical, but that he was not Biblical enough. He failed to see that part of the Biblical revelation has to do with a world view, a philosophy or point of view about how God breaks through to man. In failing to see this, he failed to see that the Biblical point of view requires something other than the utter and absolute separateness of God from man. It is not that man can find God on his own initiative, but rather that God is *always* trying to break through to man; and if man can be open to this constant and permanent divine initiative, he will be led to a knowledge of God and, in time, to a supreme revelation of His Spirit.

Actually, Barth denied nothing in the Biblical tradition, but his refusal to take a philosophical stance enabled him to hold very nearly contrary points of view, and to discuss certain elements of the New Testament like healing, and yet fail to see the implications they had for his central point of view. Barth, however, had more of a philosophical point of view than he realized. But because it was unconscious, he was not constrained by it. Certainly he was an impressive figure whose impact has been great. His influence in conservative Christian circles is tremendous today.

In actual practice there is not much choice between Barth and Bultmann in what Christians can expect from the church today. Barth would be as dubious as Bultmann about the possibility of finding interactions between matter and spirit today like those described in the pages of the New Testament. Barth believed that these amazing things did happen during the one great breakthrough, but you can't expect them now. Bultmann maintains that they simply don't happen at all, then or now.

And yet modern American Christianity is shaped to a large measure by the thinking of these two men. Probably the great majority of Protestant seminaries teach the basic framework of one of these two men, and their influence is also extending to Catholic theologians as well. Is it any wonder that ministers who come out of school with this attitude thoroughly ingrained have nervous breakdowns when they try to deal with the problems of actual men? And if ministers, or other Christians, do develop psychological problems, the church and its ministry cannot help, because their task is, they believe, only to refer such people to a psychologist or psychiatrist.

In the Catholic Church, Thomism or Neo-Thomism can hardly be described as resulting from the influence of Kant, Hegel, Kierkegaard, or others who followed after. But the tragedy is that Thomist theologians and philosophers have offered little to correct the shortsightedness of these thinkers. Even such penetrating philosophers as Jean Danielou in *God and the Ways of Knowing* and Bernard J. F. Lonergan, in his significant work *Insight*, hedge on the subject of the direct encounter with God and refuse to take the Platonic ideas or theory of knowledge seriously. Karl Rahner frankly doubts the validity of most visions and prophecies, and questions most other ways of direct human encounter with God, although he does not deny them in theory. In fact, as we have seen earlier, St. Thomas himself laid the base for the modern religious problem, and it is questionable if one can remain within the Thomistic framework and make any real contribution towards solving the present theological crisis.

The radical theologians—of whom Van Buren, Altizer, and Hamilton are a fair sampling—carry the ideas of Bultmann and Barth to their logical conclusion. They agree that God cannot, or does not break into the modern world, and so they have professed the idea that God is dead for our modern time.[22] They are honest and straightforward. They maintain that in God's absence men can only wait and hope, with the image of Jesus Christ before them. These men draw as much upon Nietzsche as upon the New Testament, but this is one consequence of existential theology.

On the other hand, there was one radical theologian, Bishop James Pike, who found that he could not look at everything in terms of logic and sense experience. After his son's death and a series of strange experiences, which are described in *The Other Side*, Pike came to the conclusion that he had been wrong, and that man may have experiences which transcend sense experience after all. And this led him back, just before his death, to taking Christian orthodoxy seriously once again.[23]

There is one very important school of thinking which we must mention, and shall discuss later, although it has not yet touched the mainstream of theological thought today. This school of logical empiricism, however, casts severe doubts upon the philosophizing of Husserl and his followers, and even upon the words of the earlier existentialists. The men of this school hold that the main task of philosophy is merely the analysis of language and experience, and they maintain that nothing is meaningful which cannot be expressed in the language of physics. Language, as they see it, consists of words that refer to things and words which refer to relationships between things. All statements that are meaningful belong to natural science. All other statements are either tautological (as in the systems of logic and mathematics), or meaningless (as in most metaphysical statements).

From this standpoint any statement about God or the Spirit which is not based on experience would be highly questionable, and this includes the statements of all the theologians we have been discussing. This point of view has been developed by Wittgenstein, Carnap, Ayer, and others of the Oxford school of philosophy. All of these men would look with real question upon the discussions of "being" and "nothing" in the thinking of Tillich, Heidegger, and Bultmann, let alone the language of Barth. Much the same conclusions have been reached independently in the United States by the general semantics movement, beginning with Alfred Korzybski. About this we shall have more to say—after we first look at still another revolution.

CHAPTER V

Opening the Door to Spirit—
A Counter-Revolution

In late years my father, as he watched the changes in the scientific world, used to laugh about a chemistry professor he had had in graduate school in the early 1900s. This man, teaching in what is still one of our best scientific schools, felt that the era of exciting scientific discoveries had ended. He was distressed that men coming into the field of chemistry would not have the challenge his generation had had, since little remained but to figure out the periodic tables a few more decimal points and fill in the few missing elements. As my father liked to point out, this attitude was held by many people at the beginning of our century.

But a new revolution had already begun, although few people were aware how quickly or how thoroughly it had started. It began overnight within certain areas of knowledge that seemed to be the property only of science itself, and almost overnight man's settled ideas about the world were swept away without his quite knowing it. In field after field scientists have discovered that man's knowledge of the world is simply not final or static in the way nineteenth century science believed. The tight, confining box of materialism, held together by precise natural laws, has come apart at the seams. And still the revolution is continuing, and men have begun to realize the magnitude and scope of the change.

But unfortunately philosophy and theology seem to have been left behind, and so a great many theologians are still trying to fit their understanding of man and his relation to reality into a framework that can no longer be supported by theory or fact; they are still battling non-existent ideas and problems. In an address to the American Psychological Association, Robert Oppenheimer—who certainly speaks with authority on the subject of physics—spoke to essentially the same problem in psychology. It is futile, he warned the psychologists, to model their science "after a physics which is not there any more, which has been quite outdated." In this address before the 1955 annual meeting, he went on:

> We inherited, say at the beginning of this century, a notion of the physical world as a causal one, in which every event could be accounted for if we were ingenious, a world characterized by number, where everything interesting could be measured and quantified, a determinist world, a world in which there was no use or room for individuality, in which the object of study was simply there and how you studied it did not affect the object, it did not affect the kind of description you gave of it, a world in which objectifiability went far beyond merely our own agreement on what we meant by words and what we were talking about, in which objectification was meaningful irrespective of any attempt to study the system under consideration.[1]

If the psychologist needs to be reminded not to base his psychology on such a framework, the theologian should also be reminded that he no longer need react to it. There is room for individual variation in a life which God has touched, in spite of the view of nineteenth century thinkers.

Since the first, almost simultaneous glimpses into the atom, into radiation, and into the psyche, in the year 1897, scientific thinkers have shown the inadequacy of that world view in seven specific ways. The first three—the work that led to splitting the atom apart, the basic thinking of Einstein, and the development of quantum mechanics—changed man's whole view of time and space and energy, and the implications of these changes have been thought out by the philosophy of science.

Next the thinking of Kurt Gödel challenged the very idea of mathematical certainty. This was followed by new ideas about evolution and purpose. Then in the field of medicine, men wrestling with some of man's most debilitating diseases found that man's body is deeply responsive to his emotions. And last of all C. G. Jung gave evidence that man's most troublesome emotions could not be healed without a completely different view of the world, taking into consideration his contact with the creative center of meaning. Those who see that religion is a vitally needed force for human life, and are concerned about freeing man's spirit from bondage to naturalism, need to know that the most advanced thinking of our time supports their efforts, rather than making them impossible. And so let us take a look at each of these revolutions within science.

93

First of all, the atom itself turned subversive with Becquerel's discovery of the mysterious ability of a package of uranium salts to expose photographic plates still in their cases. Through Mme. Curie's experiments the hard "billiard-ball" atoms of nineteenth century chemistry began to explode into a complex of particles. Far from being indivisible, the atom was composed of parts that refused to obey the laws of Newtonian physics. Thus the confident materialism of the time was shaken.

Men began to realize that their science had not given them certain knowledge, or brought them in touch with ultimate realities. Instead it had given them hypotheses or working maps to explore their experience. None of these "laws" were final; any of them could be superseded whenever new experiences required a different formulation. Man could no longer be so certain that he was *just* matter, and that spirit could have no effect upon the order of things or upon matter itself.

And then came the work of Einstein, and man's whole conception of matter and time and space, and even position as an absolute, underwent a traumatic change.[2] Through one of the greatest intuitions of all time, he came to the conclusion that space may not be what it seems in ordinary sense experience. Applying the system of geometry that Riemann had worked out simply as a possibility, Einstein found that it fitted the facts of experience. Instead of extending in straight lines indefinitely in all directions, as Euclid described in his geometry, space could be better described as curved, and it may well be that we live in a universe that is limited although without boundaries.

At the same time he saw the relation between energy and mass as interchangeable and showed this mathematically; and by this demonstration of the truth that Leibniz had seen intuitively two centuries earlier, the way was prepared for the blast at Hiroshima. In addition Einstein's study of the speed of light changed our whole idea of time, showing that there is no absolute time, but only time in relationship to place and motion, and ultimately to the speed of light. The ordinary ideas of men about the world, which had led to the certainties of so much thinking for two centuries, were turned upside down. Man lived in a strange and mysterious universe.

On the third front the attack struck again at the microcosm. In the work of Max Planck, Erwin Schrödinger, and Werner Heisenberg it was discovered that heat was not transmitted in imperceptible gradations, but in definite bundles, in *quanta*.

Further study led to the realization that no rule could be found showing how or when a quantum would be released or, in the case of radium, which atom would disintegrate when. In addition to this, it was found that mere human observation of the smallest particles of matter interfered with their actions, and so the object could not be viewed separately from the subject. The idea that man's knowledge was equivalent to the objective "thing out there" could no longer be maintained. Subject and object were each part of an interacting field.

Still further, when it came to describing the nature of atomic particles, these ultimate bits of matter themselves did not remain in Aristotelian categories, but sometimes acted like electromagnetic waves instead of like particles. Current scientific language was not adequate to describe them, and human categories did not contain them. What we had thought were unalterable mechanical laws, it now became apparent, were simply statistical averages which made sense only when applied to great masses of matter. Once more, it was clear that if one is to come close to understanding something that is actually there, he must get back to experience and use whatever language corresponds best to his experience of that thing. And as Werner Heisenberg tried to let people know, this did not apply just in the realm of physics. In his Gifford lectures, he compared "natural language" to the specific terms of science in this way:

> One of the most important features of the development and the analysis of modern physics is the experience that the concepts of natural language, vaguely defined as they are, seem to be more stable in the expansion of knowledge than the precise terms of scientific language, derived as an idealization from only limited groups of phenomena. This is in fact not surprising since the concepts of natural language are formed by the immediate connection with reality; they represent reality. . . .
>
> Keeping in mind the intrinsic stability of the concepts of natural language in the process of scientific development, one sees that—after the experience of modern physics—our attitude toward concepts like mind or the human soul or life or God will be different from that of the nineteenth century, because these concepts belong to the natural language and have therefore immediate connection with reality. . . .
>
> The general trend of human thinking in the nineteenth century had been toward an increasing confidence in the scientific method and in precise rational terms, and had led to a general skepticism with regard to those concepts

of natural language which do not fit into the closed frame of scientific thought—for instance, those of religion. Modern physics has in many ways increased this skepticism; but it has at the same time turned it against the overestimation of precise scientific concepts, against a too-optimistic view on progress in general, and finally against skepticism itself. The skepticism against precise scientific concepts does not mean that there should be a definite limitation for the application of rational thinking.

On the contrary, one may say that the human ability to understand may be in a certain sense unlimited. But the existing scientific concepts cover always only a very limited part of reality, and the other part that has not yet been understood is infinite. Whenever we proceed from the known into the unknown we may hope to understand, but we may have to learn at the same time a new meaning of the word "understanding." We know that any understanding must be based finally upon the natural language because it is only there that we can be certain to touch reality, and hence we must be skeptical about any skepticism with regard to this natural language and its essential concepts. Therefore, we may use these concepts as they have been used at all times. In this way modern physics has perhaps opened the door to a wider outlook on the relation between the human mind and reality.[3]

The same problem has also been approached from a different angle by another distinguished physicist, Friedrich Dessauer, a student of radiology. At the Eranos Conference in 1946 he presented a paper summarizing two books of his own on Galileo and Newton, concluding his comments in these words:

Any scientist or technologist who has had the good fortune to be present at the birth of a great discovery or invention will never forget this experience.... Here it becomes perfectly plain that fulfillment can come to man only after he has heeded certain requirements. Yet in many cases, and this is one of the profoundest of human experiences, it is the idea that takes hold of the man rather than the other way around. Man is overpowered by a relation, an insight. This, in a word, is *revelation*. The scientist pursues a discovery, the technologist an invention. Sometimes, in either case, the search lasts for generations. Some do not live to see it, for the road passes through centuries, or millennia. But then it is *revealed*. In the days of Nicholas of Cusa many men were aware of this. The inspired German cardinal, who in a sense anticipated the Copernican system by a whole century, regarded the investigation of nature as a form of worship, a search for the revelation of the Creator and Lawgiver in His cosmos. He found eloquent words to describe this encounter with the Creator in natural revelation. For him the study of nature was a way to God who was the fundament and goal of all things. This sentiment was almost lost when natural science departed from, or rather was thrust out of, the sphere of spiritual unity. But the insight is true: the study of nature is a journey towards the divine ideas of the Creator, a quest for natural revelation: a worship at a new altar but dedicated to the same God.

But to travel this path to the ultimate fundament is long and arduous. It leads through centuries, and the term of human life is short. Such revelation is not enough. By its very nature, man's unity demands other, nearer sources, and they can be found. There is a second level that we may call historical revelation, in which we may find the fundament through the insights of the great intellects of all peoples and all eras. For the Christian, historical revelation culminates in the appearance of the Saviour, in his words and his example, and this revelation is humanly near, it has the full living warmth of an exemplary sacrifice. Here too God is revealed. But there is still a third level of revelation to which man strives. Man strives to come closer to the fundament than the long, though kingly road of the scientist can take him in a brief lifetime, closer than the exalted but remote example of the Saviour can lead him. He desires, he yearns, he strives for personal revelation, for a closeness of his own; he longs to hear the voice of God, and that is what Kant meant when, with a shudder of profound awe, he spoke of the voice of conscience. For him, who is disposed to search, there is revelation in dialogue with God, in prayer with Him, in struggle with Him.

Man is a creature who depends entirely upon revelation. In all his intellectual endeavor, he should always listen, always be intent to hear and see. He should not strive to superimpose the structures of his own mind, his systems of thought upon reality. . . . At the beginning of all spiritual endeavor stands humility, and he who loses it can achieve no other heights than the heights of disillusionment. . . .

For man is *in statu viatoris*, in the condition of the wanderer. This metaphor seems to me to describe man's existence in the modern world better than the condition of "being thrown into existence," of hovering in fear and anxiety over the abyss of nothingness. Man is a wanderer and he has a compass if he hearkens to revelation. He senses the direction. But full arrival at the goal is denied to mortal life. Man wanders; he comes asymptotically* closer if he lets himself be guided by revelation. Each one of us, and each one of mankind, is a pilgrim to the absolute. And the absolute is not an earthly possession but a mission. Man must not lose his orientation towards it; else he is confounded and falls into the abyss.[4]

Certainly one might expect to find reflections like these, of such depth and maturity, having an effect on the leading thinkers in other fields. Instead, as we have seen, a generation of philosophers have grown who caught only the surface point— the springboard these thinkers used—and considered that man was confined entirely to sense experience. The scientists, however, with the main battle against naturalistic thinking behind them, continued to expand quite a different attitude. In the past fifteen years it has developed among a group of men who are trying to understand the significance of recent scientific discoveries for human knowing.

One of these men is Michael Polanyi, who was a distinguished scientist before he began to investigate the ways of understanding. In his larger book, *Personal Knowledge*, and in the summary of his point of view, *The Study of Man*, Polanyi gives evidence that all knowledge is an extension of the person and connected with human values. He doubts if there is any apprehension of knowledge which can be called objective, non-human truth, and this holds particularly for scientific knowledge which is the result of the scientist's passionate search.

In *Science and the Unseen World*, Arthur Eddington discussed the way man receives his knowledge of material things, and concluded that the astonishing thing is that man has been able to infer an orderly skeleton of natural knowledge, in spite of not knowing the real nature of the pieces he was trying to fit together. As Eddington points out (and as we have quoted in full in the notes), man's whole acquaintance with matter comes from some influence radiating from it, which plays on a nerve end; through a series of chemical and physical changes, mysteriously "an image or sensation arises in the mind which cannot purport to resemble the stimulus which excites it." [5] Yet these indirect communications from matter, these signals which do not pretend to tell about its real nature, give man all the knowledge he has of the physical world.

---

* Approaching, but not meeting.

Thus, as Stephen Toulmin shows clearly in his standard work on *The Philosophy of Science*, the major scientists today do not expect to produce final or invariable knowledge of the world. The physical and chemical principles they develop are simply practical aids to understanding, useful vehicles for getting about in reality. One cannot, by analogy, deduce from them anything about the ultimate nature of the universe, as so many men of the nineteenth century tried to do. Instead, another thinker has dealt a final blow to this kind of complete understanding through reason.

This fourth contribution to the revolution from within was provided by the brilliant and provocative thinking of Kurt Gödel, whose original work was published at the University of Vienna in 1931 when he was twenty-five (a year younger than Einstein when his four basic theories were published). As people understood what Gödel was formulating, his conclusion rocked the scientific world. He showed that even mathematics and mathematical conclusions cannot be regarded as certain. Even the most basic mathematical system, as he proved, assumes a set of *meta*mathematical principles upon which the system can be understood, and each attempt to verify these principles involves another *meta*mathematical assumption to be proved . . . *ad infinitum.*

Hence, according to Gödel, mathematical knowledge does not come just from the use of pure reason working according to strict logic; instead it is given by a kind of mathematical intuition. He sees mathematical concepts as realities of the same nature as Platonic ideas, as real as physical things and, like the parts of the physical puzzle, a part of reality waiting to be grasped by the exploring mind of a mathematician. As Gödel puts it,

> Classes and concepts may . . . be conceived as real objects . . . existing independently of our definitions and constructions. It seems to me that the assumption of such objects is quite as legitimate as the assumption of physical bodies and there is quite as much reason to believe in their existence.[6]

The substantial world of matter had disintegrated into particles and energies. And now the absolute certainty of man's logic and mathematics was washed away. Yet here was man, with an amazing grasp on something real enough to produce results. As Eddington had pointed out, there was one place that man did have real, and not just indirect knowledge, and that was within man himself.[7] On three fronts the revolution within science turned upon man.

Evidence About Man

The fifth break with scientific rigidity has come from the study of living things and the evolutionary process, and from the fact that the evidence does not all agree with the understanding of Darwin and his followers. Beginning with the rediscovery of Mendel's laws early in our century and a theory of mutations, these developments have been as revolutionary as anything in physics. Speaking of their significance, Erwin Schrödinger has remarked that "the theory of mutations is an atomic theory of heredity. It is for the understanding of the origin of species what the quantum theory is for physics. . . . ."[8]

More recently many scientists have taken a closer look at the long range of biological development, with similar revolutionary conclusions. Jacques Monod has carefully shown the lack of determinism in genetic events. Dr. Charles Mayo, Jr., has put his finger on the fact that nature does not develop in a smooth and even pattern as Darwin thought, but in jumps and starts. Besides this, as Loren Eiseley shows in his popular study of man's evolution, *The Immense Journey*, the mutation process apparently often prepares for an adaptation, rather than being the result of it.[9] Through anthropology, the idea of teleology (that natural process expresses purpose) has found a new place—within science itself.

This whole point of view has been clearly drawn by the scholarly Jesuit scientist, Pierre Teilhard de Chardin, in his several books. He has seen the evolutionary process as an increasing manifestation of spirit, which is always to be found in conjunction with matter. This was a carefully weighed hypothesis, derived from the almost staggering quantity of data he had amassed. It was necessary, he found, if one were trying to account for *all* the facts beginning with inorganic matter and leading to human consciousness. In his *Hymn of the Universe*, Teilhard de Chardin has also given us a clue to his own inner spiritual life and how his inner intuitions led him to the undertakings which are developed scientifically in his other writings.[10]

A colleague of mine, Dr. Ollie Backus, has summarized and pointed up this evolutionary material for religious teaching in a way that has brought home to many people its deeper meanings with great force. When the recent developments in biology and anthropology are studied in this way, as facts that have something to say, a meaning of their own to impart, it is hard to hold to the idea of a blind, purely mechanical process; this does not make sense of the data. One must consider, for instance, the role of communication developed among higher species, the function of dreaming periods in relation to arousal and protection, and not least, the often highly intelligent systems of mating. As scientific minds have come to see, the religious idea of meaning and direction in the world, the idea of teleology, is not just a harmless notion, but basic to the whole under-standing of life. A door is opened through which God, spirit, eternal life may well be influencing the world.

In the sixth area, psychosomatic medicine has struck even closer to home at the idea that man is a piece of matter, highly developed, but determined exclusively by physical causes. This was the way medicine, for the most part, had come to look on men at the beginning of our century; a patient and his disease were "things" to be treated. But man did not always react well to an asceptic, laboratory-white environ-ment, particularly when he was sick, and as certain physicians began to study this, it was discovered that emotions have a real, often very great effect on people's bodily reactions. If the goal of medicine was health, and not just research, patients had to be treated as individuals with human problems that disturbed not only their minds, but also the functioning and ultimately the organs and tissues of their bodies.

Case histories of these results were gathered together by the pioneer in this field, Dr. Flanders Dunbar, who was trained in both psychology and medicine. The evidence she assembled from all areas of medicine showed conclusively that emotional problems often reacted directly upon the body, resulting in all kinds of disease from stomach trouble to kidney and heart ailments, including lowered resistance to infections and gland-ular and respiratory problems. And even more startling, medical men came to realize that even emotions a man does not know he has—unconscious emotions—can disturb or alter bodily func-tioning.

Since the original publication of Dr. Dunbar's book, *Emotions and Bodily Changes*, two journals, *Psychosomatic Medicine* and *The Journal of Psychosomatic Research*, have been established to keep up with the growing research. At present this understand-ing is finding its place in the medical schools, and one of the leaders, Harold Wolff, has recently brought out a second edition of his textbook, *Stress and Disease.* In addition, Jerome Frank, who teaches medicine at Johns Hopkins, has written *Persuasion and Healing* to give a readable, well documented account of the subject; in it he shows the great effect a sense of meaning can have on one's emotions and thus on his health. Much of this material is also summarized in my book *Healing and Christianity.*

Thus, from a medical standpoint, it is no longer possible to consider man simply a passive assortment of physical parts, functioning in a purely material environment. His hopes and fears, even hopes and fears about transcendental things, can well change the course of an illness, and he does not always respond to laboratory treatment. Instead, his healing often requires treating him as a person with individual and religious value.

Many of these insights, of course, have come directly from the psychiatric profession, who are continually faced with the physical problems that come in the wake of neurosis and other emotional illness. With the work of Dr. C. G. Jung, who realized the importance of a mature religious orientation to mental and emotional health, it has become possible to see a bridge from the spiritual to the physical, linking the two worlds directly together. Let us turn to the work of this profound and successful Swiss doctor of the soul, in which so many of the insights we have been discussing are synthesized.

The Thinking of Dr. Jung and the Counter-Revolution

This last and most complete break with nineteenth century man and his universe has come through the efforts of depth psychologists to help sick people get over their emotional problems. And this new study, starting from Freud's first great insights into the unconscious, has made one of the most important contributions to modern thought. Where other sciences, studying the outer world, were finding that the universe is far from a causally determined system of mechanically activated matter, depth psychology was discovering even more evidence in human experience. Experiences within man himself gave direct verification of the findings of the other natural sciences.

It was Jung who developed much of this understanding, describing inwardly, within men, the processes which Teilhard de Chardin has described outwardly. He wrote with greater insight and incisiveness concerning the depth and reaches of man's psyche than any other modern student that I know of in this field. And his findings dealt with actual inner experiences which are available to all, so that their validity can be verified without going afield. For these reasons we shall go into his thought and experience at some length.[11]

Jung built on the work of others, as he clearly acknowledged, particularly of Pierre Janet and Freud. Janet's studies of hallucination and hypnotism developed from the thought of Charcot at the Salpêtrière in Paris. It was here, where formal understanding of the unconscious began, that Freud studied. Freud, however, found that hypnotism did not resolve unconscious psychic complexes; instead it was recollection of unconscious materials. And in 1897 Freud had the courage to begin studying the processes of his own unconscious psyche.

He went on to investigate the content of psychogenic symptoms, and made detailed studies of the effects of the unconscious in neurotic patients. By following one major influence scientifically through every psychic convolution he encountered, Freud was able to propose the idea of psychic causation in such a way that it had to be considered by the twentieth century world. In addition he made the most significant discovery that dreams are the best and most easily accessible means of disclosing the contents of the unconscious layer of personality. From Janet on, this work represented a break with the tradition of Wundt, who viewed the psychic only from the standpoint of consciousness.[12] Jung accepted this new, pioneering work as his starting base.

Jung also realized the philosophical implications of these ideas. In some ways his contribution may be even more important for modern philosophy—for understanding how deeply the modern counter-revolution touches men's lives—than for the field of straight clinical psychology. It is in the area of meaning, of the psychology of significance, that he made his most notable discoveries. Jung also realized that theories of the unconscious are as difficult to accept from a purely intellectual level as theories of quantum mechanics, and he often made use of the analogy between quantum mechanics and depth psychology.

While Jung did not write extensively about his methods of investigation or his basic framework, he was well aware of them, and the references pointing out the relation of his ideas to both current and historical philosophy are scattered all through his twenty volumes of writings. No other psychologist of modern times has presented his findings in philosophical perspective as Jung did, who had the interest and the knowledge.

First of all, he believed that, through the senses, man has appreciable experience of an objective physical reality. Experience alone, he considered, gives a basis for understanding this reality; mathematics and logic are valuable aids when applied to that basis. But Jung did not limit experience to the five senses. He believed that the data of experience includes both that which can be objectively verified, and also man's inner perceptions in experiences like dreams, intuitions and phantasies, which can also be studied objectively.

In studying these spontaneous encounters with the unconscious, he applied basically the same tests as the physical sciences but without the same limits: How does the experience (or experiment) work? Is it repeated? What is the result in the individual? He used a method which has been defined as "non-experimental empiricism" by Father Raymond Hostie, who described it at some length in *Religion and the Psychology of Jung*. In Jung's own words:

> Experiment . . . consists in asking a definite question which excludes as far as possible anything disturbing and irrelevant. It makes conditions, imposes them on Nature, and in this way forces her to give an answer to a question devised by man. She is prevented from answering out of the fullness of her possibilities since these possibilities are restricted as far as practicable. . . . If we want to know what these workings (of Nature) are, we need a method of inquiry which imposes the fewest possible conditions, or if possible no conditions at all, and then leaves Nature to answer out of her fullness. . . . The disadvantage, however, leaps to the eye: in contrast to the scientific experiment one does not know what has happened.[13]

Jung was fond of remarking that in clinical practice the patient and nature asked the question, in scientific experiment the scientist asked it and that there is little doubt which asks the more difficult questions. In several places in his writings he also quoted Guglielmo Ferrero's words about the necessity of such an open attitude; these two paragraphs, he felt, corroborated his own view:

> Therefore theory, which gives facts their value and significance, is often very useful, even if it is partially false, because it throws light on phenomena which no one has observed, it forces an examination, from many angles, of facts which no one has hitherto studied, and it produces the impulse for more extensive and more productive researches. . . .

Hence it is a moral duty for the man of science to expose himself to the risk of committing error, and to submit to criticism in order that science may continue to progress. A writer . . . has launched a vigorous attack on the author, saying that this is a scientific ideal which is very limited and very paltry. . . . But those who are endowed with a mind serious and impersonal enough not to believe that everything they write is the expression of absolute and eternal truth will approve of this theory which puts the aims of science well above the miserable vanity and paltry "amour propre" of the scientist.[14]

This attitude of Jung's is quite similar to that of the major scientists, as Robert Oppenheimer has shown in his comment "that when one tries to study a system there are aspects of it which are accessible to experiment but are not compatible or simultaneously accessible to experiment." [15]

Jung also accepted the Kantian idea that man has contact with two kinds of phenomenal experience, one relating to the objective, external world, the other to the subjective or psychic world. But where Kant saw only what is already conscious as belonging to the subjective, Jung considered that one's inner experience also included unconscious contents. And the experiences of this inner world were not always as personally subjective as might be thought. These contents were experienced subjectively and inwardly, but they often came into the psyche from outside of itself.

Thus Jung considered that man has contact with a real objective world, encountered outwardly—although it too is experienced subjectively—and an equally real world found within, and experienced inwardly or subjectively, both of which can be known only as phenomena and never as the "thing-in-itself." The inner or psychic experiences he described did not come from ideas or concepts created by the mind, but from psychic contents acting independently. What Jung wrote to me in 1958 summarizes his attitude towards both realities as well as anything I know of; in this letter he said:

> The real nature of the objects of human experience is still shrouded in darkness. The scientist cannot concede a higher intelligence to Theology than to any other branch of human cognition. We know as little of a supreme being as of Matter But there is as little doubt of the existence of a supreme being as of Matter. The world beyond is a reality, an experiential fact. We only don't understand it.

The failure of most people to realize that he was talking

about experiential contents and not ideas exasperated Jung. When I visited him in Zurich, there was a copy of a new book on his desk entitled *Jung and St. Paul*, and I asked him what he thought of it. His only reply was that the author had failed to grasp this most elementary point. Seldom does anyone understand Jung by merely reading him, but only by dealing directly with the realities of which he has spoken.

Jung also found himself in accord with the practical thinking of William James, whose influence he acknowledged. Like James, he believed that what works out in practice is likely to be close to the reality of things. Underlying this idea was his understanding that human life is not just a chance development in the universe, but one of the highest products of a meaningful process. What tends to further, to free and enhance human life is likely to be close to the inner meaning of the universe. Therefore, the man who lives his humanity as fully and deeply as possible is most likely to find understanding of the depth and nature of the universe, and he is also the one who expresses that central nature.

He believed that logical thinking which stepped beyond the limits of experience was always in danger of becoming nonsense on one side, or the mere subjective projection of its author on the other. The psychologist, he held, should concern himself as little as possible with metaphysical constructions; his task is with hypothetical ones, starting and ending with experience. In matters like this Jung's thinking followed the best understanding of the philosophy of science, as detailed by Cornelius Benjamin, Stephen Toulmin, Werner Heisenberg, and the schools of logical empiricism and general semantics. Let us see first what is meant by this, and then what Jung did about it.

Since experience, as he saw, is the only final determinant of knowledge, this task begins with examining the experiences—including, in the case of psychology, the experiences that may seem purely subjective and personal, but come into the psyche under their own power (autonomously) through the unconscious. The function of reason is to work out the relationship of the experiences, and to present the choices, so far as possible without eliminating logical possibilities. Reason itself gives no new, usable knowledge about the world around us.

The scientist's task, then, once the various facts of experience are assembled and put into some reasonable filing system, is to find an hypothesis in which all the facts are seen in relationship. His hypothesis may be the result of induction but more often it comes through some intuitive insight.[16] For the moment, if it tests out in experience, he sees a new relationship between the facts. But each new experience that does not fit into the hypothesis he is considering, sends him back to formulate a new hypothesis. One small repeatable fact inconsistent with the existing hypothesis may require a whole new formulation. And at this point all the possibilities of reason, including those that have been or can be developed in pure mathematics, may be needed to help fill in the gap.

The easiest example of this is, of course, the one we have been considering of the increasing knowledge of matter, beginning with the ancient idea of matter as earth, water, air, and fire. The experience of distinct atomic properties brought an understanding of matter as hard little balls of indivisible elements. Then by various stages, like the observations of Copernicus and Kepler, these were seen to be working in the macrocosm according to the laws of Newtonian physics. But then one incomprehensible fact turned up; Becquerel found sealed photographic plates exposed, in total darkness, by a mysterious substance, and the search for understanding, once more, was on. After that came the Curies, Planck, Einstein, Rutherford, Bohr . . . . . and the blast, and it was realized by even the most uninitiated that matter does not always conform to the laws of mechanics.

At the same time, beginning with Freud, men were coming to see that they themselves were not always moved about by a universal physical mechanism. Jung added his understanding of this most complex part of matter and, once again, showed that a new hypothesis, in fact a new view of the world is needed to comprehend the relation of both consciousness and the world of matter to experiences of the unconscious.

A diagram may help to demonstrate how one view of the universe has superseded the one before it, incorporating the data of older theories, and how one hypothesis follows another into the vast area of the *unknown*, which still remains beyond the latest and best hypothesis.

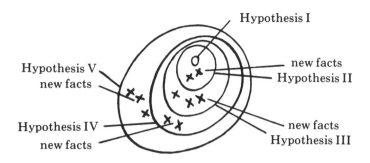

Hypothesis I: Greek science finds universe composed of earth, water, air, fire

Hypothesis II: starting from alchemy, chemists, astronomers and physicists find various elements and discover principles of physical organization, seeing the universe as matter totally determined by laws

Hypothesis III: atomic physicists, and others from Einstein on, find matter infinitely diverse in structure and organization, and see the universe as matter *and* energy governed by probability rather than by logically-proven laws.

Hypothesis IV: Freud discovers psychic causation and, still holding to determinism, sees non-material elements in the universe.

Hypothesis V: Teilhard de Chardin and Jung find life develops in relation to an infinite variety of material *and* non-material experiences, rather than causally determined, and Jung suggests a new model of the universe to explain human consciousness and energy

Jung started from the basis of nineteenth century science, and allowed the understanding of nuclear physics and relativity to open this framework up to the vitality of the vast and mobile universe that was being disclosed. As he further encountered the evidence of parapsychology in his studies, as well as in his own life and among his patients, he saw that these experiences also had to be understood in any complete view of the world. In her book, *From the Life and Work of C. G. Jung*, Aniela Jaffé, who was Jung's secretary for several years, has followed step by step the way he came to value these experiences and how his view of them was developed.

This view did not come easily or with superstitious acceptance. As Mrs. Jaffé's source material shows, Jung examined these experiences with the same care to which he subjected all data and facts, clearly feeling that a naive approach only casts further doubt on such experience and makes it harder to understand. Like certain philosophers—Henri Bergson, for instance, or C. D. Broad and H. H. Price at Oxford—he suggested that telepathy, clairvoyance and other experiences do happen, and that they operate through the unconscious reaches of the mind. Like these men, he found that the evidence required a new hypothesis, one that clearly stepped beyond the deterministic naturalism of the nineteenth century, and therefore was loaded, because the implications, in part, were theological.

At the same time, and more centrally, he was finding that the people who came to him in need of healing were the very ones who had met a dead-end because they had lost any way of relating to the unconscious from which such experiences come. Often these people were engineers and other practical scientists, whose neglect of the whole area of feeling and unconscious experience had led them to meaninglessness, and thus to neurosis, depression, anxiety, loss of drive, and even physical illness. Jung learned to listen to these people and discovered that unconscious contents were bubbling near the threshold of consciousness, and as these contents were encountered and dealt with consciously, the sick person often became well. Thus, Jung realized how closely emotions were related to images.

In this way he also discovered that images often bring contact with a world of psychic reality independent of the individual mind or personality. Jung was led to basic insights like these because he was interested in people's lives and experiences. Because he cared, and yet could listen objectively, he was able to see that men do not experience meaning only by reason. Meaning, he found, more often comes through an intuitive function that expresses itself in images and rises from the unconscious. The unconscious, in fact, has a kind of "thinking" function of its own.

In his introduction to *Symbols of Transformation*, Jung showed in detail that man is capable of two kinds of thinking. In most logic and mathematics, in most scientific, philosophical, and theological demonstrations, man uses directed, conceptual thinking, which can convey ideas by abstractions. But man also has the capacity to think in images, rather than in words and concepts. This second kind of intuitive thinking, which conveys its ideas concretely with pictures, comes from the unconscious. And this is the way man often conveys meaning, particularly his emotional meaning—through art, drama, folktales, and through mythology which expresses it in archetypal images.

Each night our dreams also present meaning from the unconscious in symbols and pictures. But we have so much lost touch with our capacity to think symbolically, to use the power of creative imagination, that we fail to understand either man's myth or his dream. Yet, as is now known scientifically, dreams go right on speaking, and those who have observed them regularly find that there is a non-rational organizing function at work within man's psyche in addition to his rational consciousness. It can also be observed that psychic contents have an objective, autonomous reality to them, much the same as man's contacts with the physical world.

Through these unconscious contents and meanings, Jung believed, men are presented with a vast psychic world, as objective, as real, as meaningful and experienceable as the material and physical world. In this understanding, he came very close to Plato's concept of the way man obtains knowledge through prophecy, dreams, healing, art and love. He saw Plato's *ideas*, not as eternal concepts, but rather as the philosophical version of his "psychically concrete" *archetypes* [17] (which we shall discuss). Indeed, in "Psychology of the Transference" and in the last pages of *Memories, Dreams, Reflections*, Jung all but embodied Plato's idea of the cognitive value of love.[18]

A New Theory of Human Personality and the World

Once Jung's basic understanding of the unconscious is considered, and one takes in the possibility that some reality may be at work in the world which is not exactly material, or rational, or simply man's subjective irrationality, then one finds that a new framework or a new hypothesis about the world is needed just to consider the evidence. Even if one simply assumes that this is true (as certain fundamentalist thinkers sometimes do), the picture of the world we are still carrying around shows no details, no facts we can even consider as related to such a possibility. But then, in the light of the scientific developments we have seen considering, perhaps we are still trying to focus on an over-exposed daguerreotype picture of the world.

Instead let us sketch in outline a new theory about man's personality and the world in which the evidence Jung offers has a place. First we shall look at a possible model or scheme, and then discuss the details.

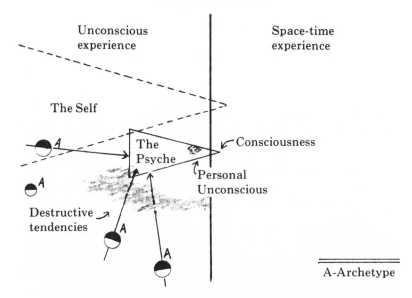

A diagram like this obviously has its faults. It is over-simplified, and only starts to map the territory and show where new resources might be found. But it does have the advantage of trying to represent the most developed points of C. G. Jung's thinking in a form that suggests where to start looking for significant data. And this is important for a particular reason. Jung's thinking continued to expand right up to his death. Rather than systematize his findings, Jung was willing to change his mind, and did so on a number of his earlier statements. Therefore, one has to look to his later writings for his most developed understanding, but on a basis of the earlier insights which he continued to find valid. Let us follow the points we have diagrammed in the model above.

1. *The Personal Unconscious:* Usually one first becomes aware of the unconscious when he realizes that some content which he knew perfectly well has slipped away from recall, and then inexplicably comes to mind. Or, a forgotten attitude becomes today's willful desire. One cannot say that such contents have disappeared, for they often exert influence on a person when he is least aware he has them. They can pop out in the most unexpected contexts, as word association experiments re-

veal. Sometimes the first awareness comes when neurosis suddenly stops a person in his tracks, making him realize that there are forces which can alter or halt his consciously willed endeavors. In fact, neurosis can sometimes be resolved in part by recalling and dealing with contents which have been lost. Freud and Jung both found dreams the royal road to discovering and understanding these unconscious contents.

Much of our behavior is the result of pressure from such contents; a slip of the tongue, missing an appointment that promised to be unpleasant, other errors or mannerisms often clearly betray the connection which the person himself may not see at all. One's dream life, however, gives a running commentary on the activity of these contents just below the surface of consciousness, and their relation to our life and behavior (and misbehavior). These are contents that were once conscious and have been repressed into the personal unconscious.

2. *The Archetypes:* In addition, there seem to be dreams with content which shows no derivative relationship to the individual ego. In one of his last published papers, "Analysis Terminable and Interminable," and also in the later *Moses and Monotheism* and *Totem and Taboo,* Freud wrote about discovering something in the unconscious besides repressed memories and the strictly wish-fulfilling activity of the id. He saw primal traces, or racial memories, that could be distinguished. These had an operating influence on present behavior, but usually in a primitive or destructive way. Jung and his followers continued to study this aspect of the unconscious and began to amass surprising information about it.

As Jung listened to patients, allowing whatever emerged from their phantasies and dreams to flow forth, he discovered all sorts of things he had never expected to find. As he told me, there had been one particular experience with a schizophrenic patient that opened his eyes. The man—a clerk with limited education, who had been in the mental hospital in Zurich for years—stopped Jung in the corridor one day and asked him to look at the sun. Jung was interested and noted his instructions, "Hold your head this way, and you will see the tube hanging down, swinging back and forth; and that is the source of the wind." It was a spontaneous vision with an eerie quality.

But a few years later Jung was startled into awareness. He was reading an obscure work by a learned philologist; there, in a language his patient had never known, was a translation of almost precisely the same vision, even to the words. It came from an ancient magic papyrus which had lain unedited for years in the Bibliothèque Nationale in Paris. This kind of experience was repeated several times during his practice, often connected in some unaccountable way with an associated outer event.

In addition, with patients coming to him from all over the world, Jung was fascinated to note how many close parallels there were in the unconscious materials of these people who often had little or no cultural relationship. He was also a student of mythology, and he discovered that the spontaneous visionary material of patients who had little or no knowledge of myths still used the themes of mythology as natural building blocks. In his *Symbols of Transformation*, based on the hypnagogic visions (those experiences one has just as one is falling asleep) of a young woman on the verge of schizophrenia, Jung described and compared the various mythical themes which came to her as dream-like images.

Through this mass of material he found distinguishable contents which appeared to impinge upon the human psyche that did not originate in either the space-time world or the individual consciousness. These contents were polar in nature. At one end they seemed to be images of pure instinctual drives, but at the other they seemed to contain spiritual reality. These contents he called *archetypes.* They broke into consciousness with a numinous attractiveness that was difficult to explain, and with a power that changed the course of a man's life. Often they were combined with elements from the personal unconscious, or at times they broke in on their own with almost no personal content at all.

Since these archetypal contents appear most distinctly in dreams and visions, or in the consciously released phantasy which Jung called active imagination, there was evidence available about these elements and their effect. This evidence showed Jung that the unconscious contains other forces besides the destructive, or simply primitive and inferior ones. He was forced to recognize that there are also creative contents that break in upon man through the unconscious which are superior to human consciousness.

For another thing, he concluded that the individual comes into life with psychic inheritance and structure as well as a biological one. Men have a potentiality for dealing with objective psychic material as well as with sense experience. While the evidence for archetypal contents in the unconscious is much less common than ordinary unconscious experience, even so it is quite a bit easier to come by than the evidence about atomic particles. Numinous archetypal experience is less rare than natural uranium salts. This is the kind of experience that the great religious leaders of all times have been describing. Jung was suggesting that men actually encounter nonphysical realities through the unconscious, which can assist and advance human consciousness. If this hypothesis is true, then the attitude of the early church towards direct religious encounters makes good theological sense, and the prophet is a natural part of life.

One can read about this experience today outside of psychiatric literature. In *The Teachings of Don Juan* and *A Separate Reality*, Carlos Castaneda has given a thorough description for anthropologists of his own encounters with this other world and how peyote and other drugs are used by medicine men among the Yaqui Indians. Mircea Eliade's *Shamanism* gives an exhaustive account of similar experiences historically, and current ones are discussed for psychologists in Charles Tart's *Altered States of Consciousness*. But the gap in communication remains.

It is difficult, as we have mentioned, to find a word in modern Western vocabulary to designate this realm. The word "unconscious" has many unsatisfactory connotations. To speak of a "non-space-time world" is hardly better. The two most adequate terms are probably Jung's word "psychoid"—meaning something more than just psychic—and the older word of the natural language, "spiritual." But "spiritual" has either lost practically all content or else, particularly in Catholic usage, it is often avoided because the word has come to imply a rationalistic attitude of separating from the world. This idea, fostered by Adolphe Tanquerey's text on ascetical theology and the spiritual life, which used to be standard,[19] is quite different from the sense in which we use "spiritual" in these pages, *that of a second and equal world of reality.*

3. *Encounter vs. repression:* Jung, for his part, sees man caught between two kinds of experience, one pointing to a world of space and time which is experienced through the five senses, and the other related to a world of nonphysical reality which he called the *collective unconscious* or *objective psyche.* Through this latter experience one comes into contact with numerous archetypal contents that are ambivalent in nature, depending largely on how the individual deals with them. The ego develops to deal with the outer world and to give a base for relationship to the objective psyche.

At first nearly any content which erupts into consciousness spontaneously will be seen as a threat and evil. The archetype

Jung called "the shadow" collects every unknown element to itself, willy-nilly. But as one learns that these elements can be integrated, he discovers that "the shadow" is often ninety percent pure gold, the source of some of one's best energy and inspiration. Ego consciousness, however, can forbid or deny such an encounter; and if it "prefers the ideas and opinions of collective consciousness and identifies with them, then the contents of the collective unconscious are repressed." [20]

If the encounter is avoided, the energy of the repressed contents adds itself to that of the repressing factor, and out of this can develop, for instance, the fanatical character of the "isms." The ego then loses its value and importance, as was the case in Nazi Germany where something like this happened. When the church stands just for a creed, "a collectively accepted system of religious statements neatly codified as potted dogmatic precepts," [20] it makes possible the repression that seeks unconsciousness, instead of trying to free man to deal with religious reality.

4. *The ego:* In all that Jung wrote about the unconscious he assumed the reality of a stable center of consciousness, an ego. His interest was in the vast domain of nonphysical reality, but primarily in exploring it with the conscious ego. Unless the ego is stable and well-developed, this is no more possible than it would be to undertake the difficult study of physical reality with one's center of consciousness at loose ends and undependable. If the ego dissolves, as it did in Nietzsche and Hölderlin, then the process of discovery ends. In his chapter on "Confrontation with the Unconscious" in *Memories, Dreams, Reflections,*[21] Jung refers to his own desperate struggle as he sought to develop and then hold onto such an ego center in the face of his own inner conflict.

His point of view at all times assumes that a stable ego base has been developed. Thus, there is no mystical doctrine in Jung's thought of the ego being swallowed by the unconscious as is found in Eastern mysticism. Instead he was considering an ego in confrontation with a content, either physical or psychic. In describing the nature of the psyche, he was quite careful to speak of two complementary experiences of its nature. Just as man's experience of the subatomic world has to be described in terms of the complementary concepts of wave and particle, so his experience of the psyche must be described in terms of a conscious ego and the unconscious. Neither one takes over direction for the other, and thus Jung considered both an adequate ego psychology and an adequate adjustment to the non-space-time field of experience necessary for maturity. Many persons misunderstand Jung simply because they do not see that he, as a psychiatrist, simply assumed that no development of the psyche is possible without a stable and well-developed ego. Therefore, during youth ego development should be stressed or unconscious content cannot be handled later in life.

Some persons have complained that the idea of man's openness to the invasion of psychic contents limits his freedom. Jung would reply that man's freedom cannot be described logically in terms of one or the other, but that man is partially free and partially unfree. It is a matter of degree and experience, not of logic. The reason for dealing with unconscious contents is to give the ego more insight and understanding and thus more freedom.

5. *Destructive tendencies:* There is, however, an aspect or element of the unconscious which seems ultimately destructive, driving men to illness and psychosis and, at times, to violence against others. It leads to disintegration and is set against wholeness. This kind of content is depicted by the witches in *MacBeth*, by Mephistopheles in *Faust*, and by the evil one so accurately portrayed in the witchcraft in the film "Rosemary's Baby." Jung has described this destructive element with terrifying reality in the chapter already mentioned of *Memories, Dreams, Reflections.*

Even if the unconscious could be anywhere nearly fully integrated, this aspect of it would remain and would have to be dealt with by the individual. Freud approached this aspect of the psyche in *Beyond the Pleasure Principle* and *Civilization and Its Discontents.* Here he described the annihilating effect of the death wish, which he saw as essentially the backward pull of the psyche, the desire to return to the deadness of inorganic matter. This is seen most clearly in suicidal people, but it is also manifested in hundreds of other ways from accident proneness to psychosomatic disease, as Karl Menninger has elaborated in *Man Against Himself.*[22]

Jung's experience made him balk at the Aristotelian position that evil is only the absence or deprivation of good, the idea of the *privatio boni*, that good naturally belongs to man. Thus he had to deal with this problem directly, and he did so as creatively as anyone in our time. He would have agreed with the author of Ephesians that "our fight is not against human foes, but against cosmic powers, against authorities and potentates of this dark world, against superhuman forces of evil in the heavens."[23] Man has to wrestle with darkness to find out its nature, and then either integrate or reject it.

Jung believed that the doctrine of the *privatio boni*, first laid down by Augustine and later developed by Aquinas, crippled man in this struggle. This doctrine deceived man about the seriousness of his struggle. "The growing awareness of the inferior part of the personality," Jung wrote, "... should not be twisted into an intellectual activity, for it has far more the meaning of a suffering and a passion that implicate the whole man." [24] Dealing with unconscious contents can be a painful process, a *via crusis* which most men will avoid if they can. This emphasis on creative suffering has much in common with the teaching of Jesus of Nazareth.

This understanding of the reality of evil has the most practical consequences. The goal of man is to become as conscious as possible, so that he can relate to the creative aspect of the unconscious and allow it to guide and transform him, separating him out from the destructiveness of elemental evil. If he remains unconscious of his psychic potential, man is likely to use his feeling of attraction, or his feelings of repulsion, as tools for projecting the contents of the unconscious out onto others. The attraction of "falling in love" can keep one so fascinated by his own psychic contents that he fails even to see the other person as he or she really is, let alone coming to know the person and relating to him.

By a similar process a race or nation can become the hated carrier of all the negative contents that we choose not to deal with; by the cults of hate and war whole peoples are turned into objects of ugliness and destructiveness that are mainly projected upon them. One can also be possessed by these destructive powers as Attila the Hun, whose name still stands for evil; they can be loosed onto wives and children, or one can even let himself be torn apart by these unconscious contents in depression, neurosis, or psychosomatic illness. On the other hand, there is always the opposite danger in repression of unconscious contents, that the energy may be switched to some conscious collectivity so that the individual is then swallowed by another "ism." Certainly, the way does seem narrow.

Jung, Religion and Spirit

6. *The self:* Jung, however, was far more interested in the creative, restoring aspect of the unconscious, the integrative complex which he called the *self.* His last major works were largely an attempt to describe this reality which leads a man to wholeness, integration and health. In these discussions of the *self,* it must be emphasized, Jung was not talking about

a concept; he was discussing experiences of an objective and autonomous (although complex) content of experience. Such contents can be discovered by one's own observation if he takes the trouble to investigate.

Jung's descriptions of these experiences have much in common with similar experiences described by the church fathers up to Aquinas. Like these men, he was interested throughout his life in what can be called religious experience, or experience of religious realities. And like them, although he did not often speak of a "spiritual world," he wrote a great deal about the positive aspects of such a realm of experience, as well as the negative ones. Even a critic of Jung like Father Antonio Moreno, who is not entirely sympathetic towards him, points out the tremendous importance of his observations in this area. In *Jung, Gods and Modern Man*, Moreno suggests that no serious student of religion can afford to neglect these findings of sixty-five years of pioneer work.

Four of Jung's statements convey his most mature and developed thought about the reality which is behind these positive experiential encounters: In his work on *The Structure and Dynamics of the Psyche*, he wrote:

> Of what lies beyond the phenomenal world we can have absolutely no idea . . . we need an Archimedean point which alone makes a judgment possible. This can only be the nonpsychic, for, as a living phenomenon, the psychic lies embedded in something that appears to be of a nonpsychic nature. Although we perceive the latter as a psychic datum only, there are sufficient reasons for believing in its objective reality. (and, again) . . . It is this clear feeling of superiority that gives the phenomenon of the spirit its revelatory character and absolute authority . . .[25]

A second and very careful expression of Jung's attitude towards the spirit is found in "The Spirit of Psychology" in these words:

> Although there is no form of existence that is not mediated to us psychically and only psychically, it would hardly do to say that everything is merely psychic. We must apply this argument logically to the archetypes as well. Since their essential being is unconscious to us, and yet they are experienced as spontaneous agencies, there is probably no alternative at present but to describe their nature, in accordance with their chiefest effect, as "spirit," in the sense which I attempted to make plain in

my paper "The Phenomenology of the Spirit in Fairy Tales." If so, the position of the archetype would be located beyond the psychic sphere, analogous to the position of physiological instinct, which is immediately rooted in the stuff of the organism and, with its psychoid nature, forms the bridge to matter in general. In archetypal conceptions and instinctual perceptions, spirit and matter confront one another on the psychic plane. Matter as well as spirit appear in the psychic realm as distinctive qualities of conscious contents. The ultimate nature of both is transcendent, that is, noumenal, since the psyche and its contents are the only reality which is given to us *without a medium*.[26]

In the last of his published works, *Memories, Dreams, Reflections*, Jung carried the same thought even further; here he wrote:

I have, therefore, even hazarded the postulate that the phenomenon of archetypal configurations—which are psychic events *par excellence*—may be founded upon a *psychoid* base, that is, upon an only partially psychic and possibly altogether different form of being. For lack of empirical data I have neither knowledge nor understanding of such forms of being, which are commonly called spiritual. From the point of view of science, it is immaterial what I may *believe* on that score, and I must accept my ignorance ... Nevertheless, we have good reason to suppose that behind this veil there exists the uncomprehended absolute object which affects and influences us—and to suppose it even, or particularly, in the case of psychic phenomena about which no verifiable statements can be made.[27]

The remark which Jung made in his British Broadcasting Company interview is almost too well known to be repeated, but it crystallizes all the other ways he tried to put this over. "Suddenly I understood that God was, for me at least, one of the most certain and immediate experiences ... I do not believe; I know. I *know*."

The task of psychological therapy from Jung's point of view is to make the individual aware of his own unique psychic structure and his relation to this storehouse of unconscious contents, releasing him from bondage to the negative and helping him relate to the creative and integrating aspects in it. The therapist then is a midwife, not one who creates in his own image. But he has a job to do—listening openly to the one who comes, knowing experientially the structure of the unconscious, the darkness that is encountered, and something of the intimations of the *self* that can come.

As the individual encounters the vast wilderness of hitherto unconscious psychic contents, he can become inflated by the positive contents, identifying with the *self* or saviour figure, and he needs the objectivity of an external standpoint. As he confronts the forces of darkness, he can be overwhelmed and feel himself alienated from others; he can experience depression, perhaps neurotic flight or withdrawal into ideas of reference, even a manic state, or the denial of reality by a dissolution of the ego. The therapist walks through this darkness with him, having withstood it himself, and allows this one, this individual, to negotiate for his own unique, creative meaning from the objective psyche. Eliade describes the same process in the training of the shaman in his book *Shamanism*.

There is another very important element, if anything the crucial element. This is *not* a process characterized by detachment and lack of personal involvement. Quite to the contrary, it is seldom possible outside of a deep concern for the other person involved in the encounter. Jung describes this element as transference, but not transference as a merely neurotic process as Freud did. Jung wrote about it in one of his more difficult essays, "Psychology of the Transference," which we have mentioned. Indeed, only as one is possessed by love can he know the reality of the self and enable another to find it. In one of the concluding paragraphs of his autobiography, he stated that love is the creator of all higher consciousness; that:

> Love "bears all things" and "endures all things" (I Cor. 13:7). These words say all there is to be said; nothing can be added to them. For we are in the deepest sense the victims and the instruments of cosmogonic "love." I put the word in quotation marks to indicate that I do not use it in its connotations of desiring, preferring, favoring, wishing, and similar feelings, but as something superior to the individual, a unified and undivided whole. Being a part, man cannot grasp the whole. He is at its mercy. He may assent to it, or rebel against it; but he is always caught up by it and enclosed within it. He is dependent upon it and is sustained by it. Love is his light and his darkness, whose end he cannot see. "Love ceases not"— whether he speaks with the "tongues of angels," or with scientific exactitude traces the life of the cell down to its uttermost source. Man can try to name love, showering upon it all the names at his command, and still he will involve himself in endless self-deceptions. If he possesses

a grain of wisdom, he will lay down his arms and name the unknown by the more unknown, *ignotum per ignotius*— that is, by the name of God. That is a confession of his subjection, his imperfection, and his dependence; but at the same time a testimony to his freedom to choose between truth and error.[28]

Love for him was as much the creative force, the beginning of any real knowledge, as for Plato.

Those who knew Jung well as a person or an analyst witness that he not only spoke of these things, he lived them. One of the most healing aspects of his therapy was that he radiated this quality. Among those who were his students, James Hillman for one has expanded this understanding of Jung in two of his books, *Suicide and the Soul* and *Insearch*.

This process of coming to creative relationship with the unconscious usually involves the whole person in contact with another human being. The process of integration requires and results in deepened human relationships. In the Bible, John put it well in his first letter when he said that no man could love God who did not love his brother.[29] Allowing one's self to have this kind of relationship is a costing experience. Often, if one is capable of it, he will find himself deluged, as men hunger so for this kind of reality. Michael Quoist gives dramatic evidence of this in his little book of meditations, entitled *Prayers*.

Jung has been accused by naturalistic scientists of being "religious" or "mystical." By rational theologians he has been accused of being naturalistic.[30] Jung maintained that he was scientific in the broad sense of the word. We have already stated that he did not describe his method carefully in any one place, but much of his use of language is reminiscent of the work of the school of linguistic analysis or logical empiricism. Let us see how the work and words of Jung fit in with the findings of these thinkers and also with the thinking of the American school of thought known as "general semantics." Then we can go on to see what kind of religious structure can be built within his basic framework.

CHAPTER VI

Spiritual Reality and the Words We Use

It may seem strange in a book on the knowledge of God to give a whole chapter to one school of none too reverent modern thought. But the school of logical empiricism not only has something important to say—it has had such an impact on other thinkers that we need to ask the reason. When one group carries as much weight as these men do today, it is not due solely to the importance of their thinking. Instead, it is more likely that these men have caught the spirit of the time, and are expressing explicitly what people already believe in less conscious ways.

My experience in a parish and in teaching convinces me that most people do see the world just about as these men do; the average person of Western European background who has not reflected deeply on his beliefs, or else had some dramatic religious experience, holds the same basic view of reality which this school has carefully elaborated. I have no general data to support this; I have tried unsuccessfully to get researchers on religious sociology to tackle the problem. However, I am quite sure that one of the problems the church is having in our day is that people accept uncritically the basic attitudes we are about to describe.

If this is the case, it is important to understand this point of view. The school of logical empiricism, or linguistic analysis, has laid out some of our basic unspoken attitudes in plain view for examination. Without meaning to, these thinkers have also pointed to a way in which these attitudes can be penetrated. This is important if religion is to be communicated.

This thinking had its philosophical beginnings around 1912, when Ludwig Wittgenstein at Cambridge began to ponder the meaning of the terms used in logic to search for truth. In his small but closely reasoned book *Tractatus Logico-Philosophicus*, he tried to show that only certain statements have logical meaning, and that much of the language used by philosophy, as well as by the ordinary person, is meaningless. As he saw it, the purpose of philosophy is to use logical forms to express meaning and clarity, and to do so, it must be able to see the limits of what can be said by being able to get back to statements that are true within themselves. Philosophy, in this view, is not a science dealing with metaphysical and ethical truths, since these cannot be expressed in language. Instead, it is an activity seeking truth essentially by playing "language games."

Between the two world wars students trying to relate philosophy to the new discoveries of physics and mathematics found Wittgenstein's thesis almost like coming up for air. Starting from a small group on the continent, the idea spread; the exodus from Germany brought leaders like Rudolf Carnap and Hans Reichenbach to this country, and others—Karl R. Popper, Alfred Jules Ayer at Oxford, Philipp Frank at Harvard—went on developing the "language game." In linguistic analysis philosophy had a plausible purpose; by using logic, mathematical language, and scientific knowledge as tools, it can arrive at word pictures in such simplified form that the actual working of language is revealed and meaning can be clearly expressed.

How can any hypothesis like Jung's, taking into account a meaningful reality apart from the space-time world, fit with the thinking of these men? In order to answer, we must first sketch their point of view in some detail, and then show how—by not being excluded—the way is left open to consider religious experiences and hypotheses, even though their meaning as direct encounters with the divine is not examined by any of the logical empiricists. To do this as clearly as we can and yet briefly, we shall consider one representative and brilliant work, *Language, Truth and Logic* by Alfred Jules Ayer, using it to emphasize more the basic tenets of this approach than its developed and finely drawn distinctions.

Truth and the Analysis of Language

According to Ayer, philosophy cannot ask, "What is truth?" because the question can only come out as, "Is this particular thing true?" Any answer must come by bringing up a proposition about it, either an analytic or a synthetic one. The main difference is that analytic propositions are valid (or false) in themselves without referring to any matter of fact, while synthetic propositions involve experience and observations. For instance, the statement "Some men are lazy" is synthetic; one has to gather this from facts about people. But saying "Either some men are lazy or none are" is certain in itself; it is a tautology or analytic proposition. It tells us nothing about "the real world out there" but only how these symbols or words are used in a certain way.

Logic and mathematics are typical systems of analytic propositions. If we multiply 7858 x 63978, we add no new information, except about the possibilities of counting. A mind that was large and fast enough would not need arithmetic. It would either see an actual quantity or arrive at the calculation as easily as we see that "2 + 2 = 4." In the same way, a mind that was infinite would have no need for logic or systems of geometry, or computer processing to land a space capsule on the moon. It would simply "see" the moment by moment positions of earth and moon and capsule and "know" the relative pull of each body and the correct speed and direction. But since our senses do not provide us with reliable information about even things right at hand, we are forced to rely on the axiomatic propositions of logic in order to figure out what it is our eyes or ears or noses have tried to tell us.

Thus, as this school holds, man has one way of reaching absolute, logical certainty. He starts with a proposition so elementary that it is true in itself,* which can be proved logically without looking at any fact outside of the symbols themselves and the ordinary steps of logical demonstration. By using similar sets of propositions mathematically, he is able to draw out their implications step by step so accurately that, as we know for instance, he is able to direct a mechanism 35 million miles away in orbit around Mars. "We see, then," Ayer says, "that there is nothing mysterious about the apodeictic (or incontrovertible) certainty of logic and mathematics."[1] Yet, Kurt Gödel's proof, which we shall come back to shortly, has revealed something quite different.

Such a logical or mathematical system, however, tells only about itself until it is related to a set of actual observations about the world. Thus the second kind of proposition, the synthetic, makes assertions about the world in which we live. We learn whether they are valid or not by verification; we go back to the experience and check out the understanding we have received from it. But only the experience of the five senses is considered by these thinkers.

Since it is impossible to verify most of the statements of metaphysics, theology, and ethics on the basis of sensory ex-

---

* An analytic proposition or tautology.

periences, we cannot say that they are true or false. We can only say that they are meaningless; they do not have experiential meaning. They may express emotion in a simple or more developed manner, but that is all. The reason for accepting the propositions of science is that they work, while the propositions of metaphysics get us nowhere and build no base for knowledge. Ayer writes:

> Actually, we shall see that the only test to which a form of scientific procedure which satisfies the necessary condition of self-consistency is subject, is the test of its success in practice.[2] (And, again) . . . The philosopher must be content to record the facts of scientific procedure. If he seeks to justify it, beyond showing that it is self-consistent, he will find himself involved in spurious problems.[2]

Thus there is no certain knowledge about an experienceable reality. We have only propositions which have either a low probability level or a very high one. We are dealing in degrees of probability in dealing with experience, not with logical certainty.

An example of Ayer's analysis will make this more understandable. He writes:

> A simpler and clearer instance of the way in which a consideration of grammar leads to metaphysics is the case of the metaphysical concept of Being. The origin of our temptation to raise questions about Being, which no conceivable experience would enable us to answer, lies in the fact that, in our language, sentences which express existential propositions and sentences which express attributive propositions may be of the same grammatical form. For instance, the sentences "Martyrs exist" and "Martyrs suffer" both consist of a noun followed by an intransitive verb, and the fact that they have grammatically the same appearance leads one to assume that they are of the same logical type. It is seen that in the proposition "Martyrs suffer," the members of a certain species are credited with a certain attribute, and it is sometimes assumed that the same thing is true of such a proposition as "Martyrs exist." If this were actually the case, it would, indeed, be as legitimate to speculate about the Being of martyrs as it is to speculate about their suffering. But, as Kant pointed out, existence is not an attribute. For, when we ascribe an attribute to a thing, we covertly assert that it exists: so that if existence were itself an attribute, it would follow that all positive existential propositions were tautologies, and all negative existential propositions

self-contradictory; and this is not the case. So that those who raise questions about Being which are based on the assumption that existence is an attribute are guilty of following grammar beyond the boundaries of sense.[3]

Ayer proceeds to show that most of the major disputes in philosophy are meaningless, as well as most theological discussions, ideas, and arguments; ethics as a science of norms also disappears. He states that

> ... although the greater part of metaphysics is merely the embodiment of humdrum errors, there remain a number of metaphysical passages which are the work of genuine mystical feeling; and they may more plausibly be held to have moral or aesthetic value. But, as far as we are concerned, the distinction between the kind of metaphysics that is produced by a philosopher who has been duped by grammar, and the kind that is produced by a mystic who is trying to express the inexpressible, is of no great importance: what is important to us is to realize that even the utterances of the metaphysician who is attempting to expound a vision are literally senseless; so that henceforth we may pursue our philosophical researches with as little regard for them as for the more inglorious kind of metaphysics which comes from a failure to understand the workings of our language.[4]

Evidently he had some second thoughts, for farther on he remarks:

> We do not deny *a priori* that the mystic is able to discover truths by his own special methods. We wait to hear what are the propositions which embody his discoveries, in order to see whether they are verified or confuted by our empirical observations.[5]

Thus Ayer, on his own, opens a loophole in the system. But after his undoubtedly correct analysis of much of philosophy and theology, he leaves people right where they are today, with the feeling that the only experiences that count are those of the five senses. How, then, can we widen this loophole for people? We shall come back to his use of the word "mystic."

These analyses of man's logic and his sense experience demonstrate how, on the basis of hypothetical, even imperfect conclusions about the world, man has been able to accomplish practical, scientific results that had existed only in imagination. This fact in itself points the way to a similarly hypothetical and empirical theology with similarly practical results for man himself. Let us see how this understanding can be developed, considering first one basic correction of the thinking we are discussing.

The Loophole

As Kurt Gödel has shown,* logic alone cannot account for the certainty man achieves by the method Ayer describes so carefully and well. Not even the simplest system of logic—arithmetic—can be proved logically within itself. Such systems apparently start from an intuition or assumption which is *given*, and on which the system is built step by step. But man has no proof that such a system is valid or valuable except to test it by making use of it in the world of experience. Thus it is not only synthetic propositions which require testing and verification. Indeed, the only way man becomes sure of any of the knowledge he is given, mathematics included, is that he has tried it and it works.

What Jung suggests is that there is equally good reason to test the belief that man is also given valuable experiences of a psychoid or spiritual reality. And Jung's propositions have already been verified by many persons who have worked with the experiences he described, and have found that there are empirical truths which can be obtained other than through the five senses. In fact, I have yet to find anyone who has investigated these experiences and hypotheses *open-mindedly* who has not found verification of them.

In addition, the same experiences often produce results that are quite observable by others. Many persons who have followed Jung's insights have returned from illness to health and well-being. They have been able to handle depression, neurosis, and come to the point where they could work more creatively than ever before. This is a success which is important. One wishes that someone might have introduced Ludwig Wittgenstein to Jung's psychology so that his life need not have been such a nightmare of depression and human alienation. As a whole it does not seem that Wittgenstein's method has had much practical human results, any more than Kierkegaard's or Nietzsche's did.

A somewhat different view of these experiences is needed, however, from the popular meaning of the word "mystical," which Ayer makes no effort to penetrate.[6] The usual meaning is that suggested by Eastern religions, of a coming into experiential oneness with all reality. This seems to be the kind of

---

* See p. 99.

127

experience Alan Watts is describing in telling about his use of drugs in *The Joyous Cosmology.* This kind of experience is given only to a few, and then only a few times in life.

But there is another, certainly more frequent experience in which the ego, by coming into contact with an autonomous, nonphysical content found in the psyche, takes in something new. The dream and the vision are specific ways in which this kind of experience happens. Mythological writing expresses the same kind of contact as does the rest of art—dramatic, plastic, or literary. It is also portrayed in certain studies of literature such as Martin Lings' profound little book, *Shakespeare in the Light of Sacred Art.*

It is just this range of experience which is seldom considered as offering direct value for human life. Some of these experiences may be seen as exciting for psychical research, or necessary for the psychiatrist to understand, or an interesting device for the movies, but they are not regarded by many people as adding anything to one's daily life. Logical empiricism goes even further and eliminates them from discussion entirely by accepting the hypothesis that only experiences of the five senses can be verified and known by man as meaningful. Instead, what we are proposing is that man has three different ways of understanding and experiencing, and that all three can be known in a meaningful way and verified, rather than only the first two. These are:

> First, the ability to make logical and mathematical propositions which are meaningful to those who understand the symbols; these symbols, however, have no relationship to our concrete experiences until they are placed in synthesis with such experience.

> Second, experiences derived from the outer, physical world which are conveyed to us through the five senses and through the sixth sense which relates one to his own body. These are always tentative and hypothetical.

> Third, experiences of an inner, psychoid world which intrude upon men with the same autonomy as experiences of the senses, and are verifiable, although in a more difficult way than verifying an observation in physical science; a discussion of these could easily be the subject for a whole book.

We can identify eight of this third group of experiences, as follows:

1. There are first of all dreams and visions, which I have described at some length in my book *Dreams: The Dark Speech of the Spirit.* Most of the ordinary hypotheses about the meaning of dreams are woefully inadequate, as Freud showed in detail in *The Interpretation of Dreams,* and they are not discussed at all in logical empiricism.

2. Next are various religious experiences, which are sometimes different in form but related to dreams, and are chiefly set apart by the fact that the experience is charged with a numinous intensity; some tremendous power seems to be breaking forth from the unconscious. This is described by William James in *The Varieties of Religious Experience,* and in many of Jung's writings. Rudolf Otto also made an excellent analysis of this kind of experience in *The Idea of the Holy,* although it was limited because Otto had no theory of the unconscious and did not consider the dream.

The mystical experience, in both the ways we have mentioned, appears as one very significant form of some contact with a transpersonal reality, and in another book I have examined experiences of speaking in tongues in some detail. I find it difficult, to say the least, to understand this experience and many of the things that continue to happen around it unless it is seen as a similar contact.[7] Experiences of healing that occur sacramentally appear to be further evidences of some touch with a creative aspect of nonphysical reality, and I have made a very thorough study of these phenomena in still another book, *Healing and Christianity.*

The need for these studies of religious experience seems obvious. Because of prejudice and the demand to be certain in some way about the existence of God, serious theologians have avoided examining this field of experience. Thinking about God is not nearly as difficult and dangerous as opening oneself to experiences of God. One runs a real risk of being misled, but a greater risk of finding that God does break through and one's human thought is not large enough to meet Him even half-way. What few theologians seem to realize, however, is how close it really is to nonsense to talk about God as an analytic proposition unless one is willing to carry his proposition over to particular experiences and run the risk of being made hash of. It is true that some people confuse religious experience and emotional excitement, but the job of the theologian is to set up criteria to distinguish these two experiences—not to eliminate encounters with God.

3. Then there are experiences of anxiety, depression, dissociation and hallucination which overwhelm the ego. These operate on their own and are experienced by far more people than admit to it in public. Although these experiences often compensate for a rigid ego development or preoccupation with consciousness, they also open people to a destructive aspect which cannot be pinned just to the individual psyche. It is often difficult to tell whether a depression or anxiety is caused primarily by personal factors, starting from a painful childhood, or by these psychoid realities, which Jesus (and the church in its strongest days) called the demonic.

Jung was forced into a study of these destructive contents, as he told me personally, because the traditional therapy has little effect in healing such illness, and at the same time the church in Switzerland would not touch these problems of the human psyche which are essentially spiritual in nature. Pastors and ministers were not interested, but Jung, with his passion to heal, had to pick up the task of dealing with invasions from this *psychoid* world. In my own counseling I have found cases where depression remains after the personal factors have been dealt with. Then one can give little help in bringing about a permanent change until the individual sees that he is attacked by forces from beyond his own psyche and must seek creative spiritual powers to aid in struggling against them.

At the opposite extreme I have found college students who think they are "sick" when in reality they are undergoing experiences much like those of the shamans, as Eliade has described them in *Shamanism*, but without any frame of reference for integrating experiences of the spiritual world. One who really knows the depth of man will realize the reality of these spiritual invasions. Personally, my own encounters with this realm have given me ample evidence of the negative side of spiritual reality to know that evil exists. These are empirical experiences which can be verified. Primitive people who have not developed stable egos are particularly prone to such experiences. Indeed these are "natural" for such collective societies.

4. Again, there is the imprint and the replay of memory, both of these inner sensory experiences, and also of those that come through the physical senses. Memories can sometimes be recalled and sometimes not, and these memories seem to have an effect on behavior whether the person is consciously aware of them or not. Man's capacity for memory is an interesting and hardly explained experience in purely physical terms,

as Arthur O. Lovejoy shows so well in *The Revolt Against Dualism.*

5. Still another strange and scarcely explained phenomenon is the ability of certain practiced individuals to turn in upon the spontaneous flow of images known as phantasy (from the Greek word for appearance). This is quite different from day dreams, in which the ego organizes memories, desires, and even these same images into a diversion, an interlude of play to get away from the concerns of the outer world. Phantasy is more spontaneous and more demanding than day dreaming. It is closely akin to the vision and has the quality of religious meditation. Myth appears to be related to this capacity. Its stories are apparently woven around phantasies which have meaning for more than one individual. The phantasy novels of George MacDonald are pure examples of this process, and it can be seen in much good literature.

6. There appears to be a similar capacity to grasp mathematical and other abstract concepts intuitively or imaginatively. Both Kurt Gödel and Albert Einstein have indicated that such concepts probably originate largely from an inner experience and perception of them, given where the capacity for pure reason creates intense interest and the ability to use and develop what is given. We have discussed Gödel's understanding of the way his own mind functioned, and Einstein's reported remark to Jung is the classic description. Asked if he had to work very hard to produce his equations, Einstein smiled. "Oh, no," he said, "I meditate and the numbers dance before me." This understanding of an intuitive basis underlying mathematical concepts follows the thought of Plato and also of the realists in the Middle Ages.

7. In the more concrete field of science, much of our knowledge also seems to come through intuitive flashes which suddenly plug in a connection or open a door on understanding. These intuitions are related to visions, but they take more the form of ideas than of straight images. Both Friedrich Dessauer (whom we have quoted) and Max Knoll, the inventor of the electron microscope, have written on the significance of this intuitive or revelatory aspect of science, and particularly about the way science itself has been changed through this process.[8]

In addition, it has been suggested by Paul K. Feyerabend, of the University of California, one of the most recent and forward-looking students of the philosophy of science, that the discoveries and the method of science both depend in large measure on freeing the imagination and learning to use it creatively.[9] This ability of man, which is stressed by so many scientific writers, appears to have the closest relation to the practice of phantasy which we have just discussed.

8. Finally, there are the extrasensory experiences reported by Rhine and many other researchers in psychical phenomena. The most common are: telepathy and precognition (experience across space and time) and psychokinesis (physical events induced by psychic factors). These experiences, which appear to be comparatively rare, are told by all peoples from the ancient Greeks to occurrences like Swedenborg's vision of the Stockholm fire, and those among the primitive bushmen, described by Van der Post in *The Lost World of the Kalahari* and *The Heart of the Hunter.* Such occurrences can also be duplicated in the laboratory situation, for instance, as in the fascinating experiments at Maimonides Medical Center in New York, reported by Montague Ullman and Stanley Krippner in *Dream Studies and Telepathy.* Instances of both kinds are cited in my book *Dreams: The Dark Speech of the Spirit.*[10]

ESP need not occur frequently to have a significant place in the development of one's world view; the significance of radium for our present understanding of matter certainly did not depend on its being found in a natural free state very often. Instead, certain persons seem to be particularly sensitive to this kind of response, and at times hypnotism seems to evoke it. It apparently does not depend on proximity in space, as the experiments conducted between Apollo 14 and earth suggest, which are described in the January 1972 issue of *Mental Health Digest.* ESP appears to be simply a fact, but one which, as yet, might as well not exist for all the difference it makes in the way most people understand the world.

Along with these capacities, men have the added ability to put words together in metaphysical constructions, based on symbols of all kinds and varying from apparent phantasy to the very rational. It is against the latter rational constructions that the logical empiricists are in such revolt, and rightly. Words can have connection with reality only when they are used to represent images which have that connection. If they do not represent either actual outer experience or some inner experience such as the above eight, then the jargon may be intoned like profound thought, but still be as non-sensical as Lewis Carroll's "Jabberwocky." * As Jung remarked about

---

*All protests on behalf of *Alice* are gratefully accepted, since Dodg-

Hegel and other modern German philosophers, the words may tell something about the personal psychology of the author but little more.

But these eight experiences, as far as most people are concerned, will have to be investigated and re-evalued to provide much connection with reality. For most people, as for the logical empiricists, an experience that has to be looked for within man can be only subjective, part of a morass of non-objectivity. These experiences, people feel, might be of interest to a few specialized scientists, but otherwise the only valid reason for investigating them is to get unbalanced people back on the right track emotionally.

If it can be admitted, however, that these eight experiences can be investigated legitimately for *objective* content, then the scope of empirical inquiry is greatly widened. The most comprehensive studies of these phenomena make it difficult, if not absurd, to derive them from ordinary sense experience, although they use elements of sense experience almost as a language. On the contrary, there is even the possibility that the form of sense experience—although not the content—may be given by and through the individual psyche. It is known that animals and pre-natal babies have physiological experiences similar to dreaming, and it can well be surmised that they are observing images. Experimental data strongly suggests that higher animals are born with a variety of images to which their actions and perceptions are related.

Some of the most recent support for this comes from experiments with certain migratory birds kept in captivity. At migration time, when the birds become very active at night, they are placed in a planetarium in special cages that record every movement, and give only a view of the planetarium stars. No matter how the axis of these stars is rotated, in the spring the birds spend all night trying to hop up the sloping sides of their cages towards the northern heavens of the planetarium; in the fall every movement is towards the southern stars, whatever the actual direction.[11] These birds seem to carry some sort of inborn images relating to the star pattern of the sky. Thus, if even birds start life able to "see" selectively, what a complex of images may possibly play into the decisions of human beings.

If this is true, an expanded empiricism is indicated. Such

son, the mathematician and logician, may have been using Lewis Carroll's nonsense verse to express much this same thing.

an approach to men's experiences could easily be the base for an empirical theology which could be grasped by anyone willing to submit to the necessary experiences and discover its truth. Many persons have discovered just this; they have asked for verification and found it as they followed the way laid out by Jesus of Nazareth and the great spiritual directors of Christianity. These persons have come to know the objectivity of the world of spirit and the necessity of dealing with it.

This encounter with religious reality is quite different from only working with ideas. If one is actually to encounter the things found in the psyche which activate men to love or hate, to arouse themselves to action or be lulled into letting go of life, he must be ready for a demanding occupation that requires commitment. There is a negative side to these contents which is dangerous. One is pushed and pulled himself, and he has to learn how to become open to the creative side. The unique quality of the religion of Jesus and his followers was the idea that each man might have his own encounter with the Holy Spirit by standing with the living Christ who has defeated evil. As the individual comes to rely upon Christ, he is able to withstand whatever he must meet.

The trouble is that after Constantine's conversion the practice changed, although the idea remained. The people in a whole culture who were not prepared to receive the reality of Christianity were forced to swallow its faith whole, and for many it was encountered as a far off idea, accepted in a spirit of expediency. But like so many great tragedies, there was the seed of something else, something on which Jung has commented frequently. A religious system grew up which was able to convey the insights of the religious encounter without exposing those who are not yet strong enough to deal with the direct divine encounter itself. A "Christian world," accepting the insights derived from Christian experience, became a theoretical possibility.

But the form that is put together to convey these insights— whether it is the idea of an omniscient, omnipresent Absolute, or an idea of the "ground of being"—still cannot be the end product. There must still be an experience, an encounter from which the insights arise if the form in which they are expressed is to have value and power. There must be someone, priest, or prophet, or seer, or shaman, who is able to encounter the experiences and mediate them to others. At the same time an empirical theology—or *any* theology, for that matter—also requires theologians who know the religious encounter as a part of their own being, and also understand it as a reality separate from oneself, which can be communicated both in words and action. The purpose of a real theology is to deal with autonomous, nonphysical realities which have actual results for human life, and to show men the evidences of these results.

There is one great difficulty with an empirical theology, however. Because it deals with qualities, rather than with measurable quantities, it is difficult to describe and communicate. As yet man has devised no form like mathematics for measuring and comparing the quality of experiences. As Kurt Gödel has suggested, it was a purely historical accident that mathematics developed along quantitative lines.[12] But because of this the scientific era from its beginning has set aside qualitative distinctions and minimized them, making it difficult to understand these distinctions. Amedeo Giorgi has shown in *Psychology as a Human Science* just how stuck we are in numerical measuring. Thus, it is important for us to reveal and describe differences in quality in order to communicate as clearly as we can the meaning of Christian experiences. For this purpose the only tool we have is careful human language. Let us look at a further understanding of this.

General Semantics and Religious Experience

At the same time that logical empiricism was developing in England, the general semantics movement grew up in the United States. Although it began outside of the academic community, and was accepted only slowly, it has had a growing influence. Its founder Alfred Korzybski believed that a wrong use of language was leading man and the culture into all sorts of difficulties. He stressed the importance of symbols in human life and development; the Aristotelian use of them, he felt, led into many dead ends.

Because men have the ability to abstract from experience and to record these abstractions, using symbols to pass on information from generation to generation, they have developed a faculty which Korzybski calls "time-binding." The same process, however, can make man the tool, rather the guide, of the symbols which are responsible for his very humanness. For this reason the general semantics movement has attempted to develop a non-Aristotelian logic based on the model of scientific procedure in order to give us instruments through which we can better use these symbols.

An empirical theology requires that we deal with a variety

of experiences which are not amenable to mathematical or quantitative reduction. Therefore, it is of the utmost importance in theology to use words and symbols carefully and descriptively of actual experiences, and avoid metaphysical nonsense. General semantics offers us some very practical tools for dealing with the qualitative with the least possible error. In presenting this material I am indebted to the excellent short summary by Kenneth G. Johnson, *General Semantics: An Outline Survey.*[13]

All symbols are abstractions. The symbol, insofar as it is a symbol, represents only an aspect of that which it stands for. This is particularly true of words, which are very abstract symbols. In spite of their importance, words are far different from things; they convey meaning only because people have agreed that a certain meaning goes along with certain sounds.

The use of words is very similar to sketching a map of a territory. While few of us would confuse a map with the roads and towns it represents, there are many who forget that the mountain passes and meadows and deserts are quite different things from the *words* which map a description around them. Sense experience itself is one level of abstraction from the outer world, and words are a further abstraction. Yet many people fall into the absurdity of identifying their words with the things which are referred to. They seem to believe, "What I say about something is what that something is." We can put this in an equation: "What I say" = what is. The absurdity of this is seen when we write the same equation in another way:

Some set of words = something that is not words.

Language involves classification, and classification is necessary if we are to reduce the manifold of experience to a manageable content. Language, however, tends to make us forget the differences between individual things, although science tells us that no two items are identical. Even the smallest quanta of energy may not be identical, and, even like atoms, the smallest particles do not seem always to function identically. All dogs are not the same . . . or men . . . or black men . . . or religious experiences. We must be careful in classifying experiences because we are abstracting and drawing the curtain on uniqueness.

A term or principle of "non-allness" is very important as a reminder that one cannot know all about anything. Empirical knowledge of either the physical or the non-physical world is never complete, and we know only a part of things. Since our knowledge is never exhaustive, we often concentrate on one aspect of an object to learn about it, purposely ignoring factors which are irrelevant to our particular interest. If this is true of studying a tomato plant or an animal, how much more true it is of knowing human beings. Similarly, if we have an experience of something transcendent (an archetype in Jung's language—an angel or demon in Christian language), or even of God, we cannot presume to know all about what we have experienced. Therefore much of what we say about an object or an experience will be tentative and subject to revision. The use of the word "all," except in specific situations, or as applied to identical, mathematical relationships, usually shows that one is not thinking or speaking very accurately.

Language tends to be static whereas life is dynamic. It is difficult in language to express progressive change. Abstractions remain fixed even though the things they are abstracted from continually change. Steve today is not the same as Steve two years ago; this is true of many objects of experience, particularly living ones. George Bernard Shaw is reported to have said, "The only man who behaves sensibly is my tailor; he takes my measure anew each time he sees me, whilst all the rest go on with their old measurements and expect me to fit them." Or, as Heraclitus reminded men in the fifth century B.C., "we can never step into the same river twice." This is difficult for us to accept and deal with linguistically, and so observations about objects and events should be dated.

Because of the structure of language we are led to confuse factual observations with inferences or assumptions about facts. This leads to a morass of confusion. A statement of fact can be made only after observation, while inferences can be made before or after having observed. There is no harm in inferences and assumptions, but they must not be confused with facts. Valid theology is built upon the converging experiences and inferences of those who have experienced numinous or religious contents. This is not much different from the way quantum mechanics has been built upon observation and inference, brought into line by going back again and again to test the actual behavior of sub-atomic particles. Theologians, thus, should be experts in religious experience, in addition to understanding the history and use of ideas and thought.

The static nature of language and its tendency towards classification tend to push us towards *either/or evaluations.* Language is full of polar opposites. Using an either/or statement tends to suggest to us that we know "all" about something. Yet the normal or statistical curve is a much better description of the way we find most things than *either/or words*. These may be valid for logic and mathematics which are not directly related to experience, but they are seldom applicable to life itself. Most of life's experiences and judgments belong to a many-point scale and cannot be squeezed into an *either/or judgment*.

Just as language has a tendency to put things together that do not belong together, it sometimes separates things which do not belong apart. Body and mind are so separated, as are time and space. Our words indicate that stupidity and intelligence, or beauty and the beast are worlds apart, but "it ain't necessarily so." Either objects or qualities may be far more closely linked than our words portray. Along with this tendency to separate things out, we also tend to look for just one cause for an event, rather than seeing that the whole field of objects forms an organic whole.

The whole problem of how things interact is very difficult to convey in ordinary language. The usual form of a transitive sentence is *actor-action-subject*. There is not the slightest hint in this grammar that the actor, too, is usually changed by his action. This is particularly true of those who think they can observe the religious experience objectively. Yet if they actually come into contact with the divine they are themselves changed. There is not even impartial observation of the smallest atom, let alone of the divine. The idea that man could be an impartial observer belonged to 19th century science, and many 20th century theologians and philosophers are still caught in this framework.

To say that subject and object interact, however, does not mean that there is no distinction between them. Rather, it is to say that man is a part of the field in which he acts. He is acted upon as he acts. These interactions are so complex that we can know only a small part of them. If God and/or teleological factors are included within the field, the complexity and depth of relationship become staggering. There are then few simple answers.

Whenever we classify we eliminate details and differences. We also forget that there are different levels of abstraction. People often get them mixed up because language makes little distinction between these various levels. Kenneth Johnson quotes from Anatol Rapoport's *Science and the Goals of Man*:

Words are abstractions made of things; reports are abstractions made of experience; inferences are abstractions made of descriptions. When people react to words as if they were things, to inferences as if they were descriptions, etc., they are confusing levels of abstraction.[14]

Johnson then asks the reader to "remember the boy who 'was'

> A menace to society.
> A thief.
> A juvenile delinquent.
> A 10-year-old boy who took some tomatoes from a neighbor's garden without asking permission." [14]

Exact communication is difficult except in the defined symbols of mathematics or in sciences which can be described in mathematical terms. As we have noted, many of the important human experiences cannot be so described. Experience has a unique subjective relationship which cannot be entirely shared —in one's own experience, a "to-me-ness." This is true of nearly all human encounters, and particularly so of meaningful ones. This is true of archetypal experience, of the dream and the religious experience, of the aesthetic experience. Where common experiences can be played upon, and re-created in imagination, the language of myth, literature, and poetry can often express this kind of meaning better than more structured words. S. I. Hayakawa has written:

> What should be understood when people tell us that the plays of Shakespeare or the poems of Milton or Dante are "eternally true" is that they produce in us attitudes toward our fellow men, an understanding of ourselves, or feelings of deep moral obligation that are valuable to humanity under any conceivable circumstances.[15]

Mathematical language can communicate specifically because it confines itself entirely to the quantitative element of an experience. But because this is seldom of any importance in the greatest experiences of life is no reason to give up on trying to communicate them. It is true that words alone cannot contain their meaning; the words must be joined to experience. For this reason it is important to work harder at coming to know human experience of many kinds—in relationship with men, with the divine, with the archetypes, with the arts. It is then our task to seek words and methods of communication which can convey and join these experiences so that we may have common ground with other people when we come together to discuss and share them. Here is one great value of myth, poetry and artistic imagery of all kinds. This is one aspect of a creative theology.

There are few words more important to understand than the verb *to know*. It can mean many different things, and when we use it we should be clear which meaning we intend. It can mean to know from experience, either outer sensory experience or inner autonomous experience. These are easy to confuse, as when we wake from a dream and do not know where we are, or, with others, when we share a common experience but unconsciously place such different values on it that a door closes between two separate experiences. If one speaks of "knowing" as if he had final, certain knowledge, it is probably from a logical point of view, and he is avoiding having to say anything about his actual experience.

Then there is knowledge which we have received through reading or listening. This is knowledge from someone else's authority, at best an abstraction from someone else's abstraction of an event. There is knowledge that you *know* you don't know. Most discoveries, scientific and otherwise, occur only when men realize that they do not know. Ignorance of what we don't know, on the other hand, can have serious results. Sometimes we "know" what is not so, and "what ails most people," as Adolf Meyer of Johns Hopkins once said, "is not that they are ignorant, but that they know too much that isn't so."

There is one last use of the word knowledge. It is used for what we believe with such conviction that we feel we "know." Many people relegate religious knowledge to this last category. Instead it belongs clearly to the first kind of knowing. Religious knowledge is genuine "knowing" of an *other* which comes to us through non-sensory experience. The task of religion is not simply to convince, but to help one relate to this *other*, to be known by it, and to know it as deeply and richly as possible.

The task of theology is to place this "knowing," this experience, within the context of man's total experience. Any philosophy which will examine and deal with all of man's experience then, most probably will become a theology as well as a philosophy. To accept the experience of the divine encounter as a part of man's life, one must shape a world view in which the concept "God" holds a very significant place, and this is theology. Let us now turn to the implications for Christian theology which can be drawn from these analyses, particularly from Jung's descriptions of men's experiences of a realm of spiritual or psychoid reality.

PART II

The Importance of Christianity

CHAPTER VII

WHAT CAN WE SAY ABOUT GOD?

Theology has often been called the science of God. It attempts to put into words what can be known about God, and then to show how this knowledge is connected with what people have learned about the world and themselves. To develop this understanding, theology has long used a "natural language," which grew up in much the same way among most peoples everywhere. But today, as we have seen, there is confusion and even despair among theologians because people find little connection between these natural words—words like "God," "soul," "spirit," "mind"—and their actual experiences of the world.

At the same time, we have found a few men trying, somewhat timidly, to relate these natural words to their understanding of the world. These are scientists like the physicist Werner Heisenberg whom we quoted at length in Chapter V.* They have found that the natural language describes the world around us better than precise scientific words like "mass," "inertia," "causality." Science itself has finally realized that such terms, while easier to deal with, are too exact and limited to describe adequately what the world is like.

Such descriptions provided the certainty and security that were needed for the growth of Newtonian physics. But the twentieth century physicist has left this far behind; he is no longer sure that he understands matter and its workings, and so he is more open to other descriptive words and to experiences which cannot be explained completely.

We have also seen that modern thinkers are increasingly less sure that men can obtain any knowledge just by thinking. If the word "God" is to have meaning, it will be the result of more than just a chain of logical thinking. If God has meaning for men's lives, this will come from a knowledge of God resulting from their experiences or encounters with the divine. Ontological analysis, deductive reasoning from first principles, or reasoning

---

* See pp. 95 f.

about purpose seen in the universe may support man's understanding of God, but the knowledge must be first given by something that man experiences. In addition, man also requires a framework or model of his understanding of the world and himself in which such experiences, such facts about God, are taken into account.

In the preceding pages we have presented such a model. If this understanding can be accepted as representing the actual way man knows himself and his world, then the idea of God can make a lot of sense; and man's theological understanding which he has built up over the ages at some cost, not only makes good sense, but deserves to be looked at carefully and given serious consideration. It may even tell something very important about the world in which we live.

The importance of such a model can hardly be overestimated. Man can collect facts and data until doomsday, but until he can fit them together into some meaningful relationship or system, he has no grasp of the whole, no understanding that can compel him to weigh and try to understand new facts. Everyone has some model, some idea of what the world is like. The important thing is to have a model that takes into account as many of the significant facts as possible, those of the scientific world as well as facts about God and God's encounter with men.

Whatever model one accepts is subject to change and correction and the one we have presented is no exception. However, the model of the world that we have presented in the foregoing pages is more adequate than the rigid and certain model which was so common in the nineteenth century and which still lies behind the thinking (or lack of it) of most people of our time. A great deal of lack of belief in our time is the result of a scientific world view which science itself has discarded.

The Model and the Experiences

According to the model we have suggested, man is not only in touch with the space-time or material world, the world of sociology and research methods and behaviorism; he is also in touch with a non-space-time or spiritual world of images and intuitions, dreams, and phantasies, myths and numinous contents which are autonomous and of more than individual significance. In each world there are vast numbers of experiences that apply just to the immediate situation, and only comparatively few that are strikingly significant for understanding the ultimate nature of that world and the course of its development. One could spend a lifetime digging up old graveyards, and never get near a fossil that had importance for anthropology. Or, he could take pictures for the family album year in and year out without spotting a trace of the radiation exposure that helped start the Curies on their search for a new element. Some experiences are simply more important scientifically than others.

The same thing is true in the psychoid or spiritual world. There are the ordinary vague dreams, the phantasies when one is quiet, say on a plane or bus, the images brought up by a folk song over the radio. Indeed, as one begins to take this other world seriously, he may be flooded by vast numbers of these emotionally charged, intangible and immeasurably volatile images. There seems about as much reason to them as the savage finds in his sensations of the physical world like watching the decaying leaves on a forest floor without understanding how this contributes to the growth of the trees themselves.

But then, unexpectedly, a numinous experience or a powerful dream breaks in upon one and strikes at the very center of his being. His former complacency is shattered, a meaninglessness is healed, an anxiety washed out, often a physical illness disappears; an inner confidence is given, a whole direction in life becomes apparent, and a secure conviction about the nature of reality is established. In other words, there are long-range and significant results in the observable, outer world.[1]

It is difficult to see how one such experience could have this kind of effect if it were purely and simply a subjective, inner experience. Such effects are quite understandable, however, in terms of the model we have presented. If these experiences are actually contacts with an objective center of meaning which men have called God, then it is not at all strange that they should have such influence and results in a man's life. In effect, a powerful new psychoid factor takes over, reorganizing an individual's whole psychic reality.

There is one major difference between experiences coming from this realm and those of the physical world. When a man sets out to discover the nature of the physical world, his own individual activity is of prime importance. He achieves results by directed, analytical thinking. It is true that this requires the help of intuition, as so many students of the philosophy of science have shown. But intuitive "inspiration" does not often come to the scientist—and it is not often used when it does come—unless he has done his homework of observing, recording, classifying, hypothesizing, analyzing and comparing. The knowledge that is given from the nonphysical or spiritual realm comes in quite a different way.

In their nature, our psyches (both conscious and unconscious) seem to be much more like the spiritual world than the physical world. The discovery of the spiritual world also takes far less effort on our part. Instead, it is thrust upon us. The central meaning of the nonphysical or spiritual world seems to wish to communicate itself to us, to convey to us some relationship with itself and some experience of its centrality and purposefulness. It is not man's ego task to storm heaven and search out such experiences, nor will searching bring much in the way of knowledge unless God is seeking to give of himself. At the same time, man must attend these experiences in which God does give of himself, trying to relate them to the rest of life, although at times even the relations are given in the experience itself.

What is required of man is the openness to allow such experience a place in his life. Then one will want to see what it means for him; and to find this out, thinking is important, but even here the experience itself is the primary guide. John Sanford in an article in *The Well Tended Tree*,[2] a group of essays into the spirit of our time, has suggested that religious experience might be compared to a scientist studying an atom, who suddenly found that the atom was reaching out to discover the scientist far more than the other way around.

Within this understanding, the pitfalls of Pelagianism and predestination are both avoided. The giving of the experience of Himself depends entirely upon God. It is up to man to supply an ego interested in receiving and integrating such experiences. Unless there is an ego strong enough to receive and to use, the giving is in vain, and most often nothing is given. No religion stresses egolessness more than Zen Buddhism, and yet the state of *satori* is only achieved as the result of the most strenuous discipline. The one-sided ideas of religious development—at one extreme, that it comes solely as the result of man's personal effort, and at the other, that man can do nothing but wait for divine intervention—are based on *either/or logic*, which is not very good logic. Because at times one side needs to be stressed more than the other, we must not be caught and carried to the point of excluding the other side entirely. Both are necessary, and the important question is: which influence has become neglected, and to what degree?

146

This question also needs to be asked individually. I remember a friend who once said to me: "I have the most extraordinary religious experiences. It would be so easy for me to be sucked in if I were not careful. If I took them seriously, I would probably end up forgetting everything I have worked for and become a one-sided religious believer." What is the stress that makes it possible for such a person to be flooded with these experiences, and yet simply ignore them? And at the same time, what is the lack in our culture that actually makes many people prefer to know nothing of such experiences, not even bothering to read about them, although, as we have noted, there are some excellent studies available? Of course, there are those who resolutely maintain that the world is flat, that certain antibiotics have no effect upon the course of disease, and that there is no such thing as man's unconscious. While most of us would scarcely admit to being so foolish about other things, we still treat these experiences, which try to touch us, as if they had no place in our lives. We shall have more to say about this later.

The experience of God does bear in upon some men, however, with enough power to make them take what is happening seriously. Often they are struck by loss of meaning, or by anxiety or depression, until they do focus attention and action upon the experience. Indeed, the very experiences of depression and anxiety can be viewed as negative religious experiences, as the anguish of the psyche which is avoiding this kind of experience, or has been separated from it by social conditioning.

For instance, a dream broke in upon the life of John Newton, a slave trader, about the middle of the 18th century; when he did not immediately follow its direction, his trouble multiplied, until he was forced to remember and reconsider. The entire re-evaluation of his life which finally resulted from this experience made him one of the most respected clerics of the Church of England, and also the author of hymns that are still being sung. A. J. Gordon was another man who had such a dream experience towards the end of the 19th century and took it very seriously; the direction it gave transformed his ministry and made him one of the most important leaders in the American church in that time. It was also in the same way that St. Theresa of the Little Flower was given the comfort that freed her from terror of the death that was to come so soon and made the last months of this young saint a blessing to herself and those around her.[3]

In less dramatic form, this is the common experience of mankind. Again and again, in groups all over the country where

I have spoken, I have had person after person come up, almost timidly, to tell me about some encounter of this sort. They want to talk with someone about the meaning they have found in the experience, which they could hardly discuss with their own minister or priest without the risk of being labeled "odd"— or even worse. Religious experiences do not belong just to the intelligent or the sophisticated. Quite the contrary, they are given to children and simple peasants, as well as to philosophers and theologians; they come to sinners bent on destruction, as well as to pious folk who feel they need no special help. This encounter is the real leveler of mankind.

A great many church people feel that such experience, without respect for intellectual, moral, or social boundaries, can have no value. This was the stand originally taken by Aristotle, who maintained, in his three little books on dreams, that God could not possibly speak through dreams: it was perfectly obvious from first principles that God would not want to communicate directly with people who were simple, or stupid and depraved. Since it was equally certain that such people had just as interesting and astounding dreams as the most intellectual and morally elite, therefore, according to Aristotle's thinking, God did not send these experiences. Modern Christianity has bought this attitude without even considering its implications.

Indeed, everything that I know of the history of religion indicates that modern religion stands isolated on this point. I know of no early culture which has not held some belief that man has direct access to the gods, to spiritual reality, through dreams and other extraordinary experiences. Usually this belief has been accepted collectively, and so long as consciousness is little developed, the experience itself is also usually given through collective means. It is the shaman, the seer, the prophet, or the medicine man, who acts as mediator between the people and direct confrontation with these realities,[4] and translates the experience and its meaning into symbolic words and actions. The body of collective belief and taboo then regulates life for the culture. The importance of this meaning is clear in primitive cultures. When these collective rituals and meanings are disturbed, the very existence of the tribe is threatened, and often the culture dissolves and the people die for no apparent reason.

In more evolved religions there is an effort to develop individual responsibility in dealing with these realities. This is probably true wherever morality has become a determining factor. Greek religion, Zoroastrianism, Islam, Vedic thought, Zen, and Christianity, all emphasize that the individual must make his own contact with the divine, while at the same time there are elements in each that cling to collective patterns. At the present time the Catholic Church is in the throes of this evolution, and is making the passage consciously from one conception to the other.

In all of these points of view, of course, there are elements that try to force a retreat to unconsciousness and collectivity, but the essential thrust in each of these religions is to individual responsibility and determination. In place of relying on law and taboo to enforce the collective values unconsciously, they seek to develop the individual's relation to God and his conscious awareness of the values that are supported and promoted by his own actions. There are few more fascinating chapters in religious history than the documents of the Second Vatican Council in which the official church council opts for individual conscience over against authority. Few Catholics or non-Catholics realize the amazing significance of these deliberations and documents.

The numinous experience not only gives meaning and value to man's life—both in the outer world as well as in his entire psychic life—it also gives direction, along with the confidence to do something about it, in fact a sense of destiny. This experience of contact with meaning and creativity also appears to be the only force that is able to stand against the destructive elements which man faces as he enters into contact with the spiritual world. Evil and destructiveness are realities in that world which man also finds when he comes into touch with this realm, and these realities have been described in various ways, besides all the infinitely varied ways they are expressed outwardly.

Originally, in primitive religions, the gods or spiritual powers are often seen as ambivalent themselves, sometimes kindly disposed and sometimes bent on man's annihilation; later these forces are divided between demonic and angelic powers. A great contribution was made to religious understanding by Zoroastrianism in Persia; this was the discrimination between the forces or powers of good and those of evil. Ahriman—the force of evil, darkness, destruction—was seen in ceaseless conflict with Ahura Mazda, the god of light. Jesus of Nazareth followed this dualistic understanding and experience, calling the dark force "the evil one." In the prayer he gave his followers, he told them to include a petition to be delivered from the evil one.[5]

149

The early church built an entire theory of salvation and atonement on the idea that, through the cross and resurrection, Jesus defeated the powers of evil, and thus he gave to those who will follow his way the confident assurance of finding their own victory in this conflict. Bishop Aulén in his scholarly work, *Christus Victor*, has shown how pervasive this idea was throughout the early church. The same conclusion is clearly delineated in the careful study of healing in the early church in Evelyn Frost's *Christian Healing*. This emphasis on the reality of evil, and the way it can be overcome, is one of the basic differences between classic Christianity and most of the Oriental religions.

Human experience bears out this conclusion about the reality of evil. In the first place, literature is filled with examples representing imaginatively how the sensitive person is subject to invasion and attack by this destructive spirit. They are found in the classics from Shakespeare's *Macbeth* and Goethe's *Faust* to Stevenson's *Dr. Jekyll and Mr. Hyde* and Tolkien's *Lord of the Ring*. And in popular literature the same thing, as Mary Shelley and Bram Stoker expressed it in *Frankenstein* and in *Dracula*, is still giving TV viewers the cold shivers.

Then there are times when this reality breaks out of man's inner world, and the images are so fully projected that they blot out all other reality, as in the witch burning that lasted almost into the 19th century, or the more recent witchhunt of Nazism with "Wotan" as god. When the church does not deal seriously with man's experience of evil, this too gains a numinous power which can burst into action in the outer world. And this is not the only result; by avoiding the reality of evil, the church also fails to deal with the realities of man's inner life, and so it does not speak to modern man in the dark night of the soul. It does not deal with man.

The Experiences in Action and Interaction

These same realities—the same powers for good and for evil that can touch man's psyche directly—can also influence the space-time or material world. Indeed just at those times when these powerful realities are being experienced most directly within one's psyche, he is likely to find them also working with observable effects in the physical world. This strange correspondence between the inner image and outer reality has been called synchronicity by Jung. In addition to events being causally influenced there seems to be a non-causal connection between experiences in the psychoid world and those in the physical one. Jung has said that non-Western man is interested in finding meaning in meaningful coincidences, while Western man is interested only in causal regularity. Jung developed a theory to account for these experiences and described many examples of them in his own life and in the lives of his patients.[6]

The same experience can be multiplied indefinitely from the sacred writing of every major religion, particularly that of Christianity, which has been called the most materialistic religion of mankind. The direct physical effects of God's power—the healings and other manifestations or signs—were described all through the Old Testament, in nearly every book of the New Testament,* and by most of the early Christian writers. Yet today it is almost impossible for us to conceive of a reality like this, existing in a world that is separate, and yet interpenetrates our own. We pass over the stories that tell of such a reality either as superstition or as the foolish ideas of uninformed men caught in an incredible world view, as myth in the "looking down one's nose" sense.

If, on the other hand, some men do in fact experience these powers directly, sometimes observing their visible influence in the physical world, then we are in quite a different position empirically. Then we are directly faced with the probability that there is a spiritual or non-material world that does underlie the physical world and is intimately connected with it, influencing this world in which we live in ways other than through the human psycho-physical mechanism. In his study of paleontology, Teilhard de Chardin found that the facts pointed to just this hypothesis. Considering the developmental process observable in nature, he found that it could not be understood, even in the first and simplest organization of matter, without taking a spiritual component into account. In all life, from the simplest to the most complex human being, some reality other than the simply physical is involved. This is the same reality, as Teilhard de Chardin and others see it, as that which influences man directly in his major religious experiences.

Of course it is difficult to see how two experiences as different as those of the material world and those of a spiritual world can be related. But this is exactly the kind of complementary experience that brings human life into being, that distinguishes "man" from "animal" by making the break from the purely instinctual, the less complex nature. In other words,

---

* See the Appendix for the numbers of examples in each book.

this is simply the way men experience the world; and—as we believe is shown by the best of available knowledge—by this means men, unlike other animals, find its meaning and what they are supposed to do about it. It is when man tries to rely just on his rationality, instead of letting his experience be the determining factor, that he falls into one difficulty or another. Then he promotes one reality or the other to the driver's seat, allowing it to govern his entire thinking, and thus his conscious actions and experiencing, and this usually results in an inadequate or faulty religious life.

On the one hand, man sometimes denies the reality of the material world, as is found in many Eastern religions, particularly those of India and those where the influence of Buddha has been paramount.[7] The physical world is only *maya*, or illusion, and so man's life in it is relatively unimportant. No wonder there has been so little development of physical science in the cultures which have been dominated by such a point of view. In the various gnostic systems the physical world was seen, not simply as illusory, but as downright evil, and the task of salvation was to free man from its attractive power and dominance. This point of view is more dangerous than putting all the stress on spiritual reality, for the gnostic puts a wall between man and his amoral physical body with its natural instincts.

Gnosticism with its rejection of the body and sexuality in particular has had more influence upon historical Christianity than we like to admit and we need to be aware of its influence, for it leads not to real religion but to mental illness. When the modern Christian denies the value of his body he is not an orthodox Christian, but is unconsciously contaminated by gnosticism. Jansenism among Catholics and Puritanism within the Protestant framework betray this influence. On the other hand, modern Western culture has taken the opposite direction, denying any reality to man's psyche or spirit. A great portion of our modern world's thinkers, from behaviorists to logical positivists, see you and me as nothing but the causally determined products of matter which can be understood completely when man's reason develops enough. Spirit is just the puff of steam from the engine as it rolls down the track, a mere epiphenomenon. This is also the official view of the Marxist state, and so the results of this point of view are on exhibit. Jung suggests that Western man is as primitive and undeveloped in his psychic development and inner life as the Easterner is in exploring the physical world.

The world into which Christianity was born had quite a different understanding of man. The central strand of Greek thinking, as well as Judaism and the Judeo-Christian view, held that man was both body and spirit, both matter and psyche, and that the two interpenetrated in innumerable ways. It thus became impossible to speak of man's religious life without at the same time speaking of what he was and what he did in the outer world. His outer actions, how he lived and treated his fellows, profoundly affected his spiritual life. And his spiritual life brought him back into the world to produce observable results (or sometimes even to find them already produced). These three points of view have all maintained the complementary nature of man's experience of reality, and this led to their postulating two different realms of experience with which man must deal—the hypothesis of a pyscho-physical dualism.

The model of reality we have presented is an attempt to show that such an hypothesis takes the totality of man's experience into consideration. It tries to account for the fact that man is influenced by both the space-time world and the spiritual or psychoid world. Since most individuals have some knowledge about the physical experiences that impinge on the psyche and some awareness of the vast number that by-pass them entirely, we have not detailed this aspect. The diagram concentrates instead on representing the realm of experience that can touch and influence our psyches directly in dreams, visions, and numinous experiences, as well as by touching the material world directly in synchronous psychic and physical events.

The essential ideas and central doctrines of Christianity make good sense in this model, as we shall show. The church's basic dogmas were developed in an effort to record the experiences of the early church. These were not worked out in solitary dialectic behind academic walls. It was the consensus of experience which determined these dogmas, not simply reason; they were worked out in the drama of the historical process by the great councils of the church. The struggle of the early church was to keep true to its experience, and this was an experience composed of complementary, if not paradoxical elements.

Early Christian Theology

These men had experienced the reality of the risen Christ, and they saw how this experience related to their knowing of the Father. They also knew the experience of the Holy Spirit. They resisted through three centuries every attempt by intellect to reduce Christ either to mere man on one side, or mere God on the other. On the one side they withstood the docetists and other early gnostics who could not see how God could be very man, and on the other they stood equally firm against the Arians who maintained that it was unintelligible to think of man as incarnating the true God. The early church was experiential in its essential outlook. It stuck to its experience when reason defied it, just as modern physics has followed truth in the same way in seeking to understand matter, or as Jung did in trying to understand the relation of the unconscious to consciousness in man. There is more which man encounters than his reason can yet account for, or than Aristotelian categories will conveniently hold.

Let us replace the Jungian terminology in our model with more familiar Christian language. Again, as we have stated before, this is only a tentative map of reality, a means of finding our way and helping to understand what realities to look for. In the first place, it is not likely to be a final model, since it is extremely doubtful that anyone but God can have final knowledge. And second, if it does actually aid in putting more of our total experience into *usable*—not necessarily understandable—form, it will undoubtedly be superseded before long by a better and more comprehensive picture of things as they are.

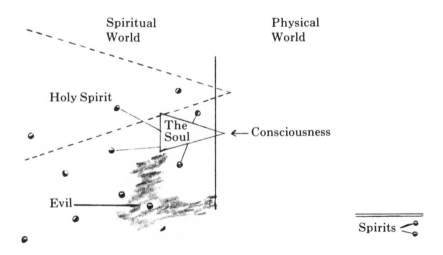

This diagram of reality agrees with the understanding of St. Augustine who had a sophisticated view of how man reacts to both the physical and spiritual world. He saw man as both body and spirit and capable of direct confrontation with either realm of reality. I have described this in some detail in *Dreams: The Dark Speech of the Spirit.*[8]

Again the schema represents man's relation to two worlds of experience—an outer or physical world and a spiritual one. The dividing line is purposely shortened in the diagram. What happens beyond the limits of the line, what interactions may go on, man cannot know because he is imbedded in the line between the two worlds. One can only speak about what happens within the realm of human experience. One's knowledge is of experiences and not of final things. Man seldom knows all.[9] Whether all things are ultimately one or many is a question that has no meaningful answer; man cannot say because the answer is not experientially verifiable.

Obviously man's psyche, in his physical body, is introduced into a physical world. Through the body man has experiences of this world that at least seem purely physical, and these he relates one to another through his rational faculty. To most people of the Western world this constitutes the totality of man. There are even some who see consciousness itself as nothing but conditioned reflexes, and so deny that the bulge of psyche into the physical world is anything but a peculiar convolution of matter. Most Thomists maintain that man is a combination of perceptive and rational psyche, but that he has no other contact with the spiritual world except when God breaks through to speak directly from the great beyond.[10] Little natural intercourse is seen then between the individual and a nonphysical world. Aristotle and Aquinas came to this conclusion for theoretical as well as empirical reasons. They believed that man could not be free if indeed man's psyche was subject to immediate infiltration by other psychic contents or realities.

But freedom is not such an *either/or* matter. There are many degrees of freedom on a many-pointed scale, starting with the almost totally determined behavior of the hydrogen atom (we are unable to talk about determinism at a lower level because our very observation disturbs the process). The scale mounts then from the determined behavior of the plant, to that of the animal, to the collective, primitive man, then to the behavior of the ordinary man in our society, and on up to men of great self-consciousness and wisdom. Rather than free or not free, men are *both* free *and* determined, and we strive for more freedom.

It is just at this point, on the question of man's freedom, that depth psychology takes off. According to the observations of both Jesus and depth psychology, man contains deeper levels than just consciousness. Jesus spoke of giving up one's life to find it, and also of attaining the single eye, indicating that man had different levels of the psyche and awareness. He also believed that a man could be beset by evil spirits which could possess the psyche and do physical, mental and moral damage to the person against his will. The person who was possessed knew that he was not in charge of his own being, but he could do nothing about it. His will was affected without damaging his powers of knowing.

From this point of view man's psyche is deeper than simple consciousness. Undoubtedly Aristotle and Aquinas had some understanding of this truth, but their stated theories implied a different picture of man, which was not clear until later. The implications did not become explicit until consciousness had been clearly defined for the first time by Descartes, and men went on to develop a one-sided attitude which neither Aristotle nor Thomas would have accepted. This attitude finally left no room for the experiences of the spiritual world that come to man—actually filter in to him—through the depth of his psyche. Yet this had been the understanding of the early church fathers, as John A. Sanford has pointed out in a careful study of their theory of knowledge.[11] Most of them clearly expressed the understanding that man received his knowledge of God and the spiritual world through the "soul" or psyche, which Jung calls the unconscious.

The Angelic and the Demonic

The question is not whether man wants to deal with the spiritual world or not—any more than he can decide whether or not to deal with the physical world. In both cases he has to learn what contents are there and how to find his way among them. In either world, if he tries to walk through without looking, he may get by, but the chances are better that he will smash into something or even be run over; and if he is driving a high-powered car . . . or a strong ego. . . .

Man is immersed in the spiritual world, and when he does not deal with its contents as consciously as possible, then they deal with him. One may project the apparently positive contents into others in the cult of romantic love or bobby-sox sentimentality. Often the hostile elements are projected into those who seem different and the result is the hate of war and race prejudice, of neighborhood bickering and church squabbles, or the picked on child in the family. Sometimes the contents of the spiritual world possess the individual, giving him an inflation, a Messiah complex that carries great, often destructive power. Or the negative forces may possess one so that he goes out to destroy, as used to be told only in "yellow journalism" or history books, but appears more and more often in our daily papers in stories like that of the Manson family.

Sometimes the negative elements seem to turn inward to attack the individual psyche; one is torn with anxiety and depression which seem to leave him powerless, and can lead to mental illness or suicide. Many people today simply try to shut off any contact with the world of the deeper psyche or soul, with the result that they are plagued by numerous anxieties and compulsions, phobias and irrationalities, which the modern church does not even try to understand, much less treat. When these tensions become great enough—although the person may not even be aware of them—they break through and are expressed in the body in some form of physical illness. The results of not dealing with the unconscious consciously are numerous and damaging, if not disastrous. Perhaps the only thing more dangerous than dealing with spiritual reality is *not* to deal with it.

One characteristic of the demonic psychic content is that it tries to possess the human psyche, while the angelic actually tries to relate to it. No matter how positive and good a psychic content appears, if it tries to take possession of the personality, its ultimate results are destructive and one is led into further unconsciousness rather than consciousness. That which comes from God brings confrontation which results in the desire to have the unifying life of wholeness that is given by the Holy Spirit. Seldom does this desire come until one has despaired of his own ability to deal with this reality from the level of ego strength and power.

What then does a man do? If he is wise and if his Christianity is vital, he turns inward and faces the depth of his soul and the world to which that soul gives access. He realizes that he is beset by a host of evil forces as real as Luther depicted in his great hymn:

> And though this world, with devils filled,
>   Should threaten to undo us;
> We will not fear, for God hath willed

His truth to triumph through us:
The prince of darkness grim,
We tremble not for him;
His rage we can endure,
For lo! his doom is sure,
    One little word shall fell him.

(Ein' Feste Burg, 1529)

The hymn ascribed to St. Andrew of Crete speaks of the same experiential reality:

Christian, dost thou see them on the holy ground,
How the powers of darkness rage thy steps around?
Christian, up and smite them, counting gain but loss,
In the strength that cometh by the holy cross.

(Early 8th century)

The New Testament is full of these realities, as are the church fathers; and, as Victor White points out in his book *God and the Unconscious*, it makes little difference whether we call them autonomous complexes or demons. The experiential content is the same for one who faces into the depth. In the appendix to my book *Tongue Speaking*, I have made a careful list of the New Testament references to the demonic and angelic. There are hundreds of references.

As a man realizes that he is beset by such powers, he soon finds that by his own ego power he cannot handle these dark and destructive forces. He also realizes that no human being can give continuous protection or defense against them. The man who has confronted this kind of darkness, dealt with this depth, must have some power to help him greater than his own ego or his own total psyche. It is God alone who can come to his aid; and that reality is there to be called upon, as the Church has maintained from its inception. The Christian is in a very different position from Job in his agony. He has the reality of Jesus Christ, who was the best of men, and who inspired men by his reality to think of him as more than man. This person Jesus met evil on the cross, was apparently defeated by it, and then rose again triumphant, thus defeating that evil dominion.

Jesus did not merely overcome evil from the outside; rather, he absorbed it into himself and transmuted it. On the cross Jesus integrated what evil could be redeemed and pushed aside the rest, and in doing so he conquered. In an individual's own confrontation with the depth of evil, a victory takes much the same course. As one finds evil which he is unable to handle, and calls upon the Spirit of the risen and victorious Christ, then that same Spirit comes into one's deepest inner being, integrates what evil can be integrated, and protects the inner being from that which cannot be integrated. Such evil, at least at this time, appears to be ultimately destructive.

The Christian has no answer intellectually to the problem of evil. He can give no reason for its existence, but he has a solution that works, one that fits the nature of the "critter"— in fact, the understanding of the human psyche we are trying to present. Operationally, when the power of the Holy Spirit comes into a life, the conflicting, like and unlike forces, converging into the psyche, are brought into harmony and wholeness, and the person is transformed morally, psychologically, and physically. He comes into harmony with Tao (as the I Ching puts it[12]), with the divine stream of things, and so is brought into harmony with God, with the world around him, and with himself. This resolution to confrontation with evil can be given by no teacher. The teacher can only point the way and help to remove the roadblocks. In this the skilled director of conscience and the psychotherapist share the same role; either one must have made the confrontation himself. Otherwise he acts as the blind leading the blind. When the clergy live up fully to the potentiality of their role, they are effective as psychological healers, as well as bringing religious and moral healing.

When I was visiting with Dr. Jung in Kusnacht in 1956, I asked him what system of psychotherapy was most similar to his. I expected him to mention some approach like Gestalt or even Adlerian psychology, but he replied: "The closest to my system of psychotherapy? . . . probably it was the method practised by Abbé Huvelin and the men like him who were skilled directors of conscience in France in the last century." [13]

This journey of confrontation is not for everyone to make alone. If one is to make this journey by himself, he must have the greatest ego strength to withstand the pressure. We shall say more later on about having companionship and a religious point of view on this "trip" inward. Jung stressed this need, suggesting in several places that the dogmatic structure of the Catholic church potentially offers the best system of relationship to the unconscious and the spiritual world that has been given to men. It offers mediation between the realm of the spiritual and man, giving protection from the destructive elements and access to the creative, and also providing a mediating priesthood. Since man needs this inward confrontation to survive, and yet only the strongest personalities can survive it without both fellowship and a point of view, the church needs to be there, giving the mediation both through doctrine and in living practice. This is the reason for its missionary activity. The church has something of reality to give which can be found nowhere else.[14]

Yet many Jews, Protestants, and now present-day Catholics, have been torn from the systematic fabric of religion and so are forced to make their own adaptation to the spiritual world or flounder. Jung discovered that many of his patients came to him simply because their lack of religious framework had made them neurotic. In talking with him I learned that he did not get into the area of meaning and religious direction because he wanted to, but because he could find no clergy who knew this realm to whom he could refer patients who needed help along these lines, and therefore he had to enter this area himself. One of Jung's friends, a Protestant minister, Hans Schaer, has described in detail Jung's convictions about the power and vitality of Christianity when it mediates a confrontation with God and gives man protection along the way. This book has the somewhat unwieldy title, *Religion and the Cure of Souls in Jung's Psychology.* Jung approved of this presentation as an adequate understanding of his religious point of view in contrast to some other published points of view which had not caught his essential idea.

It is important to realize, and we shall stress this point again, that spiritual reality is not a realm in which men can play as dilettantes; in it they find the very powers of heaven and hell. Unfortunate is the man who thinks that he can enter this realm with his own strength.

At this point a great gulf is fixed between most theology and man's experience. On one side is the theological attitude which believes that men can deal intellectually with God and evil as ideas, without being touched by them. On the other side is the experiential attitude which maintains that real theology can only be developed by men who know these realities from personal experience. To this way of thinking, which is grounded in an expanded logical empiricism, a theology that does not spring from dealing with spiritual reality is little more than an entertaining intellectual exercise. It costs nothing—beyond some ego strain—whereas experiential theology leads one into confrontation with spiritual reality, both divine and demonic, and the man who has such an encounter seldom comes away unscathed. It is no wonder intellectual theology is so much more in vogue in most Christian circles than the experiential approach. Who wants to be wounded all over again—unless in the new wounding he is healed? But then, intellectual theology seldom touches those who have been wounded and are looking for help.

Personally I blame no one for not making the individual personal encounter unless he is attempting to guide others, personally or by writing theology. The ordinary person can find his religious development transformed into lower voltage through the church, when it is alive; he can slowly work at bringing his total life into line, and if he does not make the encounter and development, the only ones who suffer are himself, his family and friends. When the theologian, however, fails to make this personal experiential encounter, then the whole of Christendom suffers and the church atrophies. Writing theology without knowing "the dark night of the soul"—which is part of the religious confrontation, as my Pentecostal friends constantly remind each other—is like trying to teach organic chemistry without ever having stepped into a laboratory.

Jung has suggested that the outer order of our world could be more peaceful if men would direct their aggressiveness inward, and there deal with their own shadowy contents. He went on to say:

> Unfortunately, our religious education prevents us from doing this, with its false promises of an immediate peace within. Peace may come in the end, but only when victory and defeat have lost their meaning. What did our Lord mean when he said, "I came not to send peace, but a sword"? [15]

God can be found immanently in the physical world, of course, and this is needed. Not only does science show the incredible intricacy of material structures, which suggests the influence by psychic purpose, but there are also strange experiences of synchronicity that indicate the influence of the world of spirit upon this world which we experience as matter. Scientists have only recently begun to study these experiences intensively. Learning about this world of experience as the scientist does is one legitimate method of coming to know God. Indeed, as Newton found, scientific knowledge can heighten men's appreciation and awe for God.

But when man becomes unduly concerned with the purely physical world of experience and neglects his experiences of transcendence, he settles for materialism and meaninglessness, and often neurosis follows. The direct experience of the spiritual world is also necessary. Or, if man is concerned only with spiritual reality and neglects the reality and importance of the physical, he can fall into gnosticism and superstition and fritter his time away, as in endless astrological computations or metaphysical speculation. Balance is difficult for men, but life does not seem to reduce to a simple, understandable oneness. Our task as Christians is to understand and value *both* the physical world *and* the spiritual one, rather than being short-changed by accepting an *either/or* value out of the duality of experience. [16]

The Christian Experience and Understanding

Let us look at some of the basic and central Christian ideas to see what sense they make in terms of the model of reality which we have proposed. My own understanding of many of these Christian doctrines came only as I began to appreciate the significance of what Dr. Jung had to say and his psychological and metaphysical hypotheses. Then I began to appreciate the wisdom and depth of insight of the church fathers of the first four centuries. I also came to see how these doctrines had undergirded the early church through persecution and conflict, giving it power so that those early Christians could actually outlive, outfight, and outdie the ancient world.[17]

Once one understands the natural interpenetration of the spiritual and physical worlds, he is no longer startled or offended by the idea of the incarnation. In a very real sense every man is spirit incarnate. As difficult as this is to describe in terms of Aristotelian thought categories, man is just such a hybrid of flesh and spirit commingled. Is it then difficult to imagine that the spirit of God himself was incarnate in one human being, first received in the womb of a woman, and then born as a human infant? The incarnation is actually the ultimate extension of the very principle of human life. People today have uncanny experiences when they encounter the realm of spirit, experiences far outside the ordinary mold. Is it then so startling that at such a time there were the star, the visions of angels, the dreams of Joseph, the coming of the wise men, the forewarning and flight into Egypt? If ordinary people have such experiences, then at a time like that . . . .

There was something beyond this, however, which gave the early Christians their doctrine of the incarnation. The apostles who had lived and suffered with this man were awed by what they met in Him; they knew that something more than ordinary

had occurred before their eyes. There was an unearthly wholeness and power to this man. Through Him they were touched
by the numinous, the transcendent, the same experience they
had in the most profound of their religious encounters. In the
healing of the sick and the demon possessed, a power of harmony
and wholeness was manifested which left them thunderstruck.[18]

And then came the resurrection. This was the confirmation
of all their deepest intuitions about Jesus. The man whom
they had followed was not conquered by men under the influence
of the Evil One, men who hung Him to a cross. And so God
wrote in actual fact in history, in the fabric of the physical
world, the mythical dream which had beaten in upon the intuition
of man from the dawn of time. What had touched man in
dream and vision and myth they now saw actualized in the
reality of the historical process. With this experience they realized that the realm of the spirit ruled over all reality, and
that in the end there was nothing to fear. Through the master
who had led them until his death, and then returned, they
could still find the same new quality of life which he had
imparted as a living man.

The actual experience of the resurrection is unquestionably
difficult to describe. But there is so much evidence about dead
persons who have returned to those for whom they cared that
people are able to deny it only by refusing to look at the
evidence. In ancient times Ambrose told of the consoling encounters with his deceased brother Satyrus. Sulpitius Severus
carefully described his vision of Martin of Tours almost at
the time Martin was dying and before the message was brought.
I have at least one modern letter describing a similar experience,
and in May 1970 an incident near Gary, Indiana, was in the
news all over the country; this was a father who was guided
by the voice of his murdered son to the killer. Particularly
at the time of death, living men seem to have the capacity
to experience the psyches of the departed directly and not
through ordinary sense experience. If this can happen when
ordinary men and women die, how much more likely it was
for this man if he actually did bear the very spirit of God
in his human body.

There is also quite a bit of evidence about collective visions,
and the resurrection appearances are easily understood as *at
least* a breakthrough of the same numinous vision to a group
of people. Jung has described how such visions can occasionally
happen in his study of flying saucers, which he sees as an
example of this phenomenon.[19] Various instances have been

reported of different men having observed the same dream. This evidence, however, does not hinder the possibility that the appearances were also objective physical experiences. If the man Jesus was truly the incarnation of the very force which had created the world, then it is not difficult to see this objective spiritual reality taking to itself the dead and torn body of Jesus and giving it new form and new splendor. Those who know anything about the "emptiness" and energic quality of matter will certainly not dismiss this as implausible. The experiences of a resurrected body, of sudden appearance and disappearance, and passing through doors, are not incomprehensible except in terms of the physics of the 19th century.

In the ascension this particular manifestation of matter returned in a blaze of glory to the creator. This experience ought not overwhelm men who understand the moment by moment creation and destruction of atoms in a star, who have seen men themselves create new atoms and turn those carefully selected ones into a blaze of energy and destructive power in the atomic bomb. If man himself can collect just the right particles to do these things, I do not find it hard to believe that God did a very similar thing in the resurrection and ascension of Jesus, rounding out his creativity by the salvation of men whom he loves.

After the ascension, the followers of Jesus were given a new awareness of the Spirit along with the almost tangible manifestation of an ecstatic speech. These men had lost everything but the hope of new life. As I have written elsewhere:

> The Jews indeed carried a burden, a crushing burden. Their task was to make God's righteousness manifest in their external lives. They carried it through suffering and exile; political subjection only intensified it. They yearned for some direct manifestation of God. While Jesus was with the group, he appeared to meet and satisfy their Jewish thirsting. But after the crucifixion and the ascension they were alone again. The only stability these men had was to sit still and wait as they had been told, both by Jesus and in a vision; being men who had known suffering and hope, they did just that. They stayed together and prayed, not knowing what might come. It was then that the experience of glossolalia first occurred. This experience was evidence to them that God's spirit was with them. It helped give them the conviction which sent them courageously into a hostile world.[20]

This was as central and vital an experience as the one Jung described as the encounter with the creative power of Spirit. One of his most important findings, which he observed again and again, was the fact that such an objective, nonphysical reality could bring wholeness, indeed health and harmony, to an individual's life once he could allow it to operate. If ordinary men, then, have experiences of a power like this, one would expect it even more for the followers of Jesus after all they had experienced and suffered. And when the Spirit and its power did break through, it came with several evidences, including the unmistakable one of speaking in tongues. Encounters with the Spirit were vital experiences which continued for these men and were passed on to their converts, often with the manifestation of tongues.

The experience of being filled with the Spirit is a kind of mysticism which is usually found only in Western thought and Christianity in particular. In it the ultimate religious experience is seen as one which does not annihilate the ego. There was a foretaste of this in the thinking of Plato, although such later Platonists as Plotinus saw the ego entirely transcended, much as in Oriental religious thought, and this in the end was picked up by the church in mystical ideas like Hesychasm. Plato, however, considered the ultimate experience to be a love relationship between the psyche and the divine, which ceases to be meaningful if the ego is dissolved. In terms of the schema we have presented, the Holy Spirit infills the psyche (covering it), bringing harmony out of the tension of discordant contents (and spirits), integrating as much of man's darkness as possible, and forming a shield against irreconcilable evil. The psyche is brought to a totally new level of reality, and far from entering into the void of nirvana, or being eliminated, the ego is transformed. It is made a harmonious part of a total human psyche, which now has a new center and focus. The old center and the new remain in relationship, a new relationship of wholeness.[21]

This experience is one of the most moving a man can sustain, but in our human condition men are not able to stay in this state. Wholeness is tasted for a moment and then becomes a goal, the end to be sought in life, and found finally in the next life. One can even turn his back completely after such an experience and reject it at any time, because there is no static end to this process. It is a *way*, not a safe harbor at the end of a journey. Whoever enters this way is faced with ever greater consciousness and the task of integrating more and more of his own darkness and the darkness of the world into such experience.

Each such experience brings a new harmony of purpose, often resulting in a sense of creative peace, and also physical healing because the tension that produces so much disease is relieved. Each experience brings greater openness to intrusions of the Spirit in dreams and visions. And it also brings greater compassion and understanding of others, changing the destructive and critical nature in each of us; one is more kind, or more firm when necessary. In fact the surest way to tell whether the Spirit had a hand in such an experience or not is to see whether the person has become more forgiving and charitable. If not, he may be possessed by some archetypal power, partial and ambivalent, instead of filled with the Spirit of God, of wholeness.

The Spirit which broke through in such a dramatic way on Pentecost resulted almost immediately in the healing of a crippled beggar, and it continued to show in the lives of Christians by such actions. It also brought them understanding of what they experienced, and the fathers of the early church developed a sophisticated doctrine of the soul of man as the mediator of the spiritual world. In his discussion of their beliefs about how the Spirit comes through to man, John A. Sanford has shown how close the ideas of these Christians are to the thinking of Dr. Jung.[22] They saw clearly that God and the world of spirit made a direct impression on man's soul. There was first the belief that Jesus was the enfleshment of the Spirit, and in addition the early church also believed that God's revelation continued in visions, dreams, intuitions, and prophecies. There was nothing far out about revelation. God had been reaching out to touch men all through the ages, and once he had broken through into historical time and space, the way was even more open for men to be touched by the reality which was revealed or unveiled. They were also in a better position, once he had broken through, to appreciate the significance of the experiences he could give them.

The experiences of individuals, shared and tested by the fellowship, gave personal guidance and understanding, as well as direction to the struggling church. Knowing as they did that God loved man enough to have become embodied in the physical world, it was not hard to believe that he would continue to break through to them in visions and dreams and prophecies. It would have been surprising if he had not. The early church apparently held little of the idea that men's brokenness and sin are so repelling to God that he will have nothing to do with them. The apostles told about God's touching their lives, not only in clear messages, but also in images upon which they had to meditate as Peter did after his dream-ecstasy in Joppa. The same tradition continued in the visions in the Shepherd of Hermas, in the account of St. Perpetua's martyrdom, among the ante-Nicene fathers, and then in all the doctors of the church.[23] With the understanding of these men that the soul participated in the spiritual world, there was no question about the need to listen to these experiences. If God or the Holy Spirit might break through at any time, it was up to those in the fellowship to be open to the spiritual world and whatever it brought in dream and vision or intuition.

There was one danger in this. Being so open to the spiritual world, one was open not just to the Holy Spirit, but to evil as well. Indeed it was expected that the more the individual was committed to the Christian community and to its life, the more his influence in the world, and more he would be selected as a target by the Evil One. The Christian would be tested again and again. As Tertullian remarked with characteristic exaggeration, the Devil was fully known only to Christians. But Christians also had the experience of being able to withstand these attacks through keeping alive and vivid the experience of the cross and resurrection.

Through the fellowship of the church, the sacraments, the symbols of the crucifixion, through experiences of healing, particularly in the laying-on-of-hands and exorcism, the Christian was able to meet evil, much of it incredibly destructive, and not go to pieces in one way or another, and from this experience the doctrine of the atonement developed. The idea of the atonement was experientially based. Somehow through the cross and resurrection the forces of evil had been turned back; man had been given protection and saved. In the crucifixion and resurrection Jesus had wrought some change in the very nature of the spiritual world, and those who were close to him shared in his victory. At present this was partial, but in the last days it would be all inclusive.

In terms of the world view we have presented, the atonement is the spiritual result of the victory Christ worked out in the physical world. Just as the outer actions of ordinary men can influence events in the psychic, nonphysical world, and even through active imagination can apparently change both psychic and physical circumstances, so here is the supreme example of a space-time happening with eternal consequences. What happened in Judaea when Pontius Pilate was procurator there has consequences in a world that is not subject to time and space, as well as in our world of the five senses. A spiritual drama was fought out and concretized in that place at that time, and so was fixed in the eternal spiritual world.

But this understanding was not conceived just intellectually, but as an hypothesis to account for the experience of freedom that men knew as they came into the Christian fellowship and found themselves no longer subject to mental and physical illness, to demons, or to simply giving up in the face of persecution. The dogmas of the incarnation and the atonement were not idle speculation invented to give comfort, but rather attempts to explain and put into wider context the incredible experiences of transformation and renewal that these men actually experienced. Since there is no space or time in the spiritual world, then there is no reason that these experiences which occurred in 35 A. D. should not occur in 315 A. D. or even 1972 A. D.

Once the possibility is seriously considered that there is a spiritual world existing alongside of the physical world, independently and in relationship with it, then the idea of life after death becomes the most natural belief. As a matter of fact, life after death then becomes the inevitable prospect which man must face whether he likes it or not. In some ways the materialistic view that sees no future but the grave is less demanding upon the human soul. If man is actually faced with continued existence, and that existence is intimately connected with how a man lives his life in this space-time world, then one's life takes on a seriousness that only very foolish men will ignore.

There are not only numbers of occurrences that men have described as coming from beyond the borders of this life, as Jung did in *Memories, Dreams, Reflections,*[24] but the resurrection itself stands for the permanence of the human soul as no other event in history. When man is conceived of as a physical structure housing a psyche that is integrated into matter but still able to relate to the independent nonphysical or spiritual world, then it is not logical to insist that the whole psyche, which has already reached out beyond the body, must dissolve with the dissolution of the body. The idea of a destiny beyond this puts man's life in quite a different perspective, giving him a very different picture of how he wants to live his life.

The sacraments of the church, in the framework of this

model, are special events through which men touch and participate in the spiritual world and its healing effects. As Jung has written,

> Baptism endows the individual with a living soul. I do not mean that the baptismal rite in itself does this, by a unique and magical act. I mean that the idea of baptism lifts man out of his archaic identification with the world and transforms him into a being who stands above it. The fact that mankind has risen to the level of this idea is baptism in the deepest sense, for it means the birth of the spiritual man who transcends nature.[25]

Again, it was just this sense of transformation which led to the doctrines that surround this sacrament, as well as to its perpetuation.

The liturgy of the Mass is such a rite, through which the individual participates in the death and resurrection of the Lord. Just as it was believed that the spirit is carried by these material bodies, and that Christ was incarnated in a human body, so in this sacrament, the living presence of the risen Christ breaks through and infuses the bread and the wine and the worshippers who have gathered to make the sacrifice. This rite becomes the place, *par excellence,* where man touches the reality of the spirit. It is a structured situation through which man may be touched and transformed by the spirit. Of this Jung has written in "Transformation Symbolism in the Mass":

> If the inner transformation enters more or less completely into consciousness, it becomes one of the vividest and most decisive experiences a man can have of his individual fate.[26]

Through the centuries this experience has kept the living mystery of the Mass alive, and from this the church developed its teaching and dogma of the Lord's Supper. Men experience something at the breaking of the bread, something real, something spiritual.

The early church was a healing community. Men and women came to the church as they had to the temples of Aescylapius, and often they were healed. As early as Plato the ancient world recognized that psychic disorder would cause sickness and infirmity in the body. It was only natural that a fellowship whose experiences brought wholeness and salvation to the psyche would bring healing to sick bodies and minds as well, and this was the experience of the followers of Jesus and the early church. These people saw sickness, not as the result of God's disfavor, but caused by the actions of the Evil One and his minions. Since the church had been given power over evil through the conquest of the incarnate Jesus on Golgotha, on this same basis it also received healing power over the mental and physical illnesses of men. The experiences of healing, which are found everywhere in the church's history, thus were interpreted within a framework essentially in agreement with the world view which we have presented in the schema earlier.[27]

We shall take up next the implications of this point of view for the practice of Christian devotion, for Christian action, and Christian education. Here again we shall consider the idea that there is a realm of experience with such power to hurt or to heal, and the fact that once one believes this, he has the incentive to spend some valuable time and effort turning to this realm in order to reach it in a creative way. In the case of relations with other human beings, once we realize that certain kinds of actions—those springing from caring and love—release other individuals from the domination of evil, just as God's loving does for us, then we can hardly avoid the supreme importance of living such a life. It is necessary if we are to keep in touch with that part of reality from which our healing flows. Both our devotion and our living of love become theologically and educationally of tremendous importance.

How easily the central dogmas of the early church fit into the double dualism which we have presented. Man is in touch with both a physical and a non-physical realm of experience. He is faced in the spiritual world with both destructive and creative forces. The basic dogmas of man's salvation flow quite naturally from this framework. The incarnation, the atonement, revelation, the sacraments, the doctrine of the Holy Spirit are all easily understandable to one who has been able to accept the basic world view which we present. Yet this world view was developed, not to support the Church's position, but rather to make sense of the realities which a psychiatrist encountered as he was endeavoring to make sick people well.

As we turn to actual practice, we find that this world view has suggestions for devotional practice and the need that it be rooted in action, and also for the crucial matter of how we can pass this information and experience on to others. In fact this view of reality holds values that pertain most specifically to education and Christian education in particular.

CHAPTER VIII

Relating to the Spiritual World

There is really no point in discussing the spiritual realm unless it can become a part of the experience of ordinary men. If this realm can only be thought about and not experienced, then it had better be left to the philosophers and the theologians while we get on with the business of adjusting our lives as best we can to the materialism in which we are irretrievably caught.

Yet the main contention of all religion is that man can come into direct and creative relationship with the realm of the spirit, that he can have its guidance and power. The purpose of any religion worthy of the name is to provide means by which this may be achieved. In fact it was because the church for the most part was not doing this that depth psychology found itself forced to enter this realm. Because the church was only talking about religion instead of providing experience with religious realities, people began to take problems of this kind to the psychologists. We have discussed the understanding Dr. Jung developed which provided his patients with the transforming power of these non-physical realities so that they regained physical and mental health. The methods he used bear a close resemblance to the methods of classical Christianity in a most vital period, and as we have seen Dr. Jung did not hesitate to call attention to this parallel. In answer to my own question he described the similarities between his method and that used by so many of the great Christian directors of conscience, particularly in nineteenth century France.

It is possible to have a sustained and creative relationship with the realm of the spirit. It is not only possible—as we shall point up later, it is imperative. Civilization—and something even more than that—hangs in the balance. Our present end-all materialism needlessly wipes out values and also what is harder to replace, the inner core of a man. By continuing on this bent we are moving towards an end very different from the promise which is actually ours and which cannot be fulfilled solely in the material world.

171

The foregoing chapters have pointed out the reality of the realm of the spirit and the fact that it can and does break into the lives of men. It is now our task to discover how this may become a continuing relationship. But before we begin there are two warnings which should be posted before the gate. The first would warn that this is not an easy undertaking. After all, the wisest person ever to speak of the religious way told his followers, "But the gate that leads to life is small and the road is narrow, and those who find it are few" (Matt. 7:14). The sustained religious encounter requires the total man. It requires more than the mind, more than the self image we usually carry through all our waking relationships; in fact the greater part of our discussion in this chapter will deal with ways in which deeper levels of human personality can be reached and brought to life. It is often easy for people to find a single-shot experience of God, at one level or another, but to live a life in which the religious encounter is an integral and daily part, this is a herculean task.

It is also far more difficult for us in our world to find a way into relationship with the realm of the spirit than it was for those to whom Christianity first spoke. Those men of the first century believed in a realm of the spirit as well as in the physical world, and the gospel message had only to convert their lives from the moral chaos in which they were living. To reach the modern man with his moral self-sufficiency (except in times of crisis) is more difficult. We have first to break through his basic philosophy of life, his fundamental world view to convince him that the world of spirit even exists, and this is a job in itself. It is really easier to change a man's morals than the basic foundations of his belief.

The second warning sign states that this way is not only difficult but dangerous. If Jesus and the church are right, then the spiritual realm abounds in evil powers and forces as well as benign ones. If it is entered lightly, or without the right preparation, or for the wrong motives, the results are likely to be quite unpleasant, for the individual is open to becoming inflated by what he finds. The power which is available can then be used for ego ends rather than for God. And God will not be mocked. These people become caught by what beckons them, and they are ultimately touched by real tragedy, though it may appear to outsiders more often ridiculous than sublime. But whether it is a balding choirmaster escaping with his one and only Venus or a frustrated feminine "politician" with self-righteous visions of power over everyone but herself, or the great Nietzsche sucked in by his images of the superman, the elements of personal disaster are present. Perhaps the major difference is that some are forced into real contact with the outer world of people and material things, while others become so fascinated by the realm of spirit that they are inundated by it and lose this contact. When this happens, they go mad. Like Nietzsche they are drowned in the unconscious, in the vast and unfathomable realm of the spirit.

Probably there is reason for the concern which some psychiatrists show when people seem to become too much interested in religion. It is not too much religion, however, but the wrong kind of religion which helps a man towards madness. Even a small amount of that kind can do the trick. But mature religion, with its emphasis constantly *balanced* between the material and the spiritual, is our best insurance against these dangers. It leads away from madness to psychological maturity and sanity.

This is one thought we shall be stressing as we discuss some rules or methods for relating to the spiritual world. The great value of Christianity is that it is the most materialistic of all religions; it emphasizes the spirit, but within the framework of the material world. Christianity is never one-sided or unbalanced when it follows Jesus of Nazareth. Its central message is that God became man, that spirituality indwelt the flesh and the two realms came together. This continues to be expressed in the central service of Christianity, the eucharist or communion service, in which bread—from the grain grown by the sweat of man's toil in the fertile, dark earth—and wine— pressed from the fruit of the green vine—are made carriers of the very powers of spirituality. Christianity in its classical forms always stresses the material as well as the spiritual. It is not a purely "spiritual" religion.

Strangely enough, this is one reason so many moderns are dissatisfied with it. These people want to be *all one thing,* preferably *not* the selves of which they are conscious. If they look for a religion which is all spirit, they run the full gamut of danger we have described. And if they turn back to the Protestantism which our generation learned to think of as "modern Christianity," they are in danger of falling into the same trap unconsciously. How, then, does the mature Christian find acceptance of himself as he actually is, in relation to the world of spirit as it really exists? What follows are basically the rules of the game for making this encounter.

These twelve rules have been culled from a great deal of experience; in the case of my own, they spring mainly from my Christian heritage, from years of reading the devotional classics and the Bible. They have all been tested in the crucible of my own struggles, though I am often faulty in observing them. What I have learned from depth psychology has brought out some of the suggestions which I might otherwise never have noticed in my heritage, and pointed up and sharpened others. In certain instances I use the language of depth psychology because it is fresher, and it breaks the habitual pattern in which so much of our Christian heritage is encased, a pattern which can keep us from true understanding.

The fact that there is a close relation between depth psychology and living Christianity is remarked on more and more often today, particularly by psychiatrists. Their methods are very similar, as Dorothy Phillips has suggested in her excellent anthology, *The Choice is Always Ours,* and much of the important work in psychology and psychiatry today is leading directly to a deeper appreciation of the New Testament and its message. From the religious side John Sanford, for one, has described in *The Kingdom Within* how depth psychology can shed light on our Biblical heritage. For my own part I have a deep respect for Carl Jung simply because he opened my eyes to the depth of Jesus of Nazareth, if for no other reason.

In addition, for nearly twenty years I have been talking with people who have come to me seeking help. These rules have been filtered through their experience and are largely the result of their comments and responses. I have learned as much from them as from any of the other sources.

Of course there is overlapping among the rules; the process we are discussing is a living, organic one, relating to the spiritual side of life which can never be analyzed conclusively. These rules are not a blueprint for assembling a sealed-in relationship with spiritual reality. There is no such blueprint, and rules are to be used in this area with caution. These are suggestions for action. They are not a philosophical system, or a set of principles merely to be thought about. Their real value lies in being tried out. Some of them call attention to practices which are avoided by many people, usually at a cost of escaping the divine encounter as well. We come to this encounter, to a living relationship with the spiritual realm and its power, not by thinking, but only as our spirits, our total psyches go into training. These rules are much like the practical ones which athletes must follow; they are empirical rules for spiritual training.

Rule 1. Act As If the Spiritual Realm Exists

The first rule of the religious way may seem self-evident, but often the most transparent ideas are the very ones we miss. Before one can go very far spiritually, he must accept at least tentatively that there is a realm of the spirit, that there is something to explore. This open attitude is very necessary. It is like prospecting; no one ever brought in a wildcat well or hit a bonanza who did not accept the possibility that there was some oil or some gold to be had. Much the same holds true for the spiritual realm. If a man does not even dream that there are vast caverns beneath the surface of life, he is not very likely to find an entrance to them. One must be prepared first for the possibility that there is something of reality beyond this material world.

This is something on which a person stakes his life and his action simply because it might be true. If he has to be absolutely sure before acting, then he will wait forever. Conviction about this realm, what we often call faith, comes with discovering its reality, and this takes action. We have much to learn from the physical scientists and their sincere, their dogged pursuit of the hypothesis. When it comes to the spiritual realm, are we willing to try the same way of action? It does not matter too much what we believe in our heads, anyway. What is important is how we act. If the spiritual world is there, and we refuse to look for it simply because we do not think it exists, then we take the course of believing negatively. We do nothing, discover nothing, and this reality has its way with us willy-nilly. But there is a stronger kind of belief, which is expressed, not in words or in thinking about what to believe, but in action. The man who takes the chance that the spiritual realm does exist, who acts upon that hypothesis as best he can, then has every chance of finding this realm and being able to relate to it in a sustained and creative way. And this is possible for all of us. Any man can enter upon this religious way no matter what he thinks or doubts.

Rule 2. Undertake the Quest With Serious Purpose

The religious quest is a serious undertaking. Joy and light-heartedness are the end results of the successful religious encounter, not the attitudes with which it should begin. Instead

175

the realm of the spirit must be approached with earnestness. Those who enter it lightly or out of idle curiosity usually end with a stomach ache, wondering why the endless cotton candy turned poisonous. Jesus told his followers to seek, and ask, and knock, and God would give the Holy Spirit in the same way that we give good gifts to our children when they ask for what they need. He also told the disciples to keep on praying like the widow who brought her claim for justice into court so many times that the merciless judge finally gave in just to get rid of her. Perhaps the access which we desire can be given only to those who are strong enough to be persistent, because they are also strong enough to withstand the overwhelming marvels of this realm.

There are enough legitimate ways to begin this journey, however, to provide access for all of us who do find the need to establish relationship with this realm. People are sometimes led to it by a quite unexpected experience of the spirit. Popping perhaps out of some ordinary situation of daily life, it breaks in on them suddenly and without preparation, and has so much meaning and power that it draws them to seek further and further. Their lives, which had been drab and stale, become unexpectedly filled with numinosity and power and new life. They then start the quest with the earnest wish to have constant relationship with the very ground of being; their entry is the desire to maintain this kind of living.

For others of us there may be the second way of obedience to our religious heritage; we are quietly called to this encounter by a deep and persistent inner voice without our knowing exactly why. This entry is through listening and obeying the prick of an inner demand, sometimes like a poke in the rear, which will not let us alone unless we go this way. The first was the way of Paul and Francis of Assisi, and many of the great saints of the church. The second is probably the way of more of us. It was the way described so well in Acts 10, in the story of Cornelius. This first century Gentile knew that he needed something, and he went on being faithful in his prayers and continuing his acts of charity and kindness until one day God sent an angel to prepare him to receive Peter who came with instructions. One must never underestimate the power of this way of entry—the faithful, continuous, daily religious practice. It is often this kind of practice which brings a transforming religious encounter to set fire to our lives. But this way is still not always enough for some of us.

Some people find their way to the religious undertaking

through despair, and this is another legitimate way. There are some of us who have plumbed the depth of life and found it meaningless. We have worked to produce something which never quite comes off. We have taken the philosophers in stride and found that they are dust and ashes. We have experimented with physical pleasure to the point of satiety, until there is no place to run. And so we turn to the one aspect of life which we have left out, God. It was in this way that St. Augustine started his spiritual quest which was to shape the course of Christian culture for centuries.

In much the same way neurosis can also be a starting place from which people go on to search towards God. While this, of course, may be a part of despair, it is a further step in which life falls in on the individual and he cannot function as he wishes to. The neurotic person is incapable of finding his way; he is lost and oppressed by anxiety and guilt and fear. It is then that God is often able to find the neurotic crack in our personalities and reach us through it. Luther's spiritual trek may well have begun in this way, and from what we know of Baron von Hügel this was undoubtedly the beginning of his search as well. Very likely the common attitude of people towards despair and neurosis needs to be reconsidered; these conditions may be the unavoidable pains of spiritual rebirth, rather than just fearful symptoms of mental weakness.

Finally there are those sensible few who simply reflect enough about life to realize that all is not well with them. They set out to find some meaning, some purpose and destiny which cannot be found in the material world, and so this search leads them ultimately to the religious way. This was apparently the way of Justin Martyr, of Cyprian, and also of others in the modern world as well.

All of these approaches have something in common. They all partake of a deep humility, a deep inner sense that something is lacking within the searcher, something he has not found which makes him less than half a man. This humility is essential for the successful quest. The man who is perfectly adjusted to this world and completely comfortable in his grey flannel suit can rarely be touched by God. Indeed no one gets very far on the spiritual journey who does not have the genuine and deep inner motivation of the man who can say, "Something is lacking in me which I must somehow find."

It should not be hard at this point to see that people can get into this spiritual venture for some very wrong reasons. A person who thinks merely that it looks like fun may suffer far worse than disillusionment. Jaunting into this vast realm of impersonal, collective values is like putting out to sea in a pleasure craft; the feelings and images produced here move men like ocean tides and storms, and they can wreck a life that is not prepared for them. Nor can one slip into the religious way as an escape from the responsibilities of outer physical life without heading straight for psychosis. In fact this is in itself a fairly good definition of mental illness, this substitution of one reality for the other, becoming absorbed in the realm of the psyche in order to leave the unpleasant realities of the material world behind.

Neither is it wise to approach the spiritual realm simply because someone else is doing it. What is good for one person is not always good for another, and the way one man goes about his religious adventure may be deadly spiritual poison for another. Last, and perhaps lowest on the list, is the sheer foolishness of going the religious way just because some well-wisher has advised it. We are hardly wise enough to run our own lives even with the best counsel and guidance we can get, without offering casual guidance to others. These facile suggestions often come from someone who is not even well acquainted with his own inner psychic life, and amount to nothing more than a dare to try what the adviser is afraid to do himself. "Thou shalt not remove thy neighbor's landmark" (Deut. 19:15), might well be accepted as the eleventh commandment, just as valid for the territory staked out for us within as for our homestead in the material world.

The genuine religious quest, then, is marked by a serious searching and so by a deep humility. It is never an offhand or frivolous undertaking; men who go this way know their real need for the assurance and joy which are its end result.

Rule 3. Seek Companionship and Spiritual Direction

Since the religious enterprise is a serious and also dangerous undertaking, one needs all the best help he can obtain in finding his way. The unconscious or the spiritual realm is no place to traverse alone. Even though it is the source of the consciousness and culture we do know, it is still the unknown which does not even speak our language. These realities can be very threatening and the way among them very difficult, and this is no wonder. They range from the most primal instinct to the complexity of a psychic image like the New Jerusalem, and they supply the power for human life; yet they are not at our command. As we spell out the rules which follow, we shall see how often it is helpful to check our own findings and experiences in this realm with another understanding person. This is necessary if we are to keep from losing our way or from becoming too engrossed in the realm of the spirit.

Indeed I would suggest that everyone who is serious about relating to the spiritual realm find himself a spiritual director, if there were more men trained and experienced in this way. Undoubtedly the person who feels this need strongly enough will find one, but if not, one must find some friend with whom he can speak of the deeper and more mysterious experiences which come to us all as we go deeper and farther in the spiritual realm. Nor is this wishful thinking. So often one feels alone in the spiritual quest; yet in every community there are others who are seeking, perhaps not in exactly the same way, but seeking none the less. And whoever they are, their feeling of isolation is the same. I have known no one following this way who was not grateful to be able to talk of his deeper and more valuable experiences of this realm, which he had kept concealed for fear of being misunderstood and mocked. The person who is sensitive, who continues to keep his eyes and his heart open, usually finds another like himself with whom he can share.

Still, there are times when the way becomes so difficult that one must have help. At these times the person who is sincere and earnest will find someone to guide him; if one knocks, the right doors do open. In a way it is much like the story of an Indian guru and the man who sought him out to ask how to find God. The holy man looked incredulously at the pilgrim and asked several times if he were really in earnest. Each time the man protested, "Yes, yes! There is nothing in the world I want more than to find God." Finally the old teacher strode out into the Ganges with him and looked him sternly in the eye. "Are you sure? Do you really want to find God?" he asked. "Oh, yes!" came the answer, and the teacher plunged him under the water and held him there until the last bubble of air came from his hapless lips. Then the guru let him come up, gasping for breath. "And what do you want now, more than anything else?" the guru asked. "Oh! for a breath of air!" the man gasped. And the guru came back dryly, "When you want God that much, you will find him."

Spiritual direction, like God, is found when the need is there.

It may cost time, or money, or travel, but it is found. Among the particular instances which I recall, one happened several years ago in an isolated university town where neither religious nor psychological guidance of this kind was available. A friend teaching there, who was searching and in deep need at the time, joined with her associates to find a new approach in their work with children and the correction of certain problems. This group studied religious and other approaches, including what Carl Jung had to say. They concluded that they must first come to know themselves, and so, without any do-it-yourself text, they began to turn inward and then to act as therapists and spiritual directors for each other. By sharing deep personal insights and experiences, and also studying together, these individuals came into an amazing contact with the world of spirit which has continued. Besides developing new techniques in their field which have since become widely accepted, they continue to see the results in their own lives and in the lives of others. Many people have my friend to thank because she realized the need for spiritual direction and did something about it.

Anyone who really seeks for direction will find it. Sincere, insistent and continued seeking open the door. Jung once remarked that one usually obtained the analyst (or spiritual director) he deserved. Perhaps our sincere seeking determines what we will deserve.

It should be noted that all the saints had their confessors, and those in monasteries their directors of conscience. Those who have been the most serious and have gone the farthest on the inner spiritual journey have all sought and found such help. It is almost invaluable. Simply the fact of seeking such direction contributes much to one's humility, because it is an outer demonstration of one's inner deficiencies. The one warning which I must give is to use care in the selection of a spiritual director. Only the person who has had direction himself can safely direct others. The blind cannot lead the blind without falling into one pit or another.

Rule 4. Turn Towards the Inner World Through Silence and Introversion

The practice of introversion is probably the most basic and fundamental rule of the spiritual encounter. It is the process of turning in upon one's self and away from the material world of people and things, and this is the germ of prayer, the beginning of communion with the nonphysical world. Without the practice of introversion there can be no real growth in the realm of the spirit. Until we turn our backs on the outer physical world, we cannot become free of the idea that there is really nothing special within man. Only as we do turn away from the material world does the world of inner reality come before us. It is in this inner world that we have direct experience of the Spirit and receive its power.

Most modern life is a studied attempt to avoid ever being alone, faced with the reality of the inner world. Just imagine how a line-artist like Steinberg might sketch the day of the average man, beginning with the moment a disc jockey connects with him to awake him in the morning. He may stay wrapped in gentle music while his razor whirrs, and then the news bombardment begins. He gets his breakfast in between skeins of words—headlines, box scores, political phrases, and a running commentary from his wife probably like a cartoon outside. He drives to work joined to the radio again, and switching over to concentration on a job even requires the help of pipeline music. With lunch he is fed conversation and business problems like spaghetti, and there is only one difference at dinner. He chops the family threads off to change over to TV or perhaps a meeting. Only when he drops into bed, too tired even to dream, do the conscious lines stop radiating, and if he cannot sleep there is the ever present sleeping pill or tranquilizer to remove the necessity of a night-time encounter with silence. The next day the routine starts over, and if there should be any interstices, the picture is quickly finished by simply adding squiggles to the lines and calling them recreation.

In such a life the Spirit has no chance of breaking through except in sickness or old age, and then who heeds its call? This kind of living tells more about our beliefs than anything we can say. It expresses our doubts about the value of the spiritual realm almost beyond argument. Until we cease this busy-ness which is an all-consuming activity, there is no chance for any sustained spiritual encounter. As long as we keep riding off in all directions at once, like the perfect English gentleman in Edward Lear's *Nonsense* story, we are not very likely to start our own inner journey.

This is almost exactly the story of one clergyman who came to Jung suffering from a nervous breakdown. The story he told was a simple one, familiar to so many of us; he had been working fourteen hours a day and his nerves were shot. Jung's instructions were also quite simple. He was to work only eight hours and then go home and spend the evening quietly in his study, all alone. Since the man was in real agony, he made up his mind to follow the prescription exactly. After he had worked his eight hours, he returned home, had his supper, and then went into his study and closed the door. And there he stayed for several hours. He played a few Chopin Études and finished a Hermann Hesse novel. The next day was the same, except that during his time alone he read Thomas Mann and played a Mozart sonata. On the following morning he went back to see Dr. Jung who asked him how he felt.

When he complained that he was no better, Jung inquired just what he had done, and heard the recital. "But you didn't understand," Dr. Jung told him. "I didn't want you with Hermann Hesse or Thomas Mann, or even Mozart and Chopin. I wanted you to be all alone with yourself." At this the poor man looked terrified and exclaimed, "Oh! but I can't think of any worse company." To which Dr. Jung gave his classic reply: "And yet this is the self you inflict on other people fourteen hours a day."

The results of real silence can be amazing indeed. I remember particularly the experience of one young man, not quite nineteen, who had come to me in a bad way, completely uncertain about his future. He seemed to do everything he wanted not to do, and had no energy for the things he really wanted to do. I suggested that he go up to a mountain cabin for several days to get away from what had become pointless busy-ness. There was no one he could talk to there, and he was to do nothing and eat lightly. He went, and stuck it out for thirty-six hours. This was all he could stand, but he came back on the second day with a dream which revealed the depth of himself and showed him exactly what was wrong. As a result—the direct result of his spending time alone—he was able to start off on the right path again.

This practice of silence or introversion as a religious discipline is particularly important for people who are caught up almost totally in the outer material world. It must be understood very clearly, however, that it is not for all people at all times. For the person who is not doing enough in the outer world, who is tempted to withdraw and look only for satisfaction inwardly, the discipline of introversion can be harmful. Its purpose, of course, is an adequate relation to both the inner and the outer worlds, and, like most of these rules, it is a general prescription which must be fitted to the individual and his own need. Here again is an indication of how valuable it is to have another person, an objective observer, with whom one can discuss these facets of his spiritual life. This is often the only way to keep from getting off on the wrong track and becoming set in it.

For most of us relationship with inner psychic reality is a practical impossibility until all outer activity has come to a halt. And this includes whatever consciously directed work we do alone, like figuring and planning. We have to learn to be alone *and useless*, to do nothing, in order to open the door to a different level of reality, a level not directed by conscious activity. Real progress on the spiritual road begins only when we learn to be still and passive. It may even be hard for some people to remember a day which they spent alone in this manner. Perhaps it was during an illness, for sickness does have value in the fact that it brings our outer activity to a grinding halt.

All the masters of the devotional life prescribe silence and passivity as an utter necessity for spiritual growth. Fénelon even directed that one should never speak if it is possible to keep silent. Among the philosophers Carlyle advised: "Do thou thyself but hold thy tongue for one day: on the morrow, how much clearer are thy purposes and duties; what wreck and rubbish have these mute workmen within thee swept away, when intrusive noises were shut out!" [1]

One of Kierkegaard's most delightful passages suggests that most men are like a kind of social bird that promptly dies when it has to be alone. In *The Sickness Unto Death* he went on: "In the constant sociability of our age people shudder at solitude to such a degree that they know no other use to put it to but (oh, admirable epigram!) as a punishment for criminals." [2]

And from the practical side there is support for the discipline of silence which undoubtedly goes back at least to the commandment about keeping holy the Sabbath day. It has been expressed in action in the submission of the Trappist monks to a life-long vow of silence and in the finding of the Quakers that silence is the center around which they can best come into God's presence. Like the tradition of silence before and after the services in certain churches, each of these practices conveys the same truth and meaning which are also expressed by writers speaking from many points of view, for instance Anne Morrow Lindbergh in her *Gift from the Sea*. What they all agree to is that this inner life, the world of spirit, can be discovered only through the practice of introversion or silence.

How long the silence need be, or how often, each individual

will discover for himself. But first he must find time for it. When a person claims that he is just too busy to do so, then usually he *is* too busy! There are as many ways of finding the time as there are hours of the day. For one friend of mine an early hour of the active day was best, and if the telephone rang during her quiet time, she simply told the caller, matter-of-factly, that she had someone with her and would call back. Other people really require the silence of the night, or a place that is free of interruptions, and the way one finds the time makes very little difference.

I find I need a time each day lasting from fifteen minutes to an hour. I also need a time weekly of an hour or so to collect the tattered fragments of my life, and at least once a year I need a day or two alone to center down and see who I am and where I am going, to find out what God wants of me and to get my priorities straight. *What is important is whether one does or does not find and keep a time of silence or introversion, because this is a good measure of just how sincere one is in making the divine encounter.*

Out of this silence come stirrings which we did not know existed within us. The bridge which introspection forms opens the depth of man to be known, and strange, hidden things come up, some of them wonderful and others shocking to discover. In the silence, when there is no one else to hold accountable, and no busy-ness to act as a cloak of self-deception, it is impossible to be dishonest. Fears and remembrances may then be stirred up which we must share with a friend or spiritual director. For such a time is the real beginning of an entrance into the spiritual realm.

Here a prayer group of like-minded people can be invaluable. Two or more people can gather together in silence and share what comes out of it. Many persons find it easier to be silent with others than alone. They are not only able to become genuinely silent more quickly with others, but they create a fellowship in this way which can also help them towards great spiritual maturity.

Rule 5. Learn the Value of Genuine Fasting

Along with silence and introversion, indeed a part of the same process, belongs fasting. In introversion we turn our minds and spirits away from occupation with the outer world; in fasting we turn our bodies away from the world. It is so easy to be self-indulgent, to take exactly what we want, when we want it. If we are to go on the spiritual way, we might as well, like Jesus, expect this self-denial. He did not say in the Sermon on the Mount "if you fast," but "when you fast," assuming that anyone who took His message about this way seriously would be fasting. It is true on the other hand that He was not noted for His abstinence, as were John the Baptist and his followers. The fact that one fasts certainly does not mean that he cannot enjoy a good meal.

It simply is an actuality that persons who have seriously entered upon the spiritual way find that a period of fasting is a great aid to them. It clears the mind and heart; it opens avenues of realization and thought which before were closed. I do not know why it is true, but those who try fasting find it liberating and helpful. Somehow as the body and mind both give up the expectation of business as usual, it becomes easier to enter into the reality which is not physical. Fasting also helps us to develop discipline and self-control, qualities which are highly important on the religious journey. Real self-indulgence, which makes a one-sided person more one-sided, is one of the easiest ways to cut the religious journey off short.

This is another rule, however, which must be carefully tempered by understanding of the circumstances of the individual's life. Fasting is especially helpful to persons who are too much caught up by satisfaction in the physical world, but it can be quite dangerous for one who is depressed or has already separated himself considerably from outer things. The withdrawn or depressed person can be dragged further down into his problem by fasting, as medical men have pointed out. Here is another crucial point on which it is so helpful to talk about one's spiritual life with some other person who is aware of the problems. Some of us, in fact, have a real need simply to express enjoyment of outer sensations. But for Americans there is one excellent reason for fasting, which I have finally come to see is also a religious reason. We are the best fed and most poorly nourished nation on earth, according to physicians, heart specialists included. Over-eating is probably responsible for ten times the death caused by drinking or narcotics, and the man who has eaten himself to death is no longer in a position to undertake the religious encounter in this life; even more, I doubt if he is in the most favorable condition to continue it in the next.

Rule 6. Learn to Use the Forgotten Faculty of the Imagination

The process of introversion also involves the discovery of one faculty which we have almost lost as a religious practice.

This is the faculty of imagination, and these two are indeed linked together. Through imagination in silence one allows the images of the inner world to become real within him, and it is in this way that one comes into contact with a level of reality altogether different from the outer world. The religious process of introversion does not go very far without imaginative thinking, and certainly no one can develop this faculty without the time of silence in which to practice it.

Here we must first point up the difference between classical Christian meditation and the devotional practices of the major Eastern religions. In Eastern thought the individual is seen as emptying himself of all emotion and images. The goal of most Eastern meditation is a union with the godhead in which the ego is dissolved and the path towards this is the suppression of images. This is true in the practice of yoga, most kinds of Buddhism and Zen in particular. In transcendental meditation so popular among modern youth the same practice is used. Christian meditation is more materialistic! One's total psyche is involved and this necessarily involves the use of images and emotions. I have discussed this matter at some length in an article in *Lumen Vitae*.[3]

Christian meditation usually goes from a mood or feeling to an image which is then dealt with imaginatively. Or it can start with an image which is allowed to be suffused with emotion so that the entire being of the individual is involved. This can start with, for instance, the image of Mary and Joseph making their way towards Bethlehem, the feeding of the five thousand, the raising of Lazarus, or meeting the risen Christ at the empty tomb. In each case it is necessary to learn how to use the imagination, and this we shall take up quite fully later on. Although some forms of Christian mysticism have spoken of the dissolving of the ego, the most orthodox speak rather of the relating of the individual with God. As long as love is a part of the relationship, there has to be something left to love.

This kind of thinking is very different from the process of rational thought in which we are schooled almost exclusively. Rational thinking—directed, analytical thought, proceeding by logical reasoning from a basic concept—is probably the most valuable tool of our present culture. It has given us our science, our philosophy and theology as we know them today. As this analytical power has been turned upon matter, the physical world has yielded up many of its secrets. But, as any basic scientist knows, there is another kind of thinking which is equally important to science, and it is even more important and basic to human life. Rational thinking cannot spin out the intuitions upon which science is based, and it certainly does not reveal the secrets of the inner world. This takes another kind of thought —thinking through images rather than concepts, thinking which is passive rather than active, which follows a meaning that seems to be independent of the rational mind. From this have come our great works of art and poetry, and it is this thinking which unlocks the secrets of the inner world.

One must learn this second kind of thinking if he is to discover the realm of the spirit. In fact it takes as much learning to develop the imagination as it does to develop the rational mind. As a race we have nearly forgotten how to use this power to think symbolically rather than rationally. And so we no longer have direct contact with spiritual reality, for this contact, as Aquinas so clearly suggested, is made through the faculty of imagination. This is unquestionably the reason we have so much difficulty understanding our dreams. Dreams are symbolic communications; like art and music, they represent imaginative thinking, and learning to appreciate them helps to awaken the faculty of imagination.

There are many different ways in which we can use the faculty of imagination. As a beginning one can simply chart the flow of phantasy which comes as he turns inward, observing what passes before the screen of consciousness. After he has developed the necessary skill—and considerable skill and practice are required—one will find that the images which pass before him are not just a jumble of fragments, but that they tell stories, have meaningful connections, and bring one into a strange and wonderful world. Jung, who studied the phantasies of people from all over the world, found this typical of them whatever the backgrounds and experiences of the people.

Imagination used in this way takes us into a realm of the spirit as independent, as autonomous and as meaningful as matter and even more complex. Such imagining might be described as waking dreaming, for it has the same significance as the dream and the same independent way of speaking about men's lives. From my own use of it, which has included recording one long fantasy which I stayed with over a period of years, this can be one of the most meaningful experiences of one's life. To put it mildly, this is one sure way of taking a person out of his rut, and here again one is grateful for wise spiritual direction. These strange productions come from the unconscious, the realm of spirit which is so close to us but from which most of us have separated ourselves. To understand them we need counsel and wisdom, for a dilettante here can step off into deep and dangerous water. Here again we need the close companionship of another traveler on the way, a spiritual director or friend to whom we can talk and listen.

One can also use this faculty in reflecting upon the events and experiences of his own life. Imagination can cast meaning into a life in much the same way that light brings out the detail in a picture which looks like a meaningless blob in partial darkness. For instance one may feel oppressed and sit quietly waiting, seeing nothing but an impenetrable grey cloud. Suddenly he sees that it is *not* black, that there must be light somewhere; and imagining its source, he begins to see images. As they flood in, the cloud is pushed back and he is freed. Or at other times he may realize how self-satisfied and cocksure he has been, and become more ready to take whatever adversity he must face.

I recall how impressive one such experience was for a woman with whom I was counseling some years ago. She was a person who was never satisifed with her adjustment in social situations, and driving home with her husband from a convention weekend, she was scolding inwardly because for once she had just been herself and had escaped from the group activities. Becoming utterly still at last, she suddenly saw herself clinging to the face of Boulder Dam, and knew that she had been diving for a penstock and had narrowly missed finding the opening and being sucked through the power plant and converted into energy. At that moment her tension was relieved and she began to see her way clearly. The number of examples that can be found like these is almost endless, and yet they would barely suggest the ways in which imaginative thinking can be turned upon one's own life and used practically.

Another most practical and helpful use of the imagination is in one's reading. So often we read only with our heads and not with our hearts. We tear into a book rather than letting it open an inner depth for us. It is as if we had spied some rare mountain goats and could choose whether to shoot one on the spot and tear it apart for food, or to follow them and let them lead us into their mountain fastnesses. The first kind—studied, discursive reading—fills the bill for an immediate, already well-defined hunger, but imaginative reading is of the latter kind. Actually, it grazes and munches, slowly, selectively. Most of us, as Baron von Hügel once suggested, would die of malnutrition if we tried to be like cows in our reading. We would probably go into such a fit over each morsel we could not eat that we would obtain no value from the nourishing parts. And yet imaginative reading has to be done very much as a cow grazes, skipping through what we cannot digest and stopping to munch on the parts we can eat. It is a way of reading which has to be learned.

The value of this way of reading can be discovered by applying it to many, many different works; it can reveal the spiritual truth in Greek tragedy, or even in *The Catcher in the Rye*, but the imagination is undoubtedly most fruitful when turned towards spiritual books. Since the Bible is the one book that most of us would say we know, or ought to know, it may be well to take our examples from this one source. And certainly the Bible is a book which requires something more than ordinary discussion. When Zen or the Vedanta Sutra come up over cocktails, I should be happy to see a copy of the Bible on the coffee table as well, but less happy to find it considered a kind of accomplishment. No other book is so much a part of the foundation of our culture, and none contains so much to feed the soul as does the Bible. As soon as one is able to appreciate its full impact, he certainly should read it right through.

Reading the Bible unimaginatively hardly touches its real worth. I remember very well one friend, a very smart fellow, who felt that he ought to add reading the Bible to his many accomplishments. He read it very carefully, analytically, and when he got through he could have passed a theological school examination on Bible content. But the main thought that stayed with him from his reading was that the stories were rather far-fetched to have much meaning for anyone today. He had not allowed the words of the book to work as a leaven in him, and he might just as well have read the World Almanac for all the religious value he received.

Two examples will suggest the possibilities of imaginative reading and the insights which the New Testament can provide. For one, the story of the Good Samaritan is known to us all. We have no trouble hearing its outward message, the obvious moral that we should be as kind to other people as the Samaritan was to the man set upon by thieves.

When one enters into the story in depth, he sees—actually looks at—this man lying by the road, and wonders what part of himself this is, lying there with his jaw bashed in and his clothes torn half off. And the thugs that rolled him, what unknown men are there inside himself who are so desperate? He really tries to see these different parts, and especially who it is that will try to save him. Is it the priest, who pauses just long enough to murmur his conventional attitude, "Poor fellow, probably drunk." Or the Levite, the picture of rectitude, who knows it is good business to be impeccable? No, these two get by as quickly as they can, and he is still lying there when the despised outlander happens along the road, and stops. Where does he belong in one's life, this Samaritan for whom no one has a good word, but who still stops to save what has nearly been killed in one?

What is the despised part of *me* which has the power to save me if I will let it? As I step into this story imaginatively, with all the parts of myself called into play, I not only understand the depth of the man who told it, but my own life comes into perspective. Indeed the reason for the timeless application of the parables of Jesus is that they speak to the deepest levels within each of us, which touch the realm of the spirit. For this reason these stories can be healing even when we do not completely understand them.

We can use the same imaginative reflection upon events in the life of Christ, and this suggestion need carry no implication that they were not historical happenings. On the contrary it can re-enforce the record as actuality. If one sees the life of Jesus as myth lived out in history, then the events of his life have both an outer meaning and an inner one. As they are touched by imagination, the depth of inner meaning that is revealed makes them real in our lives and they become more possible, not less.

Let us take for a second example the story of the raising of Lazarus, in which it was told first that Jesus was summoned because of Lazarus' illness, and He tarried in coming. When at last He reached the bereaved sisters, they told Him reproachfully, "Lord, if you had come, Lazarus would be alive." And after He had spoken to them about what it meant to be truly alive, Jesus went to the tomb, where He wept. Then He turned to the crowd of mourners and told them to take away the stone. He had to insist, because they protested that the body had been buried for four days and had begun to decompose. With the tomb open, Jesus prayed a prayer of certainty and called out in a loud voice, "Lazarus, come forth!" And Lazarus came forth, still bound in his burial wrappings, and Jesus spoke to the people again with His final command of "Unbind him."

Here we have a story which I happen to believe is historically true, and is also myth. In spite of the fact that myth is a naughty word in many religious circles today, let us see what actually comes out of imaginative thinking about these events. So often when we ask God to take over—whatever the guise we are seeing Him in—He seems to tarry. He waits, needlessly it seems, until what is sick in us has died: our hope, our courage, our capacity to love may be sick unto death. And when this part of us needs to be resurrected, then we learn what it means to be alive—on faith, like even the closest-drawn contract. While parts of us are blaming fate, we still must go to the tomb, and weep over the person that is no longer alive in us, and ask clearly for obstructions to be removed.

The trouble with so much religion today is that it tries to avoid the dead parts of our lives. If we avoid them, we need not weep. If we avoid them, we need not come into relationship by demanding to be helped actively. If we avoid them, we can do without the courage it takes to face the stench that goes with death. But then we also do without the transformation.

To come alive we have to be sorry for the dead part of ourselves, sorry enough to say what needs to be done, and strong enough to face up to the evil which caused the death. We have to be sorry enough so that we want life and will pray for it. Then, with faith and certainty, we can call out in a loud voice, and the dead within us comes forth, still in the cyst that was forming, and we are ready for the final action of setting it free. Nothing is completely dead within us, so dead that it cannot be raised. And this story puts the question: What is the dead Lazarus within me? What part have I allowed to die so that I am living only as a partial human being, busy getting more and more set in my own one-sidedness?

When this meaning unfolded before my imagination, I prepared two sermons on the story. Shortly after they were preached a young man with whom I had been working for some time without much success came to me with a dream. In it one of his brothers had died, and he had stood by the casket and raised the dead youth to life. With the realization that this was a part of himself which had been dead (his capacity to reach out to another in love), he went at the job of bringing this boy back to life in himself, and he was successful. The story and the dream were the turning points in this young man's life, both of them based on an imaginative reading of the Bible.

This boundless mine of precious material is available for any of us to work. For instance, one might read Numbers

13—seeing himself as one of Moses' spies in the promised land—and begin to wonder if it is always necessary to feel like a grasshopper among giants who have "arrived." Another person might even find himself in the Christmas story itself, perhaps first wishing he could get into the inn, and then turning to the stable with its animals and a few none-too-bright shepherds, wondering what it means to him that this was the place of the birth, the place where even the Magi came to bring their gifts. Indeed there is no limit to the depth of insight which can come from these pages when they are read with living imagination.

When one imagines one's self at the various resurrection appearances and allows these events to be recreated within him, he finds that something of the wonder and healing of those events begin to take place in his life. If one is inflated, he need only wait before the three crosses of Golgotha to touch within himself the deep, tainted stream of destructiveness in human life that made these crosses possible. But unfortunately, the church has often dwelt too much on this one image, when most of us probably need more often to spend an hour with the men who brought the paralytic to be healed by Jesus, or listen in depth to one of the parables. With the help of John Sanford's *The Kingdom Within*, the deeper meaning of the parables of the kingdom can be tapped by any of us who really wants to touch this level.

This way of penetrating the depth of the Bible is *in addition to* intellectual analysis. Again it is not a matter of *either/or*, but of using *both* practices. Imagination provides the reason for spending effort on intellectual and critical understanding. Once one has been touched by these living images, then he wants as good knowledge as possible of what Jesus actually said and did. But unless the events have transforming power, why bother?

At times one must start from the other side, from his own darkness and trouble. Almost all of us have times when we are seized by pain and agony and realize that the trouble has little to do with outer causes and events. It seems to rise from within. In order to deal with this inner darkness, I find that I must allow the mood to be turned into an image or series of images. But before one can do this, he must admit the possibility that there is an evil force or reality (the Evil One) which can attack us. Indeed the further advanced one is, the more likely he is to be the victim of these attacks; so long as one is in the hands of "his satanic majesty" attacks are not particularly necessary. One must also first be sure that he gets enough rest and nourishment.

Then the task is to use the imagination, and this takes time. Perhaps the first question is: "What does this fear or anger or depression look like?" Quite spontaneously the realization will come that there is something beyond one's ego trying to possess him. Instead of saying, "I feel worthless and depressed," or "I have no value and I hate the way things are," one says, "Something is telling me, 'You are no good to anyone,' or 'You ought to go out and hurt and destroy.' " There is a whole world of difference between these two statements. With the first statement, one is caught in a circular self-accusation from which there is no escape; with the other, one knows that he is fighting something and has a chance.

There is no harder work than taking time to sit and listen to these forces that would disrupt one's inner life. Whenever one tries, the voices laugh and mock, telling him that this is a silly game and that he is stupidly wasting his time. Or, one may see the image of himself being dragged through slime and trampled in the mud by some witch-like, some vicious creature. Another time one can find himself in a barren desert sitting on a dump heap of broken adobe bricks, the squashed bulk of a washing machine and an old car door—alone under a burning sun. There is no more demanding work, nothing that takes more courage and faith.

One must know these voices and images that can some time say, "Go out and destroy something," as they did to the college student who shot and killed at random from the tower of the University of Texas at Austin—"Kill just to destroy." Only by taking the time, by allowing these images to appear and listening to these voices, can one come to the realization, however tragic it seems, that no one can deal with these things by himself. One realizes that in his own power he is helpless, lost.

It is then that he can turn in the same way, in imagination, to the power of the conquering Christ who is beyond space and time. In the slime he realizes that Christ came to save him and the presence of Christ comes and lifts one out of the mud. Sitting on the dump heap one imagines a spring of living water suddenly flowing up from the desert floor and the Christ coming to give one a cup of cold water. Or, one asks the Christ to come and silence the voices of vengeance and destruction that shout for us to harm and destroy. The strange thing about this use of imagination is that it works.

Coming out of the imagery, one finds that the hate and fear and depression have disappeared and he can function again. When one has experienced the creative reality of Christ's spirit in this way, one no longer believes in Christ; one knows Him.

In dealing with the forces that disrupt one's inner life, it is helpful to realize that some things which appear very negative are in reality creative parts of oneself which he has rejected. Within the psyche we are faced with both a personal and a collective "shadow," as well as with naked, irreducible evil. In his chapter on "Shadow, Destructiveness, and Evil" in *Power in the Helping Professions*, Adolf Guggenbühl-Craig has made this point well, suggesting how much real wisdom is needed to distinguish between these two kinds of disrupting forces.

Some people who are afflicted with darkness find that wearing a cross helps greatly in calling upon the restoring and recreative power of the Christ. There on the cross the forces of evil tried to strike down the best of men, God's Son. They failed. The cross is the sign of His triumph over those forces and it helps one participate in this victory at the present time. This is not magic but the creative opening of the spiritual realm by imagination.

A somewhat similar use of images has proved valuable in psychotherapy. The therapist leads an individual or a group through a series of images, perhaps starting with dull and meaningless ones and leading to images of hope, light and inspiration. This has also been tried as a way of leading prayer groups. Essentially the same method was used by Ignatius Loyola in *The Spiritual Exercises*, which proved a source of strength to the Jesuit community for centuries. The Jesuits, I understand, are now returning to a use of a modified form of these exercises after having abandoned them in a modernistic fling.

One of the most interesting and creative uses of meditation through images was suggested by Aldous Huxley in his novel *Island*. In her biography of him, Laura Huxley also tells how he spoke to his dying first wife, urging her through images out in the quest of a new level of life and reality. More recently Keith Kerr has written of using symbols in a similar way to ease his twenty-one-year-old son through death; the description in his paper, "Terminal Illness Counseling—The Death Experience," is both realistic and moving.[4]

Agnes Sanford shows how much more effective praying for the sick can be when one uses imagination. By imaging the person well rather than sick, one can help to bring the creative power of God flowing through the person for whom he prays. She describes this use of imagination in several books, particularly *The Healing Light* (which has gone through thirty-plus printings), *Behold Your God,* and in her novels *Oh, Watchman!* and *The Lost Shepherd.*

John S. Dunne has also described at some length how one can "pass over" into another life. In *The Way of All the Earth* and *A Search for God in Time and Memory,* he allows us to share in his own imaginative entry to another realm. Here he has re-enacted the process of imaginative prayer or meditation, when one's mind is allowed to wander among the images that rise from the depths within him.

When one prays in this way, his intercessions and praise and petitions then flow not from the head, but from the heart, the center and seat of spiritual life. These images, as they are offered to God, then represent more than just the thoughts that are already in consciousness, because they come from the center in which consciousness is born. The person who prays in this way finds that people are brought to his attention who need not only prayer but also one's loving action and concern. He also finds that he can hold meaningful dialogue with God, for these images which flow through the imagination are the means by which God most often speaks to us, opening new feelings and fresh understanding, and even at times those strange, inexplicable perceptions that make us know the reality of the world beyond this life. Imagination is the door out of silence into the inner realm of the spirit in which we can meet and commune with God.

Rule 7. Keep a Journal

Keeping a religious journal of the events along this spiritual journey is almost as important as having the experiences. A journal like this is used to record one's thoughts and intuitions, his experiences of both high moments and valleys of despair, the insights and turmoils, the imaginings, and the phantasies that come to him. These things are not recorded in order to impress anyone or to get something published, but rather because these are the experiences through which we contact a realm different from the material one, and its communications are the most valuable we can receive. If the realm of the spirit is real, and we do not record our contact with it, then we merely show how little we value this aspect of reality. And there is a very practical side to this as well.

Only if these experiences are recorded can we go back to them to see the effect of our contact with this realm. My own journals of other years are reread, sometimes with amazement at how much I have actually changed and how easy one insuperable problem or another has become. Or again I see the same persistent problem needing imagination and the full force of my effort and understanding. And there are also new insights waiting, which I had not understood before, but which now turn a floodlight of meaning on my life.

Equally important values come simply from writing this kind of journal. A process of clarifying goes on when in the silence one sets down the concerns which seem to overwhelm him; just in the act of writing one is able to stop "squirrel caging" and see things in perspective again. This kind of writing keeps us close to reality and helps to protect us from the dangers of the spiritual encounter. Nor does the phantasy which we get down on paper ever have quite the danger of a phantasy which is kept just in our heads. If one is becoming lost on an isolated mountain top, for instance, a record of his experiences will make it easier to see a way out. Or again, if imagination shows one that he actually looks on himself as a grasshopper up against a world of giants, then this image is far easier to handle when it is tied down in writing. The "grasshopper complex" can lead to transformation when it is looked at objectively and can be discussed with a friend or spiritual director.

One last value in keeping a journal is a strange one. The more serious attention we pay to these depths within ourselves, carefully recording the insights and phantasies that come, the more significant and valuable is the material we are given. The realm of the spirit responds to concern; its secrets are revealed to the one who pays attention to them. The lives of those who have sustained a real encounter with the realm of the spirit all manifest this truth. Almost every great spiritual leader has used some means, such as the journal we suggest, to help trace out and understand the things he discovered. Some tool like this is indispensable, and for us the journal is unquestionably the best way to concretize the spiritual endeavor. It offers a continuity which men need today, and it is the clearest demonstration of their earnestness and their conviction that this undertaking is essential to their lives. Many people have told me that the most valuable suggestion I ever made was to keep this day-by-day account of one's spiritual life. The journal can be the sacrament of one's spiritual life.

Rule 8. Keep a Record of Dreams

Keeping a record of one's dreams is actually a part of the journal we have been discussing, but it is such an important part that we shall take it up separately. Indeed a record of dreams will show even those who find it difficult to use imagination that there are elements of another world working within them. And when a person knows this, then it behooves him to take his own dreams seriously so that he will not neglect the very guidance and direction of God. As we have shown, he will be in good company in seeing dreams as the voice, the puzzling dark speech of God. In other times and ages Christians listened carefully to their dreams, while in our time it is the scientific community who take them seriously. Jung suggested the value which psychiatry places on dreams when he wrote of Freud: "By evaluating dreams as the most important source of information concerning the unconscious processes, he gave back to mankind a tool that had seemed irretrievably lost." [5] As Christians we also need to regain this lost understanding.

It is difficult to get any access at all to one's dreams unless he first records them, and does this soon after awakening. The images that filter through this screen within us contain a rich and strange symbolism which most people have begun to forget by the time they are fully awake. Even after many years of keeping track of my own dreams, I find that unless a dream has had particular power for me, by mid-morning I will have forgotten ninety percent of what it was about. In fact one must write as a good reporter does, factually and with all the detail he can remember. More than this, the record should be as continuous as possible if one is to have any real idea of the variety and breadth of his dreams, or of their complexity and mystery. Continuity is also wise because of the fact that certain dreams may be repeated, and these dreams, which call attention to persistent problem areas in our lives, may well be God's repeated call to us.

But how, then, does one begin to understand them? The meaning of dreams is revealed through the same faculty which can unlock the treasures of the Bible or other works of religious devotion—the imagination. What has come from the depths requires the help of the same depths for its explanation. One goes back to the same silence from which the dream has come, in the way we have discussed, letting his imagination play over the dream figures and images. As associations with other areas of life form, there come flashes of insight, clear meanings, even rational direction for one's life. The same journal in which these are recorded may also offer a well of understanding. What finally comes out, however, the actual interpretation of a specific dream, is subject enough in itself for another book. My own study of dreams in the context of Christian history, *Dreams: The Dark Speech of the Spirit*, gives some concrete suggestions on how to deal with interpretation.[6] John Sanford's *Dreams: God's Forgotten Language* shows how helpful understanding dreams can be in solving one's personal and spiritual problems. For the present discussion two short examples will have to suffice.

At a conference not long ago I gave two lectures on dreams, and the following morning a woman came to me to talk over the strange dream she had had that night. In the midst of it, she told me, she found herself holding a lamb in her arms, and was about to put it down when she discovered that it had long, sharp claws. In reality the woman had not seen a lamb in ten years and had never even imagined one with claws! As we talked about her associations we realized that for her the lamb stood for harmlessness, her own harmlessness. She saw, before I said a word about it, that her apparently gentle, easy nature had long and dangerous claws. She was not as harmless as she thought, the dream told her, and for this woman it had provided the deepest kind of insight.

The other dream, brought to me by a young man, shows how important the very short dream can be. It often has a clarity and significance greater than long involved dreams, and, like this one, is more insistent on a hearing. "I have lost my I. D. card, and find that my mother has taken it," he reported. As we talked about the dream together, it became apparent to him for the first time that he had lost his identity to his mother and that he must begin to break away from her if he were ever to grow up and become a man. In this way the reflection of another person on a dream will often unlock its meaning for us. We have difficulty in understanding our own dreams because they come to us from *our* unconscious, that part of ourselves or of another reality of which *we* are not aware. Here again the help of the spiritual director is often invaluable.

Even if one does not view dreams as the voice of God speaking to him, it is not difficult to see that they are a reflection of the deepest levels of ourselves, portraying a side of us that we can see in no other way. There is no surer way of breaking through the set forms of the outer material world into the realm of the spirit than by the careful recording of our dreams. This is the most certain door to the discovery that there is more in this realm than we can imagine, for it leads first to a confrontation with parts of our own selves which we have never even noticed.

Rule 9. Be Honest With Yourself

Utter honesty is the next prerequisite for those who would come to the divine encounter and have their lives transformed by it. Only the person who is honest can enter safely into the realm of the spirit and deal with it. All others are either turned away or they find themselves entangled and enmeshed in the darker sides of spirituality, for God does not like false faces. He demands that the total man come before him. He wants us to present our whole selves, not just the fragment that we think we are. This is one reason so many people fail utterly in the spiritual encounter. They leave behind the most important parts of themselves and confront the spiritual realm simply as a mask. They get very little contact because they touch it with only one facet of themselves.

Besides this, God can hardly transform us by his spirit if we do not present the parts of ourselves which need transformation. In fact, God is most polite. He seldom breaks in upon us until we open ourselves to him, and so repression of the less pleasant parts of our personalities separates us from him for sure. Since it is up to us to bring what we are, like it or not, to the meeting, this takes honesty. Few men allow themselves to know what they are, what lies hidden within them, and when men do not face themselves, they cannot meet God.

We forget the real meaning of the commandment about taking God's name in vain, that this is a commandment to truth and honesty. We shall not take the name of the Lord *in vain*. We shall swear only to the truth, and be open to the fact that we cannot know it in entirety. And this, as we all know when we reflect on it, begets inner honesty from which outer honesty and truth flow naturally. "To thine own self be true, and it must follow, as the night the day, thou canst not then be false to any man." (Hamlet I, iii)

I have seen many people with their masks down, and I have never yet seen any who was not infinitely more attractive and beautiful unmasked than masked. The ugliness we often see in the naked soul is far more than made up by its native beauty, which is more wonderful and attractive than any other creation of God. When a man finally opens up the depth of himself to me I cannot help but love what I see. So I believe it is with God. When a man comes before Him in utter honesty, nakedly himself, there is a response on the part of God which opens channels of contact between God and man. This is the truth which C. S. Lewis told with such bold imagination in his magnificent novel *'Til We Have Faces.*

When I am discouraged with the state of my soul and wonder how God can put up with me, I am always heartened by the transparent honesty of Paul at the end of Romans 7. There he cries out: "The good which I want to do, I fail to do; but what I do is the wrong which is against my will . . . miserable creature that I am, who is there to rescue me out of this body doomed to death?" [7] If God accepted Paul, he can accept us too! How God longs for us to be honest with ourselves and with Him that He may respond to us all.

A spiritual director is needed as much in the pursuit of inner honesty as anywhere in our spiritual journey. It is so easy for us to deceive ourselves. Our closeness and our blindness hide the most obvious faults from our own eyes, and the spiritual director who accepts himself as he is can help us to face them honestly without poking the sore appendix. Since he does not have to hide from himself, he can be matter-of-fact, and neither gingerly nor destructive, in letting other people see the distasteful parts of themselves. The dream, properly understood, is also an enforcer of inner honesty, and sometimes a ruthless one. Yet the dream, while picturing us as we really are, never reveals more of ourselves than we are able to bear. We can ill afford to do without either relationship, for whatever helps us to come to an inner integrity, an inner honesty, also helps us along the spiritual journey.

Rule 10. Let Your Life Manifest Genuine Love

Many of the rules which we are discussing are the same for all religious groups, but there are at least two of them which are uniquely Christian. The religions which are concerned solely with spirituality do not place an emphasis on either the use of imagination or the rule of love. Love is the relating of an inner attitude outwardly. For the Christian it is an inner religious attitude, an attitude towards the whole of himself which he is openly asking God to give him. It is the act of living in relationship with others as God lives with us. We are not worthy to be given the intimate, total fellowship with God in the realm of the spirit which is indeed given to those who turn with openness toward him, and yet this is given. One of the cardinal principles of Christianity is that what we have received freely, we should give freely. As St. Catherine put it, the only way that we can give back to God what he has given us is to give the same unmerited compassion and love to another human being. But this attitude flows from a whole personality, not from just the spit and polish, and others like Baron von Hügel go further, adding that it is our task to love the unlovable even as God has loved us. Wherever Christianity has been alive and creative we find this same emphasis. Putting love into action is the one significant way we human beings are given to express our gratitude, and like humility, gratitude is the rock bottom foundation for every rule for the spiritual encounter.

The importance of love is central in the teaching and, even more significantly, in the life of Jesus. In Paul's writings—who, like Peter, felt that love covers a multitude of sins, the word love may be substituted anywhere for the Holy Spirit with little change in meaning; it is the action which most nearly characterizes the Holy Spirit. The catalogue of those who have maintained the centrality of love is endless. In our time Kagawa, Starr Daily, and Agnes Sanford have again called attention to it. Agnes Sanford writes that love is the essential quality of the healing power which operates through the Christian.

If this is true, then what are we to understand from it? Why should the outer actions of our lives have such an influence upon our capacity to confront the inner realm and experience it? Principally this is because the inner realities are different from the outer ones. They are not governed by mechanical laws, even to any degree, and for this reason they do not reveal their deepest meanings indiscriminately to everyone who searches. God, who is at the heart and center of psychic reality, is never pressed into confrontation; rather he gives of himself when and where he will. Nor can the approach to the spiritual realm be made with just the mind and consciousness. It involves the total psyche—hence the extreme importance of honesty—and love conditions the nature of the psyche, shaping it into the kind of instrument which is able to deal with the realm of the spirit. The door to the center of this realm is love, and we do not find it unless our lives are turned in that direction. It is as if we approached this door, which is love, each one with a key which he has been required to shape out of his own life, and if it does not fit, the door will not open.

As a matter of fact, those who spend their energies in spiritual activity without any effort to shape their lives in the pattern of love may experience the power of nonphysical reality, but it can well be from the demonic forces which dwell there instead of divine ones. If we become spiritual and hate, we can become the agents of some particular hatred in a most powerful and destructive way. We had better not doubt the reality of the forces of evil. When one who expresses spirituality is not motivated by love, his life can be taken over by the negative and wrathful side of spiritual reality, and he then becomes its tool. How well Charles Williams has portrayed this truth in *Shadows of Ecstasy*.

On the other side, the man who genuinely expresses love may have no sense of contact with the realm of the spirit; he may have no ecstatic experiences, and may think his life humdrum and dull. Yet he may be nearer to the angelic and expressing its essence and centrality more than the spiritual man who does not love. It is not necessary to be conscious of God to have His life in us. There are many, like St. Martin, whose way of simple kindness and concern is rewarded by the presence of the Christ. Martin's vision, when he saw Christ and spoke with Him, came in a dream the night after he had shared his cloak with a beggar. There may also be some very surprised saints, who follow a way that seems scarcely all sweetness and light from the outside, but for them fulfills the demands of love. Like God, love will not be limited to one variety of expression; after all, Narcissus' downfall was not that he saw his own reflection, but that he found it only once and drowned in it.

Our need to manifest love outwardly also has several important corollaries. For one, the person who has made the divine confrontation can no longer live entirely for himself. He must become involved in the world, although not by taking all its burdens upon his heart. This would destroy any man. Rather he must, as the Quakers put it, find his concern, some kind of social action. This is requisite if a man's spiritual life is to continue. Indeed the continuing confrontation of the divine depends upon the sincerity and integrity with which he turns outward to share what he has found. One may enter the realm of the spirit, find the richest experiences within it, receive power which is startling and real, and still be cut off completely from that life and power if he fails to turn outward and express it.

There are dangers of falling into the brand of social action we label "do-goodism," but they are much less when we are honestly aware how much it means to us to relate to the spiritual world. Doing good loses its punch only if it is taken over by ego motives instead of springing from divine inspiration, or when it becomes such a central concern that there is no time left over for the divine encounter. The surest test is when it begins to make us irritable with our families or co-workers. Then it is time to take a good look at what we are doing, remembering that doing good is not what gets us into the kingdom of heaven; and neither does avoiding it.

Another corollary of love is our need to practice listening. By this I mean the forgotten art of listening in which one empties himself and lets the totality of another personality make an impact upon his inmost being. As one discovers the totality of the other human psyche which confronts him, he can come to know the Holy Spirit which dwells and moves in the depth of the other person's soul. One can thus come to a divine encounter through another person's soul by listening. In real listening it is because we love and want the other person to be what he is; we listen to him as God listens lovingly to us. Rudolf Steiner has explained this in part in these words:

> Only to those who, by selfless listening, train themselves to be really recipient from within, in stillness, unmoved by personal opinion or feeling, only to such can the higher beings speak, of whom Spiritual Science tells. As long as one hurls any personal opinion or feeling against the speaker to whom one must listen, the beings of the spiritual world remain silent.[8]

Even more important, there is a difference between this kind of listening, with compassion, real love, and listening with indifference, and the person talking can sense it. A story is told from one minister's sanctum which I can vouch is too true to be fiction. A man he had been counseling came in one day and sat down and did not have a word to say. There he sat for the whole hour. And when he finally got up to leave, he said to the minister, "You will never know what this has meant to me. I didn't think there was any man on earth who could stand me for an hour without saying a word." This kind of listening is not easy; it must be learned, and even then it is one of the most exhausting activities a person can undertake—demanding the total psyche—and one of the most rewarding. Actually I have found out more about God through the people who have come to talk with me than from any amount of reading. In this kind of listening one does not find it necessary to make the other person over, and through it one participates in depth of another's being, and so in the spiritual world on which his life is based.

A third corollary of practicing love is involvement in fellowship or community. This word has been spread so thin that it has come to mean a superficial kind of human relating, almost a game of keeping up pretenses. Real fellowship is anything but this. In genuine fellowship with another person in a small group (two is merely the smallest group) there is an interaction of one total person with another, without the need of pretenses or masks, in an atmosphere of acceptance and love. And, in return, acceptance and love grow out of the interaction. If this kind of give and take between real people is to be possible, rather than the meeting of masks which is all that happens in most groups, a man must know that he can let down his mask. Before one can be himself, revealing what he considers are the less attractive aspects of himself, he must know that he will be accepted and not put on display, that he can be loved just as he is.

Out of this meeting of person with person there will be conflict and disagreement. So often Christians believe that human relationships should be devoid of conflict, yet there can be no genuine meeting of person with person without friction. Jesus never suggested that there should be no conflict among human beings—only no unresolved conflicts. In fact, those who run their lives so that they avoid all conflict with other people also avoid love and real fellowship. These simply do not grow outside of total contact with another person, and this is bound to involve conflict. Love comes out of action, not ideas or thought. And action involves concrete contact and relationship. It brings one up short to remember John's statement that we cannot love God until we love our neighbor, for love is seldom fulfilled in abstraction.

Churches ought to be the place where one could find real fellowship and relationship; yet for most people they are the last place where one expects to find—or to give—it. The real person is revealed far more in the meat market and the beauty shop than in church. In church we try to be what we think we ought to be, and the other person does the same, and how utterly unreal the meeting is. There are a few churches, however, which have begun to experiment with small groups, meeting to study and discuss the basic issues of life. This kind of encounter with other human beings brings about real relationship as these people meet week after week. There is conflict and then real love. The genesis of the power and spirit of Methodism was in such groups.

There is one danger, however; such groups unlock the dynamics of the human soul and sometimes one finds pent-up psychic storms unleashed which are difficult to handle. It is a good rule to have in each group like this one person who is trained to recognize such storms and deal with them, but Christians who are so trained are difficult to find. In some way the church must provide them and learn to recapture the fellowship in which human beings relate to one another. Otherwise we lose one of the most important avenues through which the individual can come to know the spiritual realm.

An understanding of this outward or extraverted aspect of the spiritual way needs to be developed in far greater detail than the beginning we have made here.[9] Youth today are crying out against the lack of love and concern which is obvious not only in our secular society but in our churches as well. If our young people who most need the church are to be reached, it must be with a message of real love, well integrated and understood.

Rule 11. Gird Yourself With Persistence and Courage

The encounter with the world of the spirit requires great persistence and courage. It is a lifetime work. If the quest is peripheral and spasmodic one will never achieve a creative confrontation. The devotion of the atomic physicist puts most religious people to shame. In order to unlock the secrets hidden in matter these men spend a third of a lifetime in preparation, and then settle down to endless days of work and thought. How often do we find men spending this kind of time and preparation, this expenditure of energy, on the religious quest? Wherever we do, we find religious results; the divine encounter is observable and the working of the spirit becomes manifest.

Most of us want to reach up on the shelf and take our religious maturity down in a package. We want to have one religious experience, one encounter with the divine, and right off the bat become oracles of His wisdom and fountains of His grace. But the effective religious life is not created in this way; it grows slowly. God can and does give spiritual and mental healing, revelations and visions, dreams and ecstatic experiences, but the mature religious personality is never given as a gift all at once. It grows slowly, tended and aided by God and the powers of the realm of the spirit. It is this kind of religious maturity which alone has continuous power in healing the bodies of men, in cleansing their minds and directing their souls. We had better look twice at anyone who claims a religious development and powers which came suddenly as a gift. He may be deceiving himself, for the Evil One can turn out superb counterfeits in just this way, and Christians need to be able to distinguish between the true commodity, the powers of the Holy Spirit, and the imitation.

The life of St. Paul is an example in point. He had his tremendous experience on the Damascus road, and another at the hands of Ananias. Undoubtedly he was given the Holy Spirit, but when he tried to preach in Damascus, he had to flee for his life. It was not just that Saul the persecutor was still hated. Paul was not ready. Ten years of preparation and integration of his experience were necessary before Barnabas saw that Paul was prepared to bring others to the experience of God. Yet most of us are in too much of a hurry to keep going religiously; we think we can know the essence and heart of reality more easily than the physical scientist learns to know one small fragment of it. Yet the same quiet, continuous persistence, so essential to science, is the only way to a significant and fruitful encounter with the realm of the spirit. If "Patience and per-sev-erance made a bishop of his reverence," they also make saints of ordinary men.

Many men fail in the religious journey because they do not have courage. They follow all the rest of the rules, but when the going gets difficult they cannot bear the suffering which is involved. Joining together the animal and the angel within oneself is painful. Neither one can stand the other. As we bring the totality of what we are before the realm of the spirit, we begin to know real guilt. Only one who has experienced this can know how painful it is to get a clear picture of our own beastliness, our egotism, cruelty and hate—those delightful qualities which we have always managed to attribute to a few "bad guys" somewhere else in the world. It is like a bad dream to find them in one's self, and added to this is the realization that, try as hard as we may, we never finish the task of complete integration, joining the realm of the spirit with the realm of the flesh within ourselves. One often falls back into unconsciousness, and then there is shame and guilt again. Whoever seeks the religious quest will suffer the gnawing pain of his own inadequacy, and this takes courage. Many turn away from life in rigidity or in mental illness simply because they do not have the courage to bear what they are. The religious encounter forces one to bear it.

The cross stands at the center of the Christian faith. If we go the way of Jesus in the religious encounter, we will inevitably come to crosses, to suffering. As popular as crosses may be to adorn the outside, how little we like to bear them in our own hearts. But those who are not willing to bear inner suffering never find out much about the realm of the spirit. This is difficult to understand, but it seems to be empirically true. Bearing suffering, however, does not mean resignedly accepting physical illness. Even though it can bring spiritual growth when courageously borne—for God can turn even evil to good—physical illness is one of the least creative forms of suffering. It is often an outpicturing in our bodies of that which we have not faced and borne directly in our souls.

Ernest Gordon's book *Through the Valley of the Kwai* is a striking example of the power of suffering to transform men. Through the suffering of the prison camp self-satisfied, complacent young men were stripped of their conceit, their egotism, their agnosticism. They realized their need for God there in a human dump-heap in the jungles of Burma. Crushed and broken in spirit and open to God, they were touched by the power and reality of God and transformed. And that particular prison camp showed some surprising results.

One of the reasons for the success of Alcoholics Anonymous is the very stripping down which has come to most drunks when they have finally admitted that they can no longer handle their problem. Here is the genuine spiritual process at work.

The saints speak of sweet suffering. Gerald Sykes concludes in *The Hidden Remnant* that the remnant exists only because it can courageously accept suffering and bear it. The truths about spiritual growth are very real, and though they can be dressed in new language, they all come from the same depth, a depth which is immeasurable and is the only place from which God gives new life. If we wish to find this life, and to grow in the realm of the spirit, we must learn to bear real suffering; we will have to help bear with God the sin of the world, around us *and* inside us. There is no question about the value of a spiritual director when this kind of pain must be borne; it is nearly impossible to go this part of the way alone.

Rule 12. Give Generously of Your Material Goods

It is impossible to continue in contact with the realm of the spirit unless one gives of his material substance for religious purposes. It is nonsense to say that one wants the realm of the spirit and its power, that he is giving his life utterly to God for this purpose, and then spend most of his financial resources on himself and his own desires and interests. It is worse than nonsense; it is hypocrisy, and God does not have much truck with hypocrites. The spiritual realm closes and remains closed, except for occasional flashes of lightning, to those who do not give. Money is simply our congealed lives, what the world pays us for what it thinks we are worth. Unless we give of it for outer religious purposes —to the institutions which, however inadequately they are performing, are dedicated to the realm of the spirit—the religious encounter goes dead within us. One can do everything else I have suggested, and if he avoids this commitment, he might just as well have tried none of them.

It might be well to remember again the story of Cornelius in Acts, who continued faithful in prayer and in giving. Cornelius kept putting out to support the expectation he had been given, and the angel came to him with knowledge which he could get only by extrasensory perception. And though today we do not call such experiences by the name Cornelius used, they still happen among people who give themselves and their substance to support what they believe.

One of the factors which was responsible for my real interest in the spiritual life was my own practice of tithing. It was not many years ago—after I was some years into the ministry, as a matter of fact—that I heard one speaker at a clergy conference state that it was wicked to tithe. This was what I was waiting to hear, because I was feeling uneasy about the smallness of my giving. I had been looking for a good excuse. But the speaker went on to say that it certainly was wicked to tithe, for this then gave one the idea that he could pay God off with a straight tip. Right then and there I decided that I had better get into the wicked category. As I began to give one-tenth of my own income, I thought to myself: "This matter of religion really is important. I had better get deeper into the real business of it." And I started giving a great deal more time to reading the Bible, meditating on books of devotion, and praying. I found, like anyone else, that giving is a sacramental action which constantly reminds us of our commitment to God and the necessity of *our* turning to Him. When one gives to God and God's work, one is likely to give the whole effort which God requires in our relation to Him.

Conclusion

If the individual is to make contact with the realm of the spirit, the total man must give himself to this encounter. The rules which we have been outlining are directions for turning one's total life to God. Some of them point up areas of life which have been forgotten, and which, by being ignored, keep most people from making a total encounter. Thus, rules of some kind are essential to bring these parts of our lives into the total relationship. Before we turn to our conclusions about the spiritual journey, let us list the rules in order:

Act as though you believe in the spiritual realm.

Undertake the quest with serious purpose.

Seek companionship and spiritual direction for the spiritual journey.

Turn away from the busy-ness of the outer world in silence and introversion.

Learn the value of genuine fasting.

Learn to use the forgotten faculty of the imagination.

Keep a journal.

Record your own dreams.

Be as honest with yourself as you can and get someone else to help you be honest.

Let your life manifest real love.

Gird yourself with persistence and courage.

Give generously of your material goods.

These rules are the result of one man's experience with his own encounter, with psychotherapy, and listening to others. Certainly they are not infallible, and many difficulties and dangers have been pointed out. In some ways it might seem safer to avoid the spiritual realm and occupy ourselves solely with physical reality. In fact, to decide about the value of the spiritual encounter, we must first ask if this is a valid alternative.

Most people take it for granted that matter is essentially harmless. The idea is deeply rooted in our culture that if one follows matter wherever it leads, all he will find in the end are material blessings, an endless prospect of things like high-powered cars and wonder drugs. It is hard to realize how completely this is accepted, for few of us ever question whether it is safe to deal with matter as if it were the only reality. We know that our material progress has side effects —pollution, dangers of atomic waste, even of turning our planet into a wasteland. We read of the stockpile of atomic weapons, the use of napalm, the destructive possibilities of the laser ray and germ warfare. In less than thirty years our rational and materialistic culture has dragged us through wars that have created as much havoc as most of the other devastations of man put together.

Yet we try to forget the barbarities and go on treating matter as if we need look no farther in dealing with these responsibilities. By ignoring spiritual reality we put ourselves in the position of the "boy Fausts" depicted by Gerald Sykes, the scientists who are merely engaged in investigating matter and carry no responsibility for the end product. If their discoveries are turned into bombs and dropped on innocent human beings, the blame belongs to someone else; their only concern is with lifeless and inert matter.

The trouble is that when men do not deal with spiritual reality, they are then subject to its power without any control over which force, negative or positive, influences them and the way they deal with matter. They simply react, very much like the African native who has not yet come to consciousness, who seeks his "friend" with smiles and gifts one moment, only to turn on him the next, berserk with rage. As long as we remain unconscious of the spiritual realm and its archetypal powers, these forces possess our lives, determining at will how we react to the outer world.

Perhaps there are more subtle ways of running amok today, of turning on oneself (and even a fast car may be used as a lethal weapon), or of trying to possess others and destroy with words. When moments of inner darkness overwhelm a person, there is little he can do to withstand these negative powers if he is unconscious of them. Moral will may help for a time, but it is our wall of morals that breaks down before the archetypal powers, and depression, anxiety and —more and more often today—violence take over. Only one who is empowered by the creative center of spiritual reality can stand up to these forces.

Collectively we are not very different from the African native, except in the scale of our generosity and our destructiveness as a nation. At one moment we may send a boatload of food and doctors to save a people, and the next we send an army somewhere. We find little satisfaction in another nation's achievement, for we are running a race with destruction. If men do not come to know the spiritual realm and its power over them, we may well destroy ourselves and our civilization, leaving only a remnant who have found central meaning and purpose in life, and thus the way to stand up to these realities.

Is it not possible, in fact, that this encounter is man's destiny which he cannot escape? At the center of spiritual reality may well be a plan, God's design that we make the conscious effort to relate to Him, that men shall come by choice to seek God, the center of spiritual reality. One thing that suggests this most strongly is the trouble we get ourselves into when we try to escape from doing just that. Of course, it is frightening, and also difficult and dangerous, to take the lead in this. But if this is what God wants, then it is time to try to find Him.

It appears that the most critical and pressing problem of our time is a return to this experience of spirituality, not what to do about the outer physical world. Indeed when we do not contain and deal with spiritual reality within ourselves, then we project its power and attractiveness willy-nilly out into the material world. By becoming caught either in the cult of sentimental love and idolatry or in the cult of hate and violence, we not only lose the real power which is available to us as men, but we see other people only as objects which carry these archetypal powers of incredible attraction or repulsion.

So much of the time we worship the ad-man's vision of a perfect man or woman instead of worshiping God and relating to real men and women. These ideals are merely the Greek gods come to life unconsciously; Venus appears, re-named, for the airlines and Adonis returns, with clothes on, to sell us cigarettes. It is a healthy beginning when we admit consciously to worshiping them as gods. Then we do not turn this adulation on a wife or child—or even a husband—and attribute such divine qualities to a human being that he is destroyed, and with him our chance for real love. Sentimental or romantic love, which is the natural result of our ignorance of spiritual reality, restricts our view so that we have no chance to know and love the real person; we end usually in either finding nothing or in hating and warring with the other.

As the noted critic Alfred Kazin once pointed out in the *Saturday Review,* men prefer war to boredom. They come to life with power and vitality when hate is aroused in them, whether by family or neighborhood squabbles, race riots, or full-scale war. In each case the devils are out there, a legitimate target giving man a one-track job—to destroy the devils with words or knives or bombs, and thus get rid of the evil. The reason men get caught up in such outer destructiveness is that they have forgotten the inner combat with the Evil One. Those who do not believe in the world of spirit have no way of dealing with the reality of the devil except outwardly, and since this struggle demands expression, they express it out in the world. Only when we wake up to the problem spiritually, so that it can be dealt with inwardly and creatively, will we find freedom from violence, war, and the risk of total destruction.

Neither love nor violence is the total, unreasonable obsession of those who have experienced the spirit and are wise in that experience. Such men find love through relationship with reality within both themselves and those whom they love. They do not switch on the automatic pilot when some archetypal pattern whispers in sultry tones, "Now love!" They make the choice for themselves. Their knowledge of spiritual reality keeps them from destroying human beings by either idolizing or seeing them personified as demons. Such mature men of the spirit may take action, but not simply because their hormones are involved. They are able to see what is required to preserve civilization because they need not see only good at home and everything demonic in the other person.

This is a difficult and dangerous way to follow. But if it is our destiny, then we had better get on with it, for the spiritual encounter probably holds our only chance for satisfaction as men, and unquestionably our best chance for staying alive. Only God, the center of creativity, can save us and through us save our world. And in the process, those who act on the hypothesis that there is a realm in which God can be encountered are very likely to find it verified. These people, who are willing to experiment and test out their "hunch," will normally come to know God as He has promised.

How, then, can the reality of this encounter and some use of these rules be communicated to men who are searching for such meaning and purpose?

CHAPTER IX

Communicating Religion

Modern Christianity is failing to communicate itself. It is this fact that originally started us to study, and to ask why "orthodox" Christianity and its theology have so little confidence that there is anything experiential, anything real and specifically Christian to communicate. We have suggested that this is mainly due to the failure of theology to keep up with the findings in other fields, which has left a wide gap between Christian thinking and today's increasingly sophisticated understanding of man and the world. To help close this gap, we have outlined a workable, experiential theology related to facts and the newer understanding of scientists and philosophers, and we have supported this point of view by suggesting some methods by which one can try out its reality for himself and verify it.

Is there any way that we can communicate this understanding, both physical and spiritual, to those in our modern generation who are lost in doubt and fear? It would be surprising if there were not. Every world view that has grown up thus far has carried within it suggestions for its communication and for education, and so does the point of view which we have proposed.

The realism of Plato, for instance, suggests experimentation through dialogue and fellowship and an understanding of myth. The intellectualism of Aristotle and the scholastics, with their stress on the physical world of sense experience, both entail development of the individual's logical and mathematical abilities (a tendency towards exclusive emphasis on the "three R's" so that those with abilities in other directions tend to lose their value). Pragmatism in its turn puts all hands to work looking for experimental ways of releasing human potential, and progressive education is the logical result of this kind of thinking. Behaviorism, while not a very sophisticated philosophy, is still a way of looking at the world, which proposes educating individuals towards whatever goal one has in mind by shaping the conditions that stimulate these individuals. Existentialism leads to a study of the human condition and how

213

the individual can meet and deal with his own existential decision.[1]

The point of view we have sketched has all sorts of involvements with education, beginning with an understanding of how we humans communicate. Obviously, we can only begin to consider these as carefully as they need to be studied. But if the understanding of the world which we have presented is close at all to reality, then the suggestions that we have to make represent only a beginning anyway, a base that becomes valuable only as the efforts of all of us are turned to investigating, comparing and testing it in the actual experience of men.

Let us ask first: If it is true that man has a deep need to find central meaning in the world—meaning which can best be seen or discovered in the *experience* of God—and that the predicament of man today results largely from the fact that he faces an increasingly complex world with no place in its outer aspects to find such central meaning, then what does this imply for our understanding of education?

A Theology of Communication

Very likely the first thing we need is to go beyond a philosophy of education to develop a theology of communication. Man's ability to understand his place in the world appears to depend upon his finding relationship to that center of reality which suffuses and gives meaning to the whole that revolves around it. When education fails to take this *experience* of man into consideration, and ignores the strong evidence that in the long run he finds value only in this way, it cannot prepare man for his total world, but educates him only for a portion of it.

Few theologians have realized that they need to understand the educational process. Most of them have assumed that religion could be presented as a set of intellectual truths that anyone with a bright enough mind would take in and assimilate. History has not exactly demonstrated this assumption, and neither do the recent surveys of religion by social scientists, as James Michael Lee has amply documented in his several books. But there is at least a beginning, and a thoughtful one, in the late reflections of one important theologian. In his *Theology of Culture* Paul Tillich has included a chapter on "A Theology of Education," and his concluding observations are addressed as a question to Christian ministers and teachers about "Communicating the Christian Message."

Tillich discusses the three major aims of education, and points out the loss to the culture when they become separated from man's basic search for meaning. He shows how *technical* education, providing the know-how to deal with the outer world, has moved in on the *humanistic* and *inducting* goals. What passes for humanistic education today no longer seeks to develop the individual's potential, but mainly deals with forms from the past. Inducting or initiatory education, which seeks to give the individual participation in the social group and its values, is used by religious groups in a limited way. But these values are quickly lost when the adult moves into the ordinary world where inducting education is the effective servant of an industrial and technical society.

The church, as Tillich sees, must continue to introduce the growing human being to the mythical language and the power of Christian symbols. At the same time it must try to help him go beyond this induction and question it. Certainly Tillich is right in this. The collective culture, the culture which is primarily non-individual, uses inducting education to perpetuate itself, often at the expense of the individual. Individual development comes as the ideas of the collective, whether primitive or modern, are questioned.

The world view we suggest sees inducting education as a stage in the development of every individual, as necessary as the identification of the child with his family, but still preliminary to self consciousness. Where the individual is seen as having a unique relationship with the spiritual world, a unique destiny and value, education does not end with this stage. Anything that is encountered through this initiatory education may be re-examined and tested by the individual to see if it fits his experience. This is the very point at which our young people seem to be today; they are no longer satisfied with being taken into the culture, like making a fraternity.

Indeed the culture itself, to stay alive, must continue on beyond this stage. The great Catholic council in 1965, Vatican II, recognized this and came out with an emphasis on the individual which represents both the spirit of the times and the spirit of Jesus of Nazareth.[2] Just as it took almost two thousand years to realize that slavery did not belong among Christians, so it has taken very nearly the same time to understand that conscious, growing human beings need their own encounters with God, and that religion cannot be just induced and stabilized in them. If the institutional church does not wake up to this fact, it is in for even worse days than it has had. Either it must provide an experiential base which individuals can know and build on, or they will look elsewhere for this base.

A far broader technical education is also needed than the present training in the sciences, arts and engineering, which deal with only half of the reality to which man is exposed. As Jung remarked in his interview with John Freeman on the BBC film "Face to Face with Dr. Jung," the problems that are most difficult for men do not come from these areas, but rather from man's lack of understanding of himself and the nonphysical world that surrounds him. Practical technical education is needed to provide the kind of skills we have discussed in the last chapter.

In the first place man needs to learn how he can resist psychic or spiritual infections, much as he needs medical techniques to fight bacterial infections. And then, because this realm of experience is known only through the psyche, understanding of the psyche is essential so that one can see and understand his experience as clearly as possible. Man needs skills to avoid distortion in psychic perception and understanding, just as refined scientific methods are developed to avoid the distortions in ordinary seeing and hearing. It is more difficult, of course, to do this in dealing with the world of experience that comes through direct contact with the psyche, but it is possible and certainly needed. In fact, this is one of the major tasks of religion, as well as of psychology.

The base of humanistic education is greatly widened in our framework. Coming to know the spiritual world and the psyche that must receive it requires the greatest development of a person's capacities. One may have the greatest insights from this "inner" spiritual world and still not be able to distinguish what has value from that which comes from destructive spiritual influences, or from wish fulfillment and pride. And unless he can bring the insights to bear on his own life and life around him, they might as well be bubbles on a stream. To do this he has his own personality, and what speaks through it, to work with. He has to depend upon his experiences and values, his ability to work with others, comparing and then feeling his way among these experiences. Men are explorers in this world of spirit; they are like physicists looking into the atom with no microscope or tracking device except their own personalities.

The task within this framework, then, is to transmit the meanings and symbols of Christianity as best we can, while we learn new ways of approaching their source, and at the same time try to grow enough as human beings to handle the new ways of experience and what they bring. This is a big order. In fact it is far too big for men to consider if they are thinking about doing it on their own.

But that is just the point we are making. The church says that it believes in God. What we have suggested is that, if the church is willing to test this proposition in experience, it will find that God is more than just an Aristotelian category of the known world. Men will find a source of meaning and power beyond their own, power that is not just an untapped residue of their own abilities. But this cannot be communicated by any stretch of the imagination to people who also confine man to a particular slot in the easily known and predictable world. These people, who are probably in the majority inside the church as well as out of it, hold a theory of personality that keeps large areas of experience at arm's length, or farther. Before communication can begin, one has to recognize this barrier and start the job of penetrating it.

A Common Theory of Personality

Most of the people who hold this popular theory of personality would be quite upset at the suggestion that they have a psychological point of view. They consider it simply a matter of dealing with facts, and they are extremely suspicious of psychology; it might as well be a four-letter word for many. Nonetheless, these people do express a psychology, which they hold without giving it much thought. And the trouble with holding a view without reflecting on it is that the view generally controls the individual rather than the other way around. When ideas are simply assumed, they cannot be criticized or examined because one does not know that he has them; instead, he thinks they are "facts." Thus, when something seems as obvious as this idea about human beings, it is time to start doubting and questioning it.

According to this view,[3] human personality has quite a simple and easily understood structure, mostly built out of conscious exposure to things and ideas. Since man comes into the world as a blank page on which life chalks up its traces, society has two responsibilities towards him. Its job first of all is to direct the experiences of the growing human being so as to turn out a society of adults filled with the right content, and then to back this up with some system of reward and punishment. The theory of education, including all the sources, follows right in line.

The role of the educator is to feed the right mixture of appropriate experiences into human beings, much as one would feed data into a very sensitive computer. His responsibility (once this role is defined) is to select and shape the patterns of the developing person in accordance with the social pattern, or the educator's pattern, or some other standard. B. F. Skinner is explicit about the way this theory has been expected to work in practice; apply the correct "operant conditioning" and one will get the desired results. Basically Skinner considers man about as complex as a pigeon. In fact, this thinking— which has been around quite a while, although not as clearly stated as Skinner puts it—is very idealistic about being able to shape man in the most desirable way.[4] If the input is correct, he will become an acceptable, productive, law-abiding member of the group.

But if a man does not turn out this way, it is the result of either the wrong input or a perverse will. One must try to correct the conditioning, but if the individual resists and refuses to take on the correction rationally, it is concluded that his will needs to be altered. In this case the second task of society comes into play. It has the responsibility of meting out certain rewards, but more especially of punishing to produce the proper conditioning and alter the will. Individuals whose actions show that they do not have the right ideas or habits, whose will is simply perverse, must be brought into line. And if punishment fails to change a man towards a more socially acceptable pattern of behavior, then the only alternative is to banish him from the social group so that his presence will not act as the rotten apple in the barrel.

Obviously I have used a fairly heavy hand to picture these ideas. Still, this does not exaggerate the way most of our law courts, most mental institutions and prisons, and many of our schools and families have operated. Mental institutions that were run on this theory left most of their patients without hope of recovery, and most prisoners treated in this way end up back in prison, confirmed in their antisocial attitudes. As for families, the people who have come to me in real need of counseling have almost invariably come from family situations in which the basis of relationship was essentially the theory of personality I have described. Nor have churches been exactly free of this understanding and its effect on the way church people treat each other and their clergy. And there have been religious schools that followed it to the letter, even to regulating the width of the strap in the principal's office!

The trouble is that the church, by a strange alchemy, has managed to ignore the difference between this thinking and the understanding of Jesus and His followers. The church is out of touch with its own reality. Secular thinkers, as we have seen, are in touch with various parts of reality, and they have been forced to take a new look at the world and man. But the church has not realized the depth and complexity of human beings and the kind of world that touches them. Until it is willing to take the risk of breaking out of this common thinking about man, and his essentially Aristotelian and materialistic view of himself, it cannot see the depth of reality, let alone communicate this to the depth of man.

The gospel was originally spread by men who were willing to take this risk, who had no social power to depend on. Jesus and most of the leaders of the early church were outlaws from the social group, and the main reason Christianity made the imprint it did was that it had a following who cared for and were interested in one another, and because they experienced breakthroughs of power that astounded the ancient world. Paul made this very explicit in his important letter to the Romans when he summed up:

> For I will not venture to speak of anything except what Christ has wrought through me to win obedience from the Gentiles, by word and deed, by the power of signs and wonders, by the power of the Holy Spirit . . .[5]

As the French philosopher Festugière has remarked, Christians had a sense of being "members of one another. . . . If it had not been there, the world would still be pagan. And the day when it is no longer there, the world will be pagan once again." [6]

When it is understood in this way, communicating the Christian gospel has an exciting quality which is quite lacking when it is reduced to transmitting a set of propositions, or final, logical ideas. This is not only dull (no matter how satisfying it may be to the teacher), but it is seldom effective in changing people's lives and behavior. As James Michael Lee has shown repeatedly, little relation can be found between the individual's ethical and religious behavior (or practice) and what he has studied about religion and ethics.[7] Such teaching may be very close to demonic, in fact, if one feels obligated to force feed another person, who may or may not be ready for it.

Even more important, this method actually discourages learning through experience about the spiritual reality that is basic to Christianity. Quite recently a group of students in a private school realized this and tried to do something about it. They approached the woman who, interestingly enough, teaches both physics and religion in the school, and asked her why they couldn't get into religion the same way they did physics. She was fascinated by the idea of helping these high school seniors search for answers, and together they started questioning and experimenting. The church, however, has been less certain of its ground than this teacher and her students, and they found few approaches to experiences with which the group could experiment.

Many people take a nostalgic view of the way religion and culture are handed on from one generation to another within a collective social group. Primitive or collective society does, of course, transmit its culture, but usually with fear and without much regard for individual value or worth; this is the point Henri Bergson makes in *The Two Sources of Morality and Religion.* Any variation from the norm is suspect and may be suppressed by the collective group. Christianity, on the other hand, speaks of the essential value of the individual, his almost infinite depth and complexity, and of his ability to make his own contact with the realm of spirit. An understanding quite beyond the collective pattern must be transmitted if this religion of ours is to be consistent with its own genius. Where then does one start to make this effective?

Where To Begin?

Probably the best way to start today is with small groups of adults, actually study groups or classes, in which a close and caring relationship can be developed, and in which the realities we have been discussing can be talked about, but not talked to death. This takes skillful leadership because it involves the individual's acceptance of both himself and others. Only in such an atmosphere is it possible for these realities of spirit to be encountered and (to some extent) shared. It is necessary to get below the surface of the individual personality, but this is a process of discovering and accepting the realities of one's own being, not a cleaning out job like an encounter group. For this reason it takes a leader who knows and accepts himself quite thoroughly, and also grasps quite clearly the relation of psychological understanding to religious realities.

This relationship which can mesh an encounter with the realm of spirit can also be found through individual counseling where a minister or others have the desire and have had sufficient experience in this area themselves. Individuals can also be started on this way through groups who seek to meditate and pray openly together; this also requires strong leadership if it is to avoid either flying off on individual tangents or becoming bogged down in just ideas about religion.

The liturgy of the church and the central act of communion with the living presence of Christ who cares and accepts beyond all others, of course, offers the deepest and fullest encounter with spiritual realities once the individual has started on this way and is able to bring more and more of himself to the altar.

Individuals who are growing, and thus are better able to approach the realities of spirit on their own also find that they can often minister to someone else when there is need. But the small class group undoubtedly remains the best way of introducing people to this view of the world, and of exploring new material with those who wish to continue growing and building new relationships.

This requires, however, a more adult approach to Christianity than we have been accustomed to. Religion has to be seen as more than moral law or a collective pattern that can be instilled into children once and for all. There are also difficulties about getting support for such a program. When the proposal for study groups was first made to the official lay board of my own church, there was more hostility than I encountered at any other time during the twenty years I was rector there, including even the time when there was an outbreak of tongue speaking. The board did not want to spend the money to pay a competent professional educator, whose value was soon proved, both in the adult groups and also in preparing an imaginative program for children.

Why is it so likely, then, that acceptance of oneself and real concern for the other person will convey a more Christian view of the world than the best-intentioned criticism or the effort to eliminate or avoid anything unpleasant in either person? And more especially, why is effort needed on experience for adults, instead of children? Let us consider first the needs of the growing child, using a diagram similar to the one used to picture this over-all view.

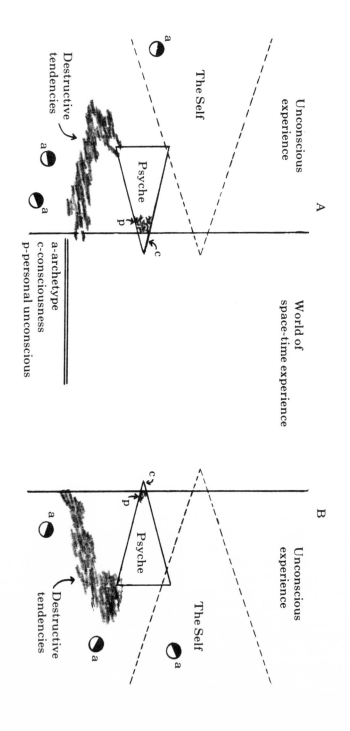

A

Unconscious
experience

The Self

a

Destructive
tendencies

Psyche

p

c

a

a

World of
space-time experience

a-archetype
c-consciousness
p-personal unconscious

B

Unconscious
experience

The Self

c

p

Psyche

a

Destructive
tendencies

a

a

Two individuals are represented, facing each other in our space-time world. Let us imagine that A is a teacher and B. a child. They have come together, Robinson Crusoe-like, on this island in space, each bringing his own complex personality structure. The adult's is more complex at the tip—the conscious attitudes and the personal memories filed away and forgotten. But each has his own early conditioning, his tendencies or type structure (probably partly inherited), his own depth of unconscious, and the child is generally more open to the realities of the spiritual world that surrounds them both.

In the Christian view we propose, the goal of the teacher—or parent or other adult—is to help the child grow so that he will become able to deal with both the outer physical world and the spiritual one that bears directly in on him. In the beginning the task is to turn the child's attention towards the outer world, helping him learn how to deal with the physical world and separate these experiences from ones of the spiritual world. But this does not mean suppressing the latter kind of experiences, for one's hope is that, when the child has matured, he will come to a relationship with the creative center of the spiritual world.

But first of all, the child needs to develop a strong center of his personality. In psychological language, he needs a well-developed ego (not in the negative sense that many religionists use this term). A strong ego, which is necessary in the outer world, is even more indispensable if the person is to encounter the spiritual world with any degree of safety. And how can something be offered to God that the person has never had? If the goal in the end is to give up one's life in order to gain it, then the beginning must be to have a life to give up. We have also discussed this in Chapter V.

As the child grows, his orientation must still be towards the outer world, building a base for his life like a pyramid, step by step. His curiosity and learning, his need for friends, for sexual identification, finally for love and the work he must fulfill, all radiate outwards. At the same time the maturity that he achieves in each of these steps depends largely on the ability of the adult opposite him, the teacher, to provide a climate of warmth and empathy. The child and young person need rules and structure to grow. The adult requires maturity and a source of inner strength to present the rules and structure so that they neither confine the growth nor warp it by too much freedom.

For the time being the young person is given his understanding of the realities of religion through story and image, symbols and myths. Then the time comes when he wishes to be separate and test what he has learned for himself. And at this point the child changes. He still needs the support of the adult who is secure in his knowledge and maturity. But from this point on a person's experience can pose the question at any time that forces him to look inward, to ask what is happening to him. This is the point that so many of our young people have reached today. It is the point at which maturity can begin, and also the point at which a person can choose his own way religiously. This is the point at which the adult who is secure himself will encourage separation and independence and testing, for each individual must make his own relationship with both the outer and inner worlds of experience.

When one does turn inward, even briefly, he usually finds destructive, annihilating aspects of spiritual reality, which are more than he can handle. His need then is for the creative spirit which is characterized by love. If he has had an accepting relationship, one of warmth and understanding and freedom, it will be easier for him to turn then for guidance. At this point the goal of the mature adult is to give him support and assurance so that he can find his own way among these realities and develop a life style characterized by mature caring for others. This is very difficult for one to communicate unless the adult has known such relationship and can exemplify these qualities himself. Can the blind lead the blind?

Such a goal is almost unknown in our culture today. Instead, almost universally, human beings are only partially accepted. Qualities of personality that are "bad," that are blamed for people's troubles, are rejected; the effort is to eliminate them. Some churches are committed to helping people look within themselves for this reason. But the basis is the antiquated theory of personality that we have discussed. The purpose is to find what is wrong in the person and get rid of it so that he can get back into operation like other normal people.

There are two results. First, one finds anger and hostility simmering within people. It often comes out in the privacy of home, and it is also seen in groups mediated for the purpose of encountering and learning something about the anger. Without a mediator who is well aware of his own hostility and quick to step in with ways of handling what comes, the net result is simply to compound the effect of these destructive forces, leaving most people worse off than ever. All of us have a natural tendency to anger and hostility. To be quite honest and genuine, we sometimes have to let it out. The person who thinks that he has none of this in himself does not know himself very well. The mature person knows his own hostility; he may not always succeed, but he at least tries to use it to serve a creative purpose (by our definition, a purpose of loving concern).

The second result of rejecting parts of the personality is to wipe out one of the most central purposes of religion in the Christian tradition. So long as being "normal" means avoiding whole areas of experience that can play into the psyche, there is no possibility of working towards wholeness of integration of the personality, the health of body, mind and soul that Jesus stressed throughout His ministry. Yet this goal itself, if intelligibly expressed, communicates the Christian spirit to men better than most of the things that fill books about God in the abstract.

For this reason, and also because so much of the young person's religious understanding is shaped by the parents, we have given first priority to groups of parents who will try realistically to accept a wider range of human experience and more of their own personalities. Indeed, so much of the child's ideas and values are formed in the home that it is even suggested in the Catholic Church that the parish grade school is not the best way to communicate religion. In order to begin to reach children, the communication of religion will necessarily be focused upon young adults and the younger parents.

This is also the most open field for religion to take hold. From high school age on most young people are trying to find their own identity; they are separating from family values and practices. It is not that they are irreligious, but rather that they are seeking the individual relation we have discussed. If they are inhibited from going their own way, they often turn irrevocably against the framework they have known. But if the church can offer experience and real relationship to these young people, particularly to those in revolt against the materialism of their parents and seeking experience in drugs, meditation, or the occult, they will be able to find the inner journey and its outer counterpart of a loving life style. At the same time, their parents, puzzled and bewildered, are almost equally ready for experience and accept

225

ance. What, then, are the most important things for a group to consider who will try to communicate this?

A Basis for Communicating Christianity

First of all we need a climate in which communication can be open. Whatever materials are dealt with, the process is one of experiencing together. This is possible only where mature Christian love—the *agape* described by Paul in I Corinthians 13—is the climate, so that the individual is opened up and this reality touches his life. Communication in this sense is more than ordinary human relationship in words and thoughts. Rather, it is communication in depth, of spirit with spirit, in which one does not so much take action as allow the Spirit that is characterized by love to act through him (as our model suggests). When Christians are effective in this way, their human love is sacramentally used, much as the bread and wine are used by the same Spirit in the Communion.

Process and content cannot be separated, however. The whole is like a three-legged stool that collapses if one leg is removed. All three legs—human beings and their ability to react, content or materials and an intellectual framework in which their meaning can be grasped, and the Spirit that enlivens both—are equally essential. But it is not an easy job to get these three into the reactor at once; this requires the best we have to give, emotionally, intellectually, and devotionally.

1. There must first be an understanding of the world which intelligent people can accept, a framework in which the materials are no longer untouchable theological ideas or actions, as most seminaries present them. For this reason it is often the hardest for us clergy to understand experiential Christianity; yet theological materials (including the model we have presented) are only a skeleton until human beings are willing to experiment with them and see what happens. And this requires a view of the world from which people can see the outcome as potentially meaningful. Thus some such model or framework as the one we offer, representing the world as accurately as possible, is essential if people are to see that there is something meaningful in their ordinary, daily lives which is beyond the space-time-material experience of the individual.

Along with this understanding, there is a need to consider how we use language to convey meaning. The rules of language that all of us have absorbed definitely favor limited communication about objects in the physical world. Perhaps our words have had to originate in this way. But when the rules for using them also make it easier to speak of one tangible thing at a time, then it means thinking carefully if we wish to discuss relations between things, or speak of something that is not sensory to begin with. One of the most interesting and liberating subjects to consider is this understanding of how words can work for us instead of helping to make us slaves of our ideas.

Much of this understanding, which we have discussed briefly, is offered by the general semantics movement in this country, and is available in simplified, outline form for general use. The handbook mentioned, *General Semantics: An Outline Survey*[8] by Kenneth G. Johnson, comes from the University of Wisconsin and includes a good bibliography. Applied to religion, the material gives a start on more open communication.

2. Understanding ourselves and how our lives are directed comes next on the specific list. And this means opening up a new possibility for anyone who looks deeply within himself. He may well find that his life is guided far more by a deep search for religious meaning and for wholeness of personality than by the outer circumstances that usually seem so significant and determining.

This is one of Jung's most basic ideas, and his *Modern Man in Search of a Soul* offers one of the best introductions to this understanding of ourselves. This should certainly be followed by John A. Sanford's *The Kingdom Within,* which develops this view by considering the meaning of the sayings of Jesus. *Creation Continues* by Fritz Kunkel [9] gives another treatment of this whole idea, and Jung's *Two Essays on Analytical Psychology,* his *Memories, Dreams, Reflections,* and later *The Way of All Women* by Esther Harding, offer additional material to build on.

3. A third essential approach is to dreams, even though this seems to mean breaking new ground to get back to the Christian understanding of them. There are certainly enough dreams in the Bible to suggest their importance. But the idea that these experiences need further understanding, as the fathers of the church considered, has not received much attention in our time.

Specifically, dreams form a bridge between the need to know ourselves and the need to know the reality, the power and direction of the Holy Spirit. With the help of dreams, the results of an encounter with God can be observed. And it is just such observable results which give meaning to the Christian framework and the effort of working towards wholeness of personality; they are basic to the communication of Christianity.

My own book, *Dreams: The Dark Speech of the Spirit*, deals with this approach, both in the Christian tradition and in the thinking of Jung, and it offers an introduction to the subject. Another valuable sourcebook is *Dreams: God's Forgotten Language*, in which John Sanford has applied a similar understanding to a group of modern dreams which brought new life and new conviction to the individuals. *The Meaning in Dreams and Dreaming* by Maria F. Mahoney offers a clear summary of Jung's understanding of dreams, which might be a valuable follow-up.

4. The whole area of healing also needs to be considered. In some churches a direct sacramental approach can be tried, and where prayer and laying on of hands for healing can be accepted as valuable, these experiences become a powerful way of communicating the Christian spirit. There is no question that healings do occur now and then, much as they are described in the New Testament, and certainly this can be convincing. Those occurring among teenage drug users through conversion experiences are one example. But this is not the only aspect that needs to be stressed. For instance, physical healing may be related to the person's wholeness, either as a prelude or as the result of his growth and integration. There are also times when healing occurs, particularly medical healing, whose value is only partly realized because the person lacks any central meaning in his life.

Much can be learned about the central meaning of Christianity by considering carefully the healing actions of Jesus described throughout the gospels. Both psychology and psychosomatic medicine also offer valuable insights; much of this material is found in *Persuasion and Healing*, a careful study by Jerome Frank of Johns Hopkins which clearly suggests the reality of Christian healing. The book I have written on *Healing and Christianity* also summarizes this material, as well as the history of healing in the church, and suggests the place of healing in the Christian world view we have proposed. Agnes Sanford's *The Healing Light* and *Behold Your God* offer an invaluable approach to the actual experience and practice.

As individuals come to appreciate the reality of the spiritual world, there are many areas, such as prayer and meditation, various spiritual disciplines, the whole charismatic movement, that groups may want to explore, as well as areas of psychology and philosophy. In fact, in one church where this program was tried, within five years hundreds of adults were coming for college level seminars, and they took home far more than book learning. The results were seen in family after family, and young people came to find out about this church which even tried to understand the ancient *I Ching*; many of them stayed to become members.

In addition, for two reasons, leaders and individuals alike will want to understand the variations and dynamics of personality structure as fully as they can. If one principal objective of Christians is to accept and express loving care for others, then it is necessary to begin to know the other person. There is not much chance of knowing another person as long as one can pick out only the similarities to oneself. Jung's understanding of personality types and differences in personality structure make it possible to know and appreciate individual differences. As we shall see, it also opens up real possibilities of a theology of communication.

Religion and Personality Type

We shall look very briefly at this understanding of personality structure because several students have written about it fully and in a clear and interesting way. Probably the best study to start with is *Introduction to Type* by Isabel Briggs Myers, which gives a clear description of the theory and method of type testing. Her *Manual: The Myers-Briggs Type Indicator* puts together the results of several years of testing and verification. Jung developed the theory in depth in *Psychological Types*, showing something of how he arrived at it, and in *Lectures on Jung's Typology*, Marie-Louise von Franz and James Hillman present a wealth of detail about individuals in relation to their type structures. P. W. Martin also discusses the theory in *Experiment in Depth*. In addition, the Myers-Briggs Type Indicator Test is readily available and easy to administer and score; with the help of Mrs. Myers' *Introduction to Type*, individuals can learn a great deal about personality type through understanding their own structures.

Jung was interested in how people functioned in the world. Starting from his original descriptions of *introversion* and *extraversion* (which have since become household words), he came to see that people also differ greatly in how they prefer to deal with their experiences. Some people are *judging* in attitude and prefer to look a situation over and come to a decision about it (and if extraverted, they will probably act; or if introverted, they generally try to get someone else to take action). There are others who would rather not reach a decision, because that concludes looking for more facts and considering all the possibilities; these people are basically *perceptive* in orientation.

In addition each of these groups is further split down the middle by the way they function in judging or perceiving. There is a *thinking* type who reaches decisions (or non-decisions) on the basis of logic and studying what is reasonable; the opposite is the *feeling* type, the person who considers the human values involved in a situation and arrives at a value-judgment (or perception) which is a structured way of looking at reality. Or again, a person (either judging or perceptive in attitude) may function mainly through either sensation or intuition. The *sensation* type gathers his impressions through the physical senses, the *intuitive* through an inner "sixth" sense, and thinking or feeling then develops as a subsidiary function. Similarly, the thinking and feeling types generally develop one of the other two—sensation or intuition—as an auxiliary. With sixteen basic combinations, the shades of difference are almost infinite.

This means that each person develops a definite strength in dealing with the world, and also a very definite weakness. The person whose strength lies in thinking is often completely unaware of human values and is utterly amazed if he finds that someone has been hurt by his logically reasoned action. A person who has developed mainly his sensation function may belittle the idea of finding something out intuitively. Certain strengths, in fact, come to dominate a culture, simply because they are valued above others by that culture.

In the introverted culture of medieval times, for instance, the introverted intuitive and feeling types were encouraged, while today the value is put on extraversion, thinking and sensation which are needed to make good business executives. The person who does not develop these strengths is left with a sore spot around the unconscious, weak function. The introverted, intuitive person knows he cannot do the things that are valued by society, and even the church. He is often a failure before he starts. Yet no one type is superior to another; they are all needed. The person who is accepted, and sees value in his dominant function, can rely on other people, and even take the time that is needed to bring his weaker side, that is unconscious and often highly creative, into play.

Religion in particular needs all the types or functions. But so often religion has been presented for only one type. When religion becomes only doctrine, a set of propositions that have to be accepted intellectually, it has little relevance or interest for the person who is interested in human values, the feeling type. When quiet and inner devotion are presented as all that matter, the person who is extraverted and sensation-oriented is not touched where he is. Or if only a need for social action is offered, the intuitive and the thinking types are lost and their interest slips away.

Instead, if religion is understood as having the central purpose of discovering how human beings can bridge a relation between God and the immediate world, then approaches of all kinds are needed. The only way that man can come to know the central meaning of the universe in any degree is to experience this power from all sides. God cannot be pinned down to a single description, and individuals of every type are needed to find approaches. Then communication between God and man becomes possible, and communication between men on every level becomes essential. Every man, just because of his difference in personality structure, becomes important as a possible avenue to God. Basically this is the meaning of a theology of communication. The New Testament expression of this is seen in the description of the Church as the 'body of Christ'—a unified organism which is able to accommodate incredible diversity; indeed, *depends upon* the diversity for its very existence.

Thus, it is essential for one to realize that he has his own individual way of reacting to the world, his own way of relating which is different from others. Once we recognize this, we will not try unconsciously (or consciously) to force others into our mold. Instead we will work towards relating to and communicating with them. There is a place for each of us, for the religious thinker, the religious activist, the expert in the devotional life, and the religious artist or builder. There are many different ways of experiencing and living the religious life, each with its difficulties and its values and rewards.

The task of the religious educator is to help each person find his own type, his own way, and to help him relate to the weaker, less conscious side from which new value can come. As Marie-Louise von Franz has remarked, one's weaker, less conscious function is like a valuable horse that cannot be whipped or trained to take the bit and saddle. With patience, one can get close enough to whisper in his ear, and even ride him without being thrown at the wrong time. But this is a complex, time-consuming business. As the way to wholeness of the personality, to relating to the unconscious where the spiritual realm can be found, it is also the business of religion, which itself is complex and time-consuming. But there is help in some of the newer thinking of education. Let us look at religious education, or the communication of religion to both child and adult, from this newer point of view.

Implementing Education of the Whole Man

There are a number of recent studies of the educational process that are valuable for the teacher or leader who wants to communicate religion as we are suggesting. In the first place, Dr. Jung has sketched out some of the implications of his point of view for education. His educational ideas are found in *Development of Personality*, volume 17 of his collected works. Frances Wickes has also written deeply and well from the same point of view; in *The Inner World of Childhood* she describes the child's development in relation to the world of autonomous or spiritual realities found in the unconscious.

Jung, however, was more concerned with the psychological inferences that could be drawn from his view. He seldom stepped into religious territory to suggest what should or should not be done, but left it to the church and those concerned with religion to put his ideas to work. As we have tried to indicate, his psychological point of view has a clearly religious side,[10] although its implications have not been worked out for religious education.

Perhaps the most important understanding for us to grasp from Jung's thinking to begin with is the complexity of man and the world around him—both physical and spiritual—and the rejection of any simple or easy educational method. And second is the importance of our job, which seems to increase its difficulty. Communication of the most elementary kind is difficult and not understood in entirety. Communication among and about human beings is even more difficult, while communication about the deepest experiences of the spirit, which are a part of man's world of experience, are the most difficult and by far the most important of all.[11]

Since the point of view we have developed is essentially empirical in the broadest sense, the religious educator who is trying out this standpoint will want the best empirical data available. Indeed he will welcome such data as an addition to his understanding of human beings and the world in which they interact. Studies like Ronald T. Hyman's *Teaching: Vantage Points for*

Study will help to direct and support his efforts in religious education. From them he will realize that fear usually inhibits learning, while a warm and accepting environment usually stimulates the learning process. He will also learn ways of checking himself and those with whom he is working to see whether he is communicating at all.[12]

From Carl Rogers' *Freedom to Learn* one also finds that an open group with genuineness and freedom of decision, as well as warmth and empathy, often enables the individual to develop his own abilities far more rapidly. Rogers supports this with data from the social sciences, as well as providing the theory and specific classroom instances. The behavioral and experimental studies of both animals and men have also produced findings which have implications for teaching and learning. The religious educator will want to know not only the results of Piaget's research, but also the religious conclusions and other inferences which Ronald Goldman has drawn from them and tested.[13]

Unfortunately Christian education has incompletes to make up in communication and educational skills and data, and it cannot make them up by continuing to cut classes, avoiding experience. As James Michael Lee points out so clearly in *The Shape of Religious Instruction*,[14] the net result has been reliance on prejudice and logical theology rather than a working knowledge, and this has not produced effective religious education. How then can we start to make up for lost time?

Teaching the Class in Religion

First of all leading or teaching an actual class in religion is not easy and cannot be done *en masse*. It is seldom possible to communicate this kind of religious approach so that it takes hold in a group of more than twelve or fifteen people. Early Christianity realized this and took time to prepare new converts. First let us compare the dynamics of this slower, more complex way of communicating religion with the ordinary ways we have known of teaching religion, again using a diagram.

We have the teacher, T, and the group members, A, B, and C. Each individual consists of both his conscious and unconscious (T', A', B', C') personalities. Each one has his own individual history, type structure, complexes, fears, desires, which appear only to a limited extent in his conscious, verbalized behavior.

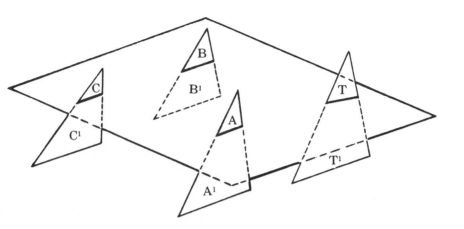

If the teacher uses what has been called the "transmission theory" of education—the idea so common among religious educators today of religious proclamation—he will structure the class situation entirely towards a conscious relationship. He will try to bring each of the conscious, rational wills to accept certain ideas about theology and morals. Each individual will then "integrate" this doctrinal system. And the teacher may well bring all the conscious personalities to perfect agreement. But the problem with this idea (besides the arrogance of assuming so much certitude) is that the moment A', B', and C' begin to exert an influence, the learning that has reached only into the conscious mind is quickly pushed aside; it has little further effect.

On the other hand, with a moralistic approach the teacher tries to shape a *total* response by each individual. By attempting to influence behavior more than the intelligence, he tries to bring all the individuals to respond in one specific way to the religious object. For instance, in the Catholic instruction modeled on St. Sulplice, every effort is made to shape the individual towards a certain pattern of "holiness." The use of devotions, the commitment to certain religious acts and practices, all the trappings of a particular religious way, all are an effort to influence A', B', and C'.

Unfortunately, the dependency needs of the teacher often force the student (particularly at certain suggestible times) to an acceptance of the pattern which still belongs only to the teacher. When the student begins to use his own individual consciousness, if he has understood the emphasis of Jesus on individuality, he is very likely to throw the baby out with the bath water. Once he feels tied down by the pattern, and realizes that this doesn't sound much like Christ, the whole enterprise is often rejected.[15]

Or again, once in a while a very skillful and capable teacher comes along who is able to reach and shape both the conscious and the unconscious in his students. But when he does this, shaping them to his own model, he cuts the individuals off from following their own direction, and real harm may be done. If the individual realizes what has been done, a reaction usually takes place; if he remains unconscious, the results may be tension, with various ways of suffering or projecting it.

Our present knowledge of the human psyche and of the total world, particularly as we have outlined it, suggests a different approach. As I see it, the immediate task of religious education is to provide the conditions in which the following six objectives can be realized.

1. The individual ego, the rational, conscious will, will be allowed to emerge in the strength of its own individuality. This means self-acceptance born of being accepted, and it is true of adults as well as children. Some adults still have ordinary maturing to achieve.

2. These developing personalities can then, within the group process, come to a natural encounter with the totality of others. In this way one learns about his own depth, as well as the depth of others, and the longing of the individual for his own wholeness may then be allowed to emerge. This is possible only if both teacher and students alike are involved in an honest encounter with each other as individuals, encountering negative elements as well as positive. This is to be understood as an important part of the religious process. If we take Jesus of Nazareth seriously, the wholeness of the person is one religious goal in itself, and this first step is an essential preparation for a later, more specifically religious encounter.

The reason Jesus spoke such harsh words about the Pharisees, and the reason he called time on men who judge others, was the same. By acting in this way they avoided any encounter with the depth of *themselves*. Self-knowledge would have changed their behavior; it is a necessity before much growth in the religious way is possible. The group encounter can show us ourselves as well as any process.[16]

3. The next step is up to the student. As he discovers the darkness within himself—elements Jung has called the "shadow"—and also intimations of the Self, he will likely want to turn inward to confront these realities within himself. It is one situation to see them in others in the group. But when he turns inward, he finds that there are dark and destructive forces bearing in upon him directly, demonic forces which he cannot control by himself.

Then the teacher's example or reassurance are needed. He must let the student know, in the way that speaks to him and his type, that he is not alone. Others have found that rational consciousness cannot handle these forces, and have sought some power other than the human. In this way, the student may find his need to encounter the creative Spirit manifested by Christ, and turn for support to this reality which Christ gave to the church to use.

We have already emphasized that this inner journey is no joy ride, and that one encounters not only elements that change according to how one deals with them, but also an aspect or content that seems to be ultimately destructive.* This content, which drives men to illness and psychosis, Jung has described in terrifying detail. Those who actually meet this reality must find some help other than human, or they are lost. Religion then becomes more than a nice additive to a well-balanced life. The teacher who would deal with this depth of the indiviual must be aware of the dangers, and at least comfortable with taking religion this seriously himself. Then he is not frightened by what the student experiences. This very calmness and assurance alone has tremendous power.

There is probably no limit to the depth and variety of individual discovery that can be made, or the ways it can be used. There are some things written on this, including those by Jung. But in the particular situation the qualities of the teacher are determining; as we look at what is required of him, let us remember that his own growth is also involved in this process.

4. A good teacher will know these inner realities well enough not to be threatened by the hostility which a student may express in any direction in the group. Even more important, he will not be threatened by the positive caring which such a situation

---

* See pp. 116 f. and 156 ff.

can constellate. The atmosphere within the class, and whether the group is left in unresolved hostility or moves towards caring, depend upon the leader, and often on his ability to seek help himself.

His conscious attitudes are not the only factor, however. His unconscious attitudes also play an important part in what the student actually takes from the learning process. If the teacher is aware of his own unconsciousness and of the forces that can play upon him from the spiritual world, he can begin to know what other attitudes he is imparting to his students along with his conscious ones. The teacher needs to know whether he is re-enforcing his teaching unconsciously, or if he sometimes imparts unconsciously the opposite of what is intended; particularly is this true of the teaching of religion.

One of my sons for a time attended an Episcopal parochial school. His teacher was a nun whose outer conscious attitude was that of warmth and concern, a delightful "Christian" person. Underneath was an opinionated and power-driven animus. This was the most negative experience this boy ever had with religion and the church, and he has not entirely recovered to this day. Again, exactly the opposite may be true. A priest who taught chemistry for a time at Groton School used to tell me with a twinkle in his eye how religion ought to be taught. Teaching chemistry with his collar on, saying nothing about religion, and caring how and what his students learned, he said, was more effective in conveying religious instruction than most of the courses in religion at the school. If this reflects on courses in religion, it need not; this is up to us.

5. The teacher will be professional in the sense that he is not in the teaching position to satisfy his own needs (and this takes a lot of consciousness). He will remain the catalyst, a part of the reaction and yet outside it, ready to be withdrawn once it has taken place. The student needs his freedom, and he needs the security of knowing that the teacher is there *when he is needed*. As the individual comes to his own ground, the teacher withdraws. He may not even be appreciated by the students. His influence will be seen by only the most perceptive, and few will realize what he has done to set up and maintain a climate of experiential learning.

6. He will also be professional in understanding his subject matter. He will have done his intellectual homework, as well as the developmental kind, so that he has an integrated understanding of *content* and how it relates to his own experiences and the experiences of the group. The teacher—in class or

home, who is trying to communicate religion in a specific way —will know what he believes and why he believes in that way.

7. One very important quality of such a teacher is the confidence which he sometimes feels—and sometimes only expresses as best he can in words and actions—that there is a creative power in the universe, a power best expressed in Christ and His Spirit, which seeks to enter into relationship with the individual, to protect and guide him towards wholeness and meaning.

Finally, there are the tools of the trade. The Bible is one which the church has provided for religious education. There is no greater help than this book when it is seen as the history of God's encounter with men. From the beginning the elements are there that one finds in himself, and most of our ways of encountering and dealing with them. In their culmination one finds the unsurpassed personality of Jesus Christ, the whole man in whom God broke through. The stories, the teachings and actions of Christ give direction to the individual search once they are seen as a guide and not as a straight-jacket. In the resurrection there is the knowledge that the world was unable to destroy the whole God-man, and this gives us the hope that there is a new life, and a great destiny, for those whose lives are open to the inflow of His Spirit.

In addition there is the history of the church, a history of numerous encounters of God with man from the end of the New Testament until the present. As the lives of Augustine, St. Francis, Martin Luther, St. Catherine of Siena, William Law, Thomas Kelly, all show, revelation continues, and men are still touched and changed. If the point of view we have presented is correct, these men have left a record of encounter which is second in importance for our guidance only to the Biblical narrative.

The liturgy is the other, double-pronged tool. In it the church acts out its own continued care for men within the family of Christ. At the same time, as Christ's central act of caring is remembered and re-enacted in the way that He suggested, He is present in continuing reality, expressed in and through the fellowship and the bread and wine. Classroom teaching can be a preparation for this experience, which itself is one of the finest ways the church communicates its message. A real liturgy, when seen in depth, is teaching *par excellence*.

Summary and Conclusions

The Christian church is needed by men today probably more than ever before in its history. For this reason we have gone over some difficult ground in these pages, to see how Christians can effectively tap and communicate the power that should be theirs to offer people who need it. To sum up, these are the suggestions we have tried to support and give body to. It is up to each of us to make them live.

1. There is a religious reality about which man desperately needs to know if he is to survive and grow in our twentieth century world. This is at least as important as any other area of learning.

2. The knowledge of this reality—like any other knowledge, scientific, mathematical, *or* religious—is given through experience. As we have seen, man's reason, his logic and rational thought are essential in order to understand his experiences, which are never given with absolute, predictable certainty. But, in spite of the understanding of some recent philosophy and theology, it is not our logic or rational thought that give us knowledge of any kind. If men are to know God, they must go back again and again to their experiences of the divine and find the knowledge that God gives to those who seek.

3. It is impossible to find this knowledge measured and packaged for ready consumption. The spiritual world requires an individual response from each of us. God requires a more individual, a more personal interaction from those who would learn of Him than do the objects of chemistry or physics or geology. Learning about God is more like learning about another human being than about things, and human beings seldom reveal themselves until the conditions are right. If God had been able to communicate himself through a law or prescription, he very likely would have done so. But there seems to be no easy, mass method of arriving at mature religious practice. Once this is deeply understood and accepted, we are not taken in by one panacea or another, but are ready to give the effort that is needed to know God.

God himself came as a person in Jesus of Nazareth, whose ministry was not limited to one way of communication. It was a ministry of exemplification, joined with acts of power and creative love, and with teaching. It was communication in the fullest sense. It resulted in a conflict with evil and death, and finally in resurrection. This was all part of the way God taught his message in Jesus Christ. God himself made a great effort. It is not our task to imitate all of this, but we need to do more than just talk about it or draw up propositional statements to be memorized. There is a Spirit which can live in and through our lives if we allow it, the Spirit sent by Jesus Christ.

4. Our central task in the church is to know and communicate this Spirit. But since the church has failed to provide either an encounter with this Spirit or the understanding that would lead to it, we must first develop the intellectual understanding and the emotional and spiritual conditions that will allow experiences of the Holy Spirit to work in and give value to our own lives. With this theological, psychological, and philosophical base, we can then get on with the task of communicating religion.

5. Genuine communication of religion, as an individualized undertaking, will try to express concern for the individual and his growth. Only so much of man's religious potential can be achieved in youth, or at any other single stage. Religious education is a life long venture. Much of the basic learning about religion will come to the child from his parents. Thus the importance of opportunities for communicating knowledge of religious realities to adults can hardly be overestimated.

In addition, one comes to know the realities with which religion deals in an individual encounter, and since the forces in the religious encounter are so complex, this communication will take place in small groups.

6. Religious education is the most demanding kind of teaching. It requires insight, consciousness, and continuing growth on the part of the teacher. He has to know not only something of the reality of the subject matter experientially and within a world view, but also a great deal about the learner and his dynamics as well. He will see himself more a catalyst, stimulating reaction within the learner and among the group, than as a reacting part of the process. This requires the greatest self-understanding and maturity.

An industrialist friend of mine once remarked that he saw his job as the primary influence in the company, as working to create the conditions whereby each individual might develop to the maximum of his potential within the opportunities at hand. This is a good description of the task of the church in its communication of Christianity. The task is to create the conditions wherein individuals, in all of their complexity, may develop so that they may come to their maximum potential, embodying as much of the Spirit of God as possible. The early church fathers held that Christ became what we are in order that we might become what He is. The task of the church is to create the conditions so that this may happen, so that through its communication men may come to know God.

There is no more important task in our modern world, and no other agency but the church exists to do it.

APPENDIX
FOOTNOTES
BIBLIOGRAPHY
INDEX

APPENDIX

References to Spiritual Experiences in the New Testament

Part I:

Number of verses referring to various spiritual experiences*

| | Number of verses | | | Descriptions of source | | | | |
	Total	Related to Spiritual Experience	Percent	Spirit	Holy Spirit	Angels	Demons	Devil
Matthew	1071	495	46%	4	8	23	26	29
Mark	678	323	48%	2	5	4	41	8
Luke	1151	555	48%	7	26	41	35	25
John	879	476	54%	2	24	5	7	12
Acts	1007	491	49%	10	72	42	19	1
	4786	2340	49%	25	135	115	128	75
Romans	433	179	41%	14	11	—	6	10
I Corinthians	437	221	51%	18	15	7	20	8
II Corinthians	257	110	43%	17	7	—	5	10
Galatians	149	59	39%	1	17	3	4	—
Ephesians	155	62	40%	—	14	—	9	6
Philippians	104	22	21%	2	2	1	1	1
Colossians	95	33	35%	1	2	2	6	1
Thessalonians **	136	57	42%	2	5	1	1	11
Timothy **	196	70	36%	1	4	2	1	7
Titus	46	12	26%	—	3	—	—	—
Philemon	25	5	20%	—	—	—	—	—
	2033	830	41%	56	80	16	53	54
Hebrews	303	130	43%	7	11	16	1	11
James	108	30	27%	2	—	1	2	4
Peter **	166	83	50%	6	11	5	3	10
John ***	132	44	33%	1	9	—	5	16
Jude	25	15	60%	—	3	2	—	2
Revelation	404	402	97%	1	1	1	—	—
	1138	704	62%	17	35	25	11	43
Entire New Testament	7957	3874	49%	98	250	156	192	172

  * Excluding references to more than one experience in a single verse.

 ** Book I and II

*** Books I, II and III

Principal Experiences			Gifts of the Spirit								Location	
Miracles, Signs, power	Healing	Resurrection, eternal life	Grace, gifts	Dreams	Visions	Prophecy	Tongues	Wisdom, knowledge	Faith	Gospel	Kingdom of Heaven	Judgment, eternal punishment
83	65	28	—	6	11	75	—	—	—	—	132	5
72	86	37	—	—	9	18	—	—	—	—	63	5
81	101	86	—	—	22	58	—	—	—	—	73	—
117	130	133	—	—	6	36	—	—	—	—	2	2
92	57	34	—	3	63	77	16	—	—	—	5	—
445	439	318	—	9	111	264	16	—	—	—	248	12
9	—	24	16	—	—	47	—	4	24	5	2	7
11	2	37	23	—	1	12	18	17	5	9	11	7
12	1	16	12	—	7	3	—	6	5	5	3	1
2	—	5	7	—	—	2	—	—	9	8	1	—
2	—	5	11	—	—	1	1	2	3	2	6	—
—	—	3	3	—	—	—	—	2	2	3	1	1
—	—	5	3	—	—	—	1	3	1	1	7	—
3	—	7	6	—	—	2	—	—	7	6	2	4
5	—	15	9	—	—	1	—	4	14	2	2	3
—	—	3	1	—	—	1	—	1	3	—	—	—
—	—	—	1	—	—	—	—	1	2	1	—	—
44	3	120	92	—	8	69	20	40	75	42	35	23
9	1	10	2	—	1	39	—	1	3	1	13	4
2	3	1	3	—	1	3	—	1	2	—	1	4
4	—	8	6	—	1	12	—	3	1	2	4	7
3	—	9	—	—	—	—	—	—	—	—	—	1
1	—	1	—	1	—	2	—	—	1	—	—	2
—	—	3	1	—	393	1	—	1	—	—	—	—
19	4	32	12	1	396	57	—	6	7	3	18	18
508	446	470	104	10	515	390	36	46	82	45	301	53

	Spirit	Holy Spirit	Angels	Demons	Devil	Miracles, signs, power	Healing	Resurrection, eternal life
Matthew	4	12	26	33	33	92	99	34
Mark	5	6	5	49	8	81	123	38
Luke	10	28	53	49	26	90	129	101
John	4	27	7	7	13	144	147	204
Acts	23	102	49	30	5	108	68	49
	46	175	140	168	85	515	566	426
Romans	17	17	1	6	11	12	—	27
I Corinthians	30	25	9	22	13	17	4	47
II Corinthians	22	11	—	5	14	14	2	23
Galatians	3	19	3	4	3	2	—	5
Ephesians	4	15	2	10	7	2	—	6
Philippians	2	2	2	2	1	—	—	3
Colossians	3	4	3	7	2	—	—	5
Thessalonians **	3	7	2	1	11	4	—	9
Timothy **	5	6	2	1	9	7	—	16
Titus & Philemon	—	4	—	—	—	—	—	3
	89	110	24	58	71	58	6	144
Hebrews	11	12	18	1	15	9	2	11
James	2	—	1	2	4	4	3	1
Peter **	7	14	8	4	12	5	—	11
John *** & Jude	3	15	5	6	23	5	—	11
Revelation	11	14	115	13	106	8	2	26
	34	55	147	26	160	31	7	60
	169	340	311	252	316	604	579	630

* Including references to two or more experiences often found in a single verse.
** Books I and II
*** Books I, II and III

Grace, gifts	Dreams	Visions	Prophecy	Tongues	Wisdom, knowledge	Faith	Gospel	Kingdom of heaven	Judgment, eternal punishment
—	9	11	76	—	—	—	—	135	5
—	—	9	19	1	—	—	—	37	5
—	—	44	72	—	1	—	—	76	—
—	—	9	39	—	—	—	—	2	3
—	7	82	87	25	—	—	—	7	—
—	16	155	293	26	1	—	—	257	13
25	—	—	49	—	4	29	10	4	9
26	—	2	33	28	40	7	9	13	8
15	—	10	4	—	7	5	9	5	1
7	—	—	2	—	1	17	10	1	—
14	—	2	3	1	5	5	4	10	—
3	—	—	—	—	2	2	5	1	2
3	—	—	—	1	5	3	2	9	—
6	—	—	2	1	—	10	8	4	6
10	—	—	2	1	5	27	4	4	4
6	—	—	1	—	2	7	1	—	—
115	—	14	96	32	71	112	62	51	30
4	—	1	48	—	2	5	2	15	6
3	—	1	5	—	2	4	—	1	4
10	2	2	18	—	4	5	4	7	12
1	—	—	4	—	—	2	—	1	6
2	1	393	30	—	3	1	1	147	76
20	4	397	105		11	17	7	171	104
135	20	566	494	58	83	129	69	479	147

FOOTNOTES TO CHAPTER I

[1] This is the view of behavioral psychology, whose best known spokesman today is Burrhus F. Skinner. Skinner has presented the basic theory in *Science and Human Behavior*, New York, The Macmillan Company, 1953, and he has carried out the implications of this understanding of human beings, first in *Walden Two*, New York, The Macmillan Company, 1960, and recently in *Beyond Freedom and Dignity*, New York, Alfred A. Knopf, 1971.

[2] Merton P. Strommen et al., *A Study of Generations*, Minneapolis, Augsburg Publishing House, 1972.

[3] Presented at the American Sociological Association meeting in Washington, D.C., August 31, 1970; see the *Mental Health Digest*, Vol. 3, No. 6, June 1971, pp. 40-42.

[4] Notably Martin E. Marty, who suggested that even if the movement did not last, "five years from now you may have some better Presbyterians because of their participation in the Jesus movement." *Time*, Vol. 97, No. 25, June 21, 1971, p. 63, where the classic remark by Robert E. Terwilliger, of Trinity Institute in New York City, was also quoted, that "There is revival of religion everywhere—except in the church."

[5] *The New York Times*, December 26, 1971, gave page one space to report in some detail on the Jesus movement organizations on certain of the leading college campuses.

[6] Jerome D. Frank, M.D., *Persuasion and Healing: A Comparative Study of Psychotherapy*, New York, Schocken Books, 1969, p. 234; also Chapter V, particularly pp. 94 ff.

[7] James J. Gill, M.D., "Religion and Psychiatry Today," *Psychiatric Annals*, Vol. 1, No. 2, October 1971, pp. 44-59.

[8] *Emphasis*, October 1970, p. 1. The local Presbyterian Synod (Southern California) also informs me that their church school enrollment had begun to decline nationally by 1959 and is continuing at a steady clip.

[9] Unless otherwise noted, these figures and the statistics that follow are taken from the *Yearbook of American Churches*, Editions for 1967, 1969, and 1971, New York, National Council of the Churches of Christ in the U.S.A., 1967, p. 218; 1969, pp. 205 and 193; 1971, pp. 216 ff. and 220 ff., and from the recent surveys by the American Institute of Public Opinion (the Gallup Poll) on religious belief, on the influence of religion, on the decline of religious and moral values, and on church attendance, as published by *The New York Times* on May 25, 1968, p. 38; August 14, 1968, p. 18; Decemer 22, 1968, p. 39; December 26, 1968, p. 21; June 1, 1969, p. 39; March 5, 1970, p. 18; April 26, 1970, IV, p. 9; May 21, 1970, p. 37; November 3, 1970, p. 37; December 24, 1970, p. 26;

December 25, 1970, p. 40; and January 9, 1972, p. 59.

[10] *The Los Angeles Times*, April 11, 1971, Section E, p. 3.

[11] *The New York Times*, August 10, 1969, p. 1.

[12] Ed. B. Fiske, "Why Priests Marry," *The Christian Herald*, July 1969; also John A. O'Brien, Ed., *Why Priests Leave*, New York, Hawthorn Books, Inc., 1969. A study by John P. Koval and Richard Bell, submitted to the National Federation of Priests' Councils, Chicago, in 1970, revealed that 10 percent of the priests active at that time were considering resigning in order to marry. In his book *The Time of the Fugitive*, Garden City, New York, Doubleday & Company, Inc., 1971, Dr. Carlo Weber has shown the importance of this movement compared with other periods in the church's history, and he opens up some significant questions for consideration.

[13] And in other places the situation is even worse, as in Quebec, the former stronghold of Canadian Catholicism; see *The New York Times*, January 2, 1972, p. 2, for the report by the Catholic Bishops of Canada.

FOOTNOTES TO CHAPTER II

[1] Otto Pfleiderer, *Philosophy and Development of Religion*, Vol. II, pp. 3 f., as quoted by John Macquarrie, *Twentieth Century Religious Thought*, New York, Harper & Row, 1963, p. 141.

[2] F. R. Tennant, *Philosophical Theology*, Cambridge (Eng.), The Cambridge University Press, 1956, pp. 324 f.; also pp. 311 f.

[3] The actual term "dispensationalism" is quite new; it came into use towards the middle of this century and first appeared in a general dictionary in 1961. Random House and G. & C. Merriam Company each give several interesting references for the inclusion of this word in their dictionaries, the earliest from a publication in 1945. Thus the meaning of this term is still being developed, and it appears that Dispensationalism with a capital "D" is becoming quite different from the older idea of a special dispensation for a limited time. I use the word in this older sense, as expressed by Luther and Calvin.

[4] Rudolf Bultmann, *Kerygma and Myth: A Theological Debate*, ed. by Hans-Werner Bartsch, London, S.P.C.K., 1957, pp. 10 f.

In criticizing the theological framework of Bultmann, we do not want to deny his great contributions to Biblical criticism. We shall say more about this later.

[5] *Ibid.*, p. 11; he also expresses the same idea in *Jesus Christ and Mythology*, New York, Charles Scribner's Sons, 1958, pp. 18 ff.

[6] Andrew M. Greeley, *Priests in the United States: Reflections on a Survey*, Garden City, New York, Doubleday & Company, Inc., 1972, p. 200.

[7] Jacques Maritain, *Challenges and Renewals: Selected Readings*, Notre Dame, Indiana, University of Notre Dame Press, 1966, Chapter 14. It may seem strange that we refer only later to the work of Bernard J. F. Lonergan, whose book, *Insight*, London, Longmans, Green

and Co., 1964, is a most profound attempt to provide an intellectual knowledge of God. He does not attempt, however, to integrate knowledge coming in ways that are not already conscious.

[8] Karl Rahner, *Visions and Prophecies*, New York, Herder and Herder, 1963, p. 21.

FOOTNOTES TO CHAPTER III

[1] These discoveries, within the last twenty years, were described in *The Wall Street Journal*, August 12, 1969, p. 1. Our own culture, however, might learn a great deal from some of the primitive peoples. The Senoi in central Malaya, for instance, have created a peaceful and crime-free culture on the basis of their sophisticated understanding of dreams and human psychology. This society, their practices and theories, have been described by Kilton Stewart, of the Rockefeller Institute, in *Creative Psychology and Dream Education*. New York, Stewart Foundation for Creative Psychology.

[2] G. E. von Grunebaum and Roger Caillois, Eds., *The Dream and Human Societies*, Berkeley, University of California Press, 1966, p. 5.

[3] C. G. Jung, *Two Essays on Analytical Psychology*, Cleveland, The World Publishing Co., 1956, pp. 215 f. (or, *Collected Works*, Vol. 7, New York, Pantheon Books, 1953, p. 203.)

[4] Ernst Cassirer, *An Essay on Man: An Introduction to a Philosophy of Human Culture*, New Haven, Yale University Press, 1944, p. 93.

[5] Mircea Eliade, *Shamanism: Archaic Techniques of Ecstasy*, Princeton, New Jersey, Princeton University Press, 1970, Foreword, p. xix.

[6] Cassirer, *op. cit.*, pp. 81 f.

[7] This was the conception of Ralph Cudworth, one of the Cambridge Platonists in the seventeenth century, as described by Lancelot Law Whyte. *The Unconscious Before Freud*, New York, Basic Books, Inc., 1960, p. 94.

[8] See particularly the Declaration on Religious Freedom, *The Documents of Vatican II*, ed. by Walter M. Abbott, S. J., New York, The America Press, 1966, pp. 675 ff., as well as various sections on the Holy Spirit.

[9] Paul Friedländer, *Plato: An Introduction*, New York, Harper & Row, 1964. There are other excellent books on Plato, among them the standard work by A. E. Taylor, *Plato: The Man and His Work*, London, Methuen and Co., 1929; Raphael Demos, *The Philosophy of Plato*, New York, Charles Scribner's Sons, 1939; John Wild, *Plato's Theory of Man*, New York, Octagon Books, 1964. Mary Renault has also written two novels which portray quite accurately the times of Socrates and Plato—*The Last of the Wine* and *The Mask of Apollo*, both of which are available in various paperback editions.

[10] One renowned student of Plato who has given careful consideration to these aspects is E. R. Dodds at Oxford. His study, *The Greeks and the Irrational*, Boston, Beacon Press, Inc., 1957, presents thoroughly documented evidence of the Greek appreciation of experience of all

kinds as, inevitably, the real source of knowledge and wisdom. Jane Harrison is another scholar who does not try to trim the Greek thinkers down to fit the ideas of nineteenth century rational materialism; in *Prolegomena to the Study of Greek Religion*, New York, Meridian Books, Inc., 1960, she offers a similar approach to Plato and other Greek philosophers.

Many Catholics are bothered by the gnostic implications in Plato. Matter is the source of evil in his thought, and this can result in unwise asceticism. This failing in Plato, however, does not negate the value of his basic world view, his basic idea of how we know and what can be known.

[11] This and the quotations that follow come from the *Phaedrus*, sections 244, 245, and 248. *The Dialogues of Plato*, tr. by B. Jowett, Oxford, At the Clarendon Press, 1964, Vol. 3, pp. 150 ff and 155.

[12] One interesting study of Indian sandpainting, *Tapestries in Sand: The Spirit of Indian Sandpainting* by David Villaseñor, Healdsburg, California, Naturegraph Company, 1966, shows how the same idea is used in Navajo religion. In his sandpainting the Navajo medicine man represents the perfect harmony which has been lost by the sick person, and the sick man is laid on the painting to absorb this harmony.

[13] Friedländer, *op. cit.*, p. 37.

[14] Published by Harcourt, Brace and World, 1964.

[15] Some Christians, however, have been embarrassed by the Platonic idea. The structure of Greek society and the low place of women both helped to force the actual love relationship into a homoerotic pattern. But this does not change the fact that the cognitive value of truly caring for other human beings (male *and* female) is central to both Greek philosophy and the teaching of Christianity. The importance of love as a divine gift that has results is shared by both.

[16] In my book *Tongue Speaking: An Experiment in Spiritual Experience*, Garden City, New York, Doubleday & Company, Inc., 1964, pp. 41 ff., I give evidence of the continued expression of this point of view in Eastern Orthodox practice, experience and understanding.

[17] See pp. 148 ff. in my book *Dreams: The Dark Speech of the Spirit*, Garden City, New York, Doubleday & Company, Inc., 1968, for a more detailed explanation of this understanding, together with the references in Augustine's works. I have also discussed here the similar understanding of Ambrose and that of Athanasius, particularly in his *Life of St. Antony*, (pp. 145 ff. and 130 ff.). In addition, Augustine's great statement of the meaning of these experiences and this understanding for men's lives is found in the final chapters of *The City of God*, Book 22.

FOOTNOTES TO CHAPTER IV

[1] The Ostrogoths, the Visigoths and Vandals had all been converted to Arianism, and as Hastings' *Encyclopedia of Religion and Ethics* points out, the orthodox Catholics even came to prefer Arian conquerers

to the pagan ones. Various writers of the time commented on the fact that Arian invaders had at least learned something of Christianity and did not destroy as wantonly as many conquerors before them had. The Arian king Theodoric, who reigned for 33 years over Italy, was praised for his moderation and for bringing peace and prosperity.

But when the Arian Lombards threatened to overrun Italy completely in the eighth century, it was the Franks, who had been converted from out and out paganism under Clovis, to whom the Pope turned for help. Under Pepin a new empire began to take shape, and by the time Charlemagne succeeded him, it was possible for orthodox, Catholic Christianity to be recognized as the established religion.

History has put so much stress on Constantine as the one man who was responsible for the ultimate acceptance of Christianity that it is sometimes forgotten that this religion of ours had to start almost from scratch again in the West. In addition, it is almost never mentioned that Thomas Aquinas—who probably did more than any other one individual to preserve Christianity for the modern world, and also to alter its basic nature—came from a family of distinguished, fighting Lombards on his father's side. One wonders how much the practical, worldly images of Arianism had been affected in this strong masculine line by orthodoxy.

[2] William Harris Stahl offers an English translation and a thorough discussion of Macrobius' work in his *Macrobius: Commentary on the Dream of Scipio*, New York, Columbia University Press, 1952.

[3] Although Augustine remained popular, it became increasingly difficult for the Middle Ages to grasp the reality that lay behind his thorough intellectual approach.

[4] See Frederick C. Copleston, *Medieval Philosophy*, New York, Harper & Row, 1961, Chapter VI.

[5] *On Prophecy in Sleep*, 464a; Aristotle, *On the Soul, Parva Naturalia. On Breath*, tr. by W. S. Hett, Cambridge, Harvard University Press, 1964, p. 383.

[6] It appears that Aristotle had also come close to the same kind of experience; only a few months before he died, he wrote in a letter to Antipater: "The more I am by myself, and alone, the fonder I have become of myths." His will also directed his executors to "set up in Stagira statues of life-size to Zeus and Athena the Saviours." Aristotle was by no means as one-sided as the modern world has come to belive.

[7] The Encyclical Letter of Pope Leo XIII "On the Restoration of Christian Philosophy According to the Mind of St. Thomas Aquinas, the Angelic Doctor," was followed in 1917 by the Canons issued by Pope Benedict XV, requiring religious students to follow the humanities with two years of philosophy and four of theology carried out accurately according to the arguments, doctrine, and principles of St. Thomas.

[8] See my discussion of this point in *Tongue Speaking, op. cit.*, pp. 186 ff.

[9] "Planet of the Apes," a film released in 1969, was a parody of ecclesiastical rigidity. The story of ape culture follows the human one;

in it the ape high priest stands for dogma over against experience. The medieval church was closer to this than we like to think.

[10] Quoted by Ernst Cassirer, *An Essay on Man, op. cit.*, p. 20.

[11] See the section on "Basic Greek," *Dreams, op. cit.*, pp. 80 ff. In contrast, modern English has the word "spiritual," which has lost most of its substance along with "angel," "demon," "appearance," "spirit," "vision." The idea that anything but the physical could touch matter is so outmoded that only archaic words are required to put this idea in historical perspective.

[12] Descartes also separated practical living and scientific thinking, holding that one need not influence the other. See his *Discourse on Method*, Part II, first rule.

[13] Helmuth Jacobsohn et al, *Timeless Documents of the Soul*, Evanston, Illinois, Northwestern University Press, 1968. The other authors are Marie-Louise von Franz and Sigmund Hurwitz.

[14] As explained by Harald Höffding, *A History of Modern Philosophy*, London, The Macmillan Company, 1935, Vol. I, p. 339.

[15] An excellent critical study of Kierkegaard has recently been done by David B. Burrell of the University of Notre Dame. His article, "Kierkegaard: Language of the Spirit," will appear as Chapter IV of *Exercises in Theological Understanding*, a volume now in process of publication.

[16] Published together as *Phenomenology and the Crisis of Philosophy*, New York, Harper & Row, 1965.

[17] See his discussion, *ibid.*, pp. 169 ff. Husserl overlooked the fact that Comte had made essentially a religious myth of positivism.

[18] C. G. Jung, "The Spirit of Psychology," *Papers from the Eranos Yearbooks*, Vol. 1, *Spirit and Nature*, New York, Pantheon Books, 1954, pp. 381 f.

[19] Paul Tillich, *Theology of Culture*, New York, Oxford University Press, 1959, p. 10. In essence Tillich sees no third possibility between an ontological and a cosmological approach to God, nor any real alternative to either naturalism or existentialism.

[20] See pp. 30 f.

[21] Karl Barth, *Church Dogmatics*, Edinburgh, T. and T. Clark, 1936-1969, Vol. III, Part 4, Section 55.1, pp. 369 ff. Other sections that show quite clearly Barth's attitude towards the Holy Spirit and any gifts or evidences of the Spirit are Vol. I, Part 1, 12.1, pp. 515 ff., especially pp. 526 ff.; Vol. I, Part 2, 13.1 and 16.1, pp. 10 f., 221 ff.; and 232 f.; Vol. II, Part 2, 33.1 and 34.3, pp. 105 f., 118 and 249 f.; Vol. III, Part 2, 46.1, pp. 332 ff.; Vol. III, Part 4, 54.3, pp. 320 ff.; Vol. IV, Part 1, 62 f., especially 64.1 and 2, pp. 648 f. and 666 ff.; Vol. IV, Part 2, 64.4 and 68.4, pp. 320 ff., 648 f.; 825 ff., and 836 ff.; Vol. IV, Part 3, 69.4, 72.4, and 73.1 f.; pp. 274 ff., 895 f. and 902 f.; Vol. IV, Part 4, 1, pp. 3 ff., especially pp. 27 ff.

[22] John A. T. Robinson discusses the radical, death-of-God theologians at some length in *Exploration into God*, Stanford, California, Stanford University Press, 1967, particularly in Chapter III, "Locating the

Reality of God." He takes a positive, and yet critical, approach to these men, but in the whole book he does not once suggest the reality of religious experience. For an entirely different approach to this thinking, see Bernard Martin's *If God Does Not Die*, Richmond, Virginia, John Knox Press, 1966; Martin is also the author of *The Healing Ministry in the Church*, Richmond, John Knox Press, 1960, in which he takes a point of view quite close to our own.

23 In *The Wilderness Revolt*, Garden City, New York, Doubleday & Company, Inc., 1972, Bishop Pike's widow, Diane K. Pike, and her brother, R. Scott Kennedy, have caught something of the reality which Pike tried to express before his death. They have taken the bulk of their book, however, to establish a "factual" base for the life and ministry of Jesus as a revolutionary leader. One wonders where the Bishop's own quest would have led, if he had come through the wilderness and his own revolt.

FOOTNOTES TO CHAPTER V

1 Robert Oppenheimer, "Analogy in Science," *The American Psychologist*, Vol. 11, 1956, p. 134.

2 For a simple and quite readable account of Einstein's thought, see Lincoln Barnett's *The Universe and Doctor Einstein*, New York, Bantam Books, Inc., 1968.

3 Werner Heisenberg, *Physics and Philosophy: The Revolution in Modern Science*, New York, Harper and Brothers, 1958, pp. 200 ff.

4 Friedrich Dessauer, "Galileo and Newton: The Turning Point in Western Thought," *Papers from the Eranos Yearbooks*, Vol. 1, *op cit.*, pp. 319 ff.

5 Arthur Stanley Eddington, *Science and the Unseen World* (Swarthmore Lectures, 1929), New York, The Macmillan Company, 1929, p. 33. As Eddington explained in detail, man can no longer look at matter as one static and knowable thing, and put the human spirit outside the pale of knowledge.

"We all share," he wrote, "the strange delusion that a lump of matter is something whose general nature is easily comprehensible whereas the nature of the human spirit is unfathomable. But consider how our supposed acquaintance with the lump of matter is attained. Some influence emanating from it plays on the extremity of a nerve, starting a series of physical and chemical changes which are propagated along the nerve to a brain-cell; there a mystery happens, and an image or sensation arises in the mind which cannot purport to resemble the stimulus which excites it. Everything known about the material world must in one way or another have been inferred from these stimuli transmitted along the nerves. It is an astonishing feat of deciphering that we should have been able to infer an orderly scheme of natural knowledge from such indirect communication. But clearly there is one kind of knowledge which cannot pass through such channels, namely knowledge of the intrinsic nature of that which lies at the far end of the line of communication. The inferred knowledge is a skeleton frame, the entities which build the frame being of undisclosed nature. For that reason they are described by symbols, as the symbol x in algebra stands for an unknown quantity.

"The mind as a central receiving station reads the dots and dashes of the incoming nerve signals. By frequent repetition of their call-signals the various transmitting stations of the outside world become familiar. We begin to feel quite a homely acquaintance with 2LO and 5XX. But a broadcast station is not like its call-signal; there is no commensurability in their nature. So too the chairs and tables around us which broadcast to us incessantly those signals which affect our sight and touch cannot in their nature be like unto the signals or to the sensations which the signals awake at the end of their journey. . . . It is just because we have a real and not merely a symbolic knowledge of our own nature that our nature seems so mysterious; we reject as inadequate that merely symbolic description which is good enough for dealing with chairs and tables and physical agencies that affect us only by remote communication." *Ibid.*, pp. 33 ff.

⁶ Quoted by Ernest Nagel and James R. Newman in *Gödel's Proof*, New York, New York University Press, 1958, p. 100, from an article by Kurt Gödel, "Russell's Mathematical Logic," in *The Philosophy of Bertrand Russell*, ed. by Paul A. Schilpp, 1944, p. 137.

⁷ See the quotation from *Science and the Unseen World*, note 5 above.

⁸ Erwin Schrödinger, "The Spirit of Science," *Papers from the Eranos Yearbooks*, Vol. 1, *op. cit.*, p. 335.

⁹ This is particularly clear in Eiseley's chapter, "Man of the Future," *The Immense Journey*, New York, Random House, Inc., 1957.

¹⁰ Besides the more personal *Hymn of the Universe*, the basic works by Teilhard de Chardin are *The Phenomenon of Man, The Appearance of Man, The Future of Man*, and *The Divine Milieu*, all published by Harper & Row between 1959 and 1966. There is also an excellent popular work by Joseph V. Kopp, *Teilhard de Chardin: A New Synthesis of Evolution*, Glen Rock, New Jersey, Paulist Press, 1964.

¹¹ The basic works of Jung are listed in the bibliography. In addition, much of this primary understanding of his thinking is found in the article we have noted, "The Spirit of Psychology," *Papers from the Eranos Yearbooks*, Vol. 1, *op. cit.*, pp. 371-444. In this paper which he gave to the Eranos Conference in 1946, Jung summarized his findings in a simple and straightforward manner, and much of the material that follows is found in this presentation.

¹² To Wilhelm Wundt, the founder of modern experimental psychology, the idea of anything being unconscious and psychic was unthinkable, as Jung discussed at some length. It is interesting to note that Husserl had been a student of Wundt and never broke with this essential concept. Through phenomenology, this idea was handed on down to existentialism, and it was held without a break until the time of Merleau-Ponty. Amedeo Giorgi, in his recent book *Psychology as a Human*

Science, New York, Harper & Row, 1970, has produced a lot of evidence from an existential point of view for criticizing Wundt's basic idea.

13 C. G. Jung, *Collected Works*, Vol. 8, *The Structure and Dynamics of the Psyche*, Princeton, New Jersey, Princeton University Press, 2nd ed., 1969, pp. 451 f., quoted by Raymond Hostie, S. J., in *Religion and the Psychology of Jung*, New York, Sheed and Ward, 1957, p. 9, from an earlier version of this paper.

14 Guglielmo Ferrero, *Les Lois psychologiques du symbolisme*, p. viii; used by Jung on the flyleaf introducing Part I of *Symbols of Transformation*, (*Collected Works*, Vol. 5, New York, Pantheon Books, 1956, p. 2), and also quoted in part (in French) in *Two Essays on Analytical Psychology, Collected Works*, Vol. 7, *op. cit.*, p. 116n.; quoted in a different translation by Hostie, *op. cit.*, pp. 12 f.

15 Oppenheimer, "Analogy in Science," *The American Psychologist, op. cit.*, p. 131.

16 Karl R. Popper discusses this point well in *The Logic of Scientific Discovery*, New York, Basic Books, Inc., 1959, p. 41. See also, Lawrence S. Kubie, "Blocks to Creativity," *International Science and Technology*, No. 42, June 1965, pp. 72 ff.

17 Jung, *Collected Works*, Vol. 8. *The Structure and Dynamics of the Psyche, op. cit.*, p. 191.

18 Jung, *Collected Works*, Vol. 16, *The Practice of Psychotherapy*, New York, Pantheon Books, 1954, pp. 164 ff.; *Memories, Dreams, Reflections*, recorded and edited by Aniela Jaffé, New York, Pantheon Books, 1963, pp. 353 f.

19 See Adolphe Tanquerey, *The Spiritual Life*, Westminster, Maryland, Newman Press, 1945.

20 Jung, "The Spirit of Psychology," *Papers from the Eranos Yearbooks*, Vol. 1, *op. cit.*, p. 428 and p. 431.

21 Jung, *Memories, Dreams, Reflections, op. cit.*, Chapter VI, particularly pp. 176-8 and 189.

22 In an unpublished manuscript on "Religion and Aggression" I have developed this point of view at some length.

23 Ephesians 6:12, *New English Bible*.

24 Jung, *Collected Works*, Vol. 8, *The Structure and Dynamics of the Psyche, op. cit.*, p. 208.

25 *Ibid.*, pp. 228 and 336.

26 *Papers from the Eranos Yearbooks*, Vol. 1, *op. cit.*, pp. 425 f.; the same passage appears in almost identical words in the revised form of this article, retitled, "On the Nature of the Psyche," in Vol. 8 of the *Collected Works, op. cit.*, pp. 215 f.

27 Jung, *Memories, Dreams, Reflections, op. cit.*, pp. 351 f.

28 *Ibid.*, p. 354.

29 I John 4:20.

30 Jung has also been accused of being a racist, and these accusations are still common, as one can see, for instance, in a recent article in *Psychology Today*. Those who make them, however, overlook the fact that Jung came to realize that he had made a mistake at the

beginning of World War II and admitted that he had been in the wrong. They also overlook the grief and personal suffering he went through. This whole question has been dealt with carefully by Aniela Jaffé in her interesting study, *From the Life and Work of C. G. Jung,* New York, Harper & Row, 1971.

FOOTNOTES TO CHAPTER VI

[1] Alfred Jules Ayer, *Language, Truth and Logic,* New York, Dover Publications, Inc., 2nd ed., 1946, p. 85.

[2] *Ibid.,* pp. 50 and 98.

[3] *Ibid.,* pp. 42 f.

[4] *Ibid.,* p. 45.

[5] *Ibid.,* p. 118.

[6] Wittgenstein, however, had his own definition of the word mystical, as anything which is not rational. Those who have written as friends of this extraordinary man tell how close he came to mental illness. Like Kierkegaard and Nietzsche, he found human relationship difficult, and his solution was to hold closely to the great insight he had received, and to develop it in as true a form as he was able. See Norman Malcolm and Georg Henrik von Wright, *Ludwig Wittgenstein: A Memoir,* London, Oxford University Press, 1962.

[7] For one thing, the number of young drug addicts who have such an experience and suddenly find themselves free of addiction without going through withdrawal symptoms.

[8] Max Knoll, "Transformations of Science in Our Age," *Papers from the Eranos Yearbooks,* Vol. 3, *Man and Time,* New York, Pantheon Books, 1957, pp. 264-307.

[9] Paul K. Feyerabend, "Materialism and the Mind-Body Problem," *Review of Metaphysics,* Vol. 17, 1963, pp. 49-66.

[10] *Dreams, op. cit.,* pp. 3, 79, 93, 146, 157, 261 ff., for instance.

[11] Stephen T. Emlen, "The Celestial Guidance System of a Migrating Bird," *Sky and Telescope,* Vol. 38, No. 1, July 1969, pp. 4-6. Dr. Emlen is associated with Cornell University in the Division of Biological Sciences.

[12] Quoted by Robert Oppenheimer in his address, "Analogy in Science," *The American Psychologist, op. cit.,* p. 134.

[13] Kenneth G. Johnson, *General Semantics: An Outline Survey,* Madison, Wisconsin, Extension Division, University of Wisconsin, 1960.

[14] *Ibid.,* pp. 16 and 17.

[15] Quoted by Kenneth G. Johnson, *Ibid.,* p. 23.

FOOTNOTES TO CHAPTER VII

[1] William James described much of the range of religious experience in his *Varieties of Religious Experience,* based on his Gifford Lectures in 1901 and 1902. Elmer O'Brien, a Jesuit scholar, has surveyed the

experiences of Christian mysticism with understanding and a light touch in *Varieties of Mystic Experience*, New York, Holt, Rinehart and Winston, 1964. The classic study of these phenomena is found in Baron Friedrich von Hügel's study of St. Catherine of Genoa, *The Mystical Element of Religion*, London, J. M. Dent & Sons Limited, 1927.

Jung also presented relevant materials all through the twenty volumes of his collected works, particularly in Vol. 11, *Psychology and Religion:West and East*, New York, Pantheon Books, 1958, and in his spiritual autobiography, *Memories, Dreams, Reflections, op. cit.* In my book *Tongue Speaking: An Experiment in Spiritual Experience, op. cit.*, modern examples from experiences in the Pentecostal movement are given in Chapters IV and V. I have also discussed the implications of religious experience for healing in my book *Healing and Christianity*, New York, Harper & Row, 1973, which also deals with some of the material we are discussing in these pages.

[2] John A. Sanford, "Analytical Psychology: Science or Religion? An Exploration of the Epistemology of Analytical Psychology," *The Well-Tended Tree*, ed. by Hilde Kirsch, New York, G. P. Putnam's Sons for the C. G. Jung Foundation for Analytical Psychology, 1971, pp. 90-105.

[3] These experiences are discussed in detail in my book, *Dreams: The Dark Speech of the Spirit, op. cit.*, pp. 183 ff.

[4] Carlos Castaneda gives a modern account of such experiences, describing his apprenticeship as a student in anthropology to the medicine man of a Yaqui Indian tribe in Southern New Mexico, in *The Teachings of Don Juan*, Berkeley, California, University of California Press, 1968, and *A Separate Reality*, New York, Simon and Schuster, 1971. The same kind of experiences in the life of an Oglala Sioux Indian are described by John G. Neihardt in *Black Elk Speaks*, Lincoln, Nebraska, University of Nebraska Press, 1961. The popularity of these books among young people shows a new openness to such experiences in our time.

Mircea Eliade has discussed the same kind of material in several of his studies, particularly *Shamanism, op. cit.*, and *Cosmos and History*, New York, Harper & Brothers, 1959. Jean Danielou also discusses the reality of the primitive encounter in Chapter I of *God and the Ways of Knowing*, Cleveland, World Publishing Co., 1965, and Jung has offered an excellent analysis of similar experience in "Archaic Man," *Collected Works*, Vol. 10, *Civilization in Transition*, New York, Pantheon Books, 1964, pp. 50 ff. In addition, Jerome Frank goes into the problem of taboo deaths in *Persuasion and Healing, op. cit.*, pp. 38 ff.

[5] The Greek words in the Lord's Prayer, *apo tou ponérou* (ἀπὸ τοῦ πονηροῦ) in Matthew 6:13, and in some ancient editions in Luke 11:4 are the same form used in other places in the New Testament to refer specifically to the devil or the Evil One. An analysis of the passages in which the word *ponéros* occurs throughout the New Testament shows clearly that it is used in the Lord's Prayer to mean the Evil One, not just evil generically.

The petitions "save us from the evil one," and "keep us safe (or deliver us) from the Evil One" are used in the recent translations of the New Testament in *The New English Bible, The Jerusalem Bible,* and the American Bible Society's *Good News for Modern Man,* and in the new paraphrased version of *The Living Bible.* But in the services of Christian churches, even in the new Protestant Episcopal liturgy, the translators evidently fear the use of these words, either because people might concretize the devil and believe he exists in physical form, or because sophisticated moderns who do not believe in such a reality might be offended. The Episcopal revisers have not been so reticent about other changes. I have discussed this matter at length in an article, "The Mythology of Evil," about to be published in *The Journal of Religion and Health.*

An excellent discussion of evil and its relation to the personal and collective shadow is found in Adolf Guggenbühl-Craig's *Power in the Helping Professions,* New York, Spring Publications, 1971, pp. 107 ff.

[6] This theory is developed in "Synchronicity: An Acausal Connecting Principle," in Jung's *Collected Works,* Vol. 8, *op. cit.,* pp. 419 ff. Probably the clearest, most readable and comprehensive account of Jung's thinking on this subject is given by Aniela Jaffé in her book *From the Life and Work of C. G. Jung, op.cit.* Many examples are also found in Jung's *Memories, Dreams, Reflections.* In his view, synchronicity and causal thinking do not replace each other; instead, much as quantum theory brings together two complementary ways of looking at heat and light, so this theory deals with an aspect of reality complementary to that of cause and effect, which is beyond our capacity to rationalize.

[7] In Bombay one is struck by the vast difference between the prosperous Parsees (the remnants of Persian religion) and the life of most Hindus in India.

[8] *Dreams, op. cit.,* pp. 148 ff.

[9] Philosophically this can be stated in the following manner: Man's ultimate knowledge is epistemological, not ontological. Man does not know noumenal reality in any complete way, but only so far as noumenal reality wishes to reveal itself. Note that the Holy Spirit is the only unlimited reality in the diagram, for this appears to be the nature of our experience.

[10] The Thomistic discussion of emotion shows the area through which spiritual influences are understood to be mediated.

[11] An unpublished manuscript on Christian epistemology by John A. Sanford.

[12] In the most ancient Chinese commentaries.

[13] I have discussed the matter of spiritual direction in a paper entitled, "Rediscovering the Priesthood Through the Unconscious," *Journal of Pastoral Counseling,* Vol. 7, No. 1, Spring-Summer 1972, pp. 26-36.

[14] I have discussed this problem in the manuscript on "Religion and Aggression" referred to above.

[15] C. G. Jung, *Collected Works,* Vol. 10, *op. cit.,* p. 224.

[16] It usually comes as a shock to the modern clergyman to realize

that he has been fed only theological ideas and given little if any direct experience. The following article was written by a minister shortly after a Conference on Spiritual Experience which I had conducted in his city; he was led to read Jung's *Memories, Dreams, Reflections,* and wrote these words which appeared in his church bulletin for February 27, 1972:

Dear Brethren,

I have been reading the delightful book of Dr. Carl G. Jung, *Memories, Dreams, Reflections.* It is written in first person and moves along in an interesting conversational style. Although Dr. Jung is noted for psychology, the book reads more like a study in spirituality. In his discussion about philosophers and some theologians he wrote: "I wondered. Evidently they know God only by hearsay." In one sentence he verbalized a feeling which I have had for the past few years but until now could never find the words to say it.

So much of contemporary writing and discussion is done within the hearsay framework, as if none of us had any firsthand knowledge of God. I have often been asked, what does the Church believe or what am I supposed to believe? It is interesting to note any appeal to authority is a hearsay appeal. Scripture has often been used as a hearsay appeal because with protestantism it became the basis for authority.

But the beauty of scripture is not its authority or its hearsay evidence but rather the opportunity to really get into the soul of the writer. By that very process one can know God. We benefit by others sharing with us their relationship to God because it gives us added tools by which we can "latch on" to our own feelings and perceptions of Him. Just as Jung's sharing gave me insight into some of my own quandaries, so too this sharing with you may open new insights into your own relationship with God.

Hence the ultimate authority is no one other than yourself, and the ultimate question is: Can I say, "I know God, and He knows me and not as a stranger."?

Fr. Weaver

[17] This section is similar to the discussion of the theology of healing found in Chapter XII of my book *Healing and Christianity.*

[18] The essential factuality of the gospel narrative has been supported with great critical acumen by Günther Bornkamm in his study *Jesus of Nazareth,* New York, Harper & Row, 1960, and by Norman Perrin in *Rediscovering the Teachings of Jesus,* New York, Harper & Row, 1967. These are among the finest studies of the gospels in recent years.

[19] Jung, *Collected Works,* Vol. 10, *op. cit.,* pp. 307 ff.

[20] *Tongue Speaking, op. cit.,* pp. 18 f.

[21] See our discussion above on Jung's understanding of encounters

with nonphysical reality, particularly the self, and the relation of the ego; pp. 114 ff. and 117 ff.

²² John A. Sanford, in the manuscript referred to above.

²³ In Chapters 4, 5, and 6 of my book, *Dreams, op. cit.*, most of these materials from the New Testament and the important fathers of the Church up through the fifth century are discussed in some detail.

²⁴ See *Memories, Dreams, Reflections, op. cit.*, pp. 100, 104 ff., and 190 ff. I have also discussed the implications of Jung's thought for Christian hope in an article to be published in the near future in *Lumen Vitae*, the journal of religious education published in Brussels.

²⁵ C. G. Jung, *Collected Works*, Vol. 10, *op. cit.*, p. 67.

²⁶ C. G. Jung, "Transformation Symbolism in the Mass," *Papers From the Eranos Yearbooks*, Vol. 2, *The Mysteries*, New York, Pantheon Books, 1955, p. 336.

²⁷ A full description of the history of healing in the life of the Church is found in my book, *Healing and Christianity, op. cit.*

Footnotes to Chapter VIII

¹ Thomas Carlyle, *Sartor Resartus*, Book III, Chapter III.

² Søren Kierkegaard, *The Sickness unto Death* (published with *Fear and Trembling*), Garden City, New York, Doubleday & Company, Inc., 1954, p. 198.

³ "The Place of Affect in Religious Education: Psychodynamics of Affectivity and Emotion," *Lumen Vitae*, Vol. 26, No. 1, 1971, pp. 68 ff. A thorough and up to date discussion of Transcendental Meditation (known to initiates as TM) is found in *The Wall Street Journal* for August 31, 1972, p. 1.

⁴ Keith W. Kerr, "Terminal Illness Counseling—The Death Experience," *The Marriage and Family Counselors Quarterly*, Vol. 7, No. 2, Winter 1972, pp. 11-38.

⁵ C. G. Jung, *Memories, Dreams, Reflections, op. cit.*, p. 169.

⁶ *Dreams, op. cit.*, particularly pp. 201 ff.

⁷ Romans 7:19 and 24, *New English Bible.*

⁸ Rudolf Steiner, *Knowledge of the Higher Worlds and Its Attainment*, New York, AnthropoSophic Press, (1947), p. 40.

⁹ I have developed this understanding a good deal farther in a paper on "The Centrality of Love," which is being prepared for later publication.

Footnotes to Chapter IX

¹ This understanding of the relation of a culture's philosophy to its thinking about education has been developed by Howard Ozmon in a very interesting and readable study, *Dialogue in the Philosophy of Education*, Columbus, Ohio, Charles E. Merrill Publishing Company, 1972.

2 The results of the Second Vatican Council have begun to appear in interesting ways. The generally conservative Knights of Columbus, for instance, recently ran an ad featuring the reality of the Holy Spirit and the pentecostal evidence of this. The ad, with its very clear and reverent statement, ran in the Sunday newspaper magazine *Parade* on April 23, 1972.

3 In my book *Healing and Christianity, op. cit.*, I have described this understanding of human beings at some length, showing how different it is from the way Jesus spoke of and acted towards men.

4 See "The Scientist as Shaman," by Malachi Martin, *Harper's Magazine*, March 1972, Vol. 244, No. 1462, pp. 54-61, for an insightful treatment of the problems that arise when Skinner, Jacques Monod and Konrad Lorenz try to play philosopher and theologian without seeing what they are doing.

5 Romans 15:18, *Revised Standard Version*.

6 Quoted from a French journal of theology and philosophy by E. R. Dodds in *Pagan and Christian in an Age of Anxiety*, Cambridge (Eng.), The University Press, 1965, p. 138.

7 See particularly "The Teaching of Religion," in the study edited by James Michael Lee and Patrick C. Rooney, *Toward a Future for Religious Education*, Dayton, Ohio, Pflaum Press, 1970, pp. 55 ff.

8 This and the books that follow will be found listed in our bibliography.

9 A reprint of Fritz Kunkel's *Creation Continues* is being prepared at the present time by Word, Inc., publisher in Waco, Texas.

10 Eve Lewis, in *Children and Their Religion*, New York, Sheed and Ward, Inc., 1962, has presented some suggestions drawn from Jung's thought in regard to teaching religion to children. P. W. Martin's *Experiment in Depth*, London, Routledge & Kegan Paul, 1955, makes other connections between the religious way and the understanding of Jung from a Quaker point of view. From the more Jungian side, James Hillman offers an approach to the religious way in *Insearch: Psychology and Religion*, New York, Charles Scribner's Sons, 1968.

11 In the conclusion of his important study of how we know, *The Revolt Against Dualism*, Arthur O. Lovejoy suggests that the only way such knowing can be described is through recourse to a myth; New York, W. W. Norton & Company, Inc., 1930, pp. 319 ff.

12 It is helpful to understand the various methods that are now being developed by educators to measure the success of the educational process. See Ronald T. Hyman, Ed., *Teaching: Vantage Points for Study*, Philadelphia, J. B. Lippincott Company, 1968, pp. 240 ff.

13 A selection of Jean Piaget's works and also the two principal books by Ronald Goldman are included in the bibliography.

14 Other books which are particularly suggestive and helpful in this area are *Research on Religious Development*, ed. by Merton P. Strommen for the Religious Education Association, New York, Hawthorn Books, 1971; Neil Postman and Charles Weingartner, *Teaching as a Subversive Activity*, New York, Dell Publishing Company, 1966; George B. Leonard, *Education and Ecstasy*, New York, Dell Publishing

Company, 1968; and Kenneth E. Eble, *A Perfect Education*, New York, Collier Books, 1968; further studies in this area are listed in the bibliography.

[15] This material is drawn from the study by James Michael Lee, *The Purpose of Catholic Schooling*, Dayton, Ohio, National Catholic Education Association Papers, 1968.

[16] In two papers as yet unpublished I have explored the use of the group process among pre-medical students, in a seminar formed for the purpose of discussing death and dying. I have also used the same process in seminars within the Program of Non-Violence at Notre Dame, set up to help these students deal more adequately with their own inner violence. The religious implications of these two, quite successful experiments are obvious.

BIBLIOGRAPHY

Edwin A. Abbott, *Flatland: A Romance of Many Dimensions.* New York, Barnes & Noble, Inc., 1963.

Franz Alexander, *Psychosomatic Medicine.* New York, W. W. Norton & Company, Inc., 1950.

Thomas J. J. Altizer and William Hamilton, *Radical Theology and the Death of God.* Indianapolis, Bobbs-Merrill Company, 1966.

The Ante-Nicene Fathers. Grand Rapids, Michigan, Wm. B. Eerdmans Publishing Company, various dates.

St. Thomas Aquinas, *The "Summa Theologica,"* tr. by The Fathers of the English Dominican Province. New York, Benziger Bros., various dates.

The Basic Works of Aristotle, ed. by Richard McKeon. New York, Random House, Inc., 1941.

Aristotle, *On the Soul, Parva Naturalia, and On Breath,* tr. by W. S. Hett. Cambridge, Harvard University Press, 1957.

W. F. Arndt and F. W. Gingrich, *Greek-English Lexicon of the New Testament and Other Early Christian Literature.* Chicago, University of Chicago Press, 1957.

Gustav Aulén, *Christus Victor: An Historical Study of the Three Main Types of the Idea of the Atonement.* New York, The Macmillan Company, 1951.

Alfred Jules Ayer, *Language, Truth and Logic.* New York, Dover Publications, Inc., 2nd ed., 1946.

John Baillie, *Our Knowledge of God.* New York, Charles Scribner's Sons, rev. ed., 1959.

————, *The Sense of the Presence of God.* New York, Charles Scribner's Sons, 1962.

Lincoln Barnett, *The Universe and Doctor Einstein.* New York, Bantam Books, Inc., 1968.

Karl Barth, *Church Dogmatics,* tr. and ed. by G. W. Bromiley and others. Edinburgh, T. and T. Clark, 1936-1969.

————, *Epistle to the Romans,* tr. by Edwin C. Hoskyns. London, Oxford University Press (H. Milford), 1965.

A. Cornelius Benjamin, *Science, Technology and Human Values.* Columbia, University of Missouri Press, 1965.

Nicolas Berdyaev, *Dream and Reality: An Essay in Autobiography.* London, Geoffrey Bless, 1950.

————, *The Meaning of the Creative Act.* New York, Collier Books, 1962.

Henri Bergson, *The Two Sources of Morality and Religion.* New York, Henry Holt and Company, 1935.

Black Elk, *The Sacred Pipe: Black Elk's Account of the Seven Rites of the Oglala Sioux*, ed. by Joseph E. Brown. Norman, University of Oklahoma Press, 1970.

Dietrich Bonhoeffer, *Act and Being*. New York, Harper & Brothers, 1962.

——, *Letters and Papers from Prison*. New York, The Macmillan Company, 1953.

Günther Bornkamm, *Jesus of Nazareth*. New York, Harper & Row, 1960.

C. D. Broad, *Lectures on Psychical Research*. London, Routledge & Kegan Paul, for the International Library of Philosophy and Scientific Method, 1962.

Carl Brumback, *Suddenly . . . from Heaven: A History of the Assemblies of God*. Springfield, Missouri, Gospel Publishing House, 1961.

Martin Buber, *The Prophetic Faith*. New York, The Macmillan Company, 1949.

Rudolf Bultmann, *Existence and Faith: Shorter Writings of Rudolf Bultmann*, tr. by Schubert M. Ogden. New York, Meridian Books, Inc., 1960.

——, *Jesus Christ and Mythology*. New York, Charles Scribner's Sons, 1958.

——, *Kerygma and Myth: A Theological Debate*, ed. by Hans-Werner Bartsch. London, S.P.C.K., 1957.

David B. Burrell, "Kierkegaard: Language of the Spirit," *Exercises in Theological Understanding*. Chapter IV (in process of publication).

Joseph Campbell, *The Hero with a Thousand Faces*, New York, Meridian Books, 1956.

Rudolf Carnap, *Introduction to Semantics and Formalization of Logic*. Cambridge, Harvard University Press, 1959.

Ernst Cassirer, *An Essay on Man: An Introduction to a Philosophy of Human Culture*. New Haven, Yale University Press, 1944.

Carlos Castaneda, *A Separate Reality: Further Conversations with Don Juan*. New York, Simon and Schuster, 1971.

——, *The Teachings of Don Juan: A Yaqui Way of Knowledge*. Berkeley, University of California Press, 1968.

Leon Christiani, *Evidences of Satan in the Modern World*. New York, The Macmillan Company, 1962.

Frederick C. Copleston, *Aquinas*. Baltimore, Penguin Books, Inc., 1961.

——, *Medieval Philosophy*. New York, Harper & Row, 1961.

Harvey Cox, *The Feast of Fools: A Theological Essay on Festivity and Fantasy*. Cambridge, Harvard University Press, 1969.

Iris V. Cully, *Imparting the Word: The Bible in Christian Education*. Philadelphia, The Westminster Press, 1962.

Jean Danielou, *God and the Ways of Knowing*. Cleveland, World Publishing Co., 1965.

Raphael Demos, *The Philosophy of Plato*. New York, Charles Scribner's Sons, 1939.

The Philosophical Works of Descartes, tr. by Elizabeth S. Haldane and G. R. T. Ross. Cambridge (Eng.), at the University Press, 1967.

The Documents of Vatican II, ed. by Walter M. Abbott, S. J. New York, The America Press, 1966.

E. R. Dodds, *The Greeks and the Irrational*. Boston, Beacon Press, 1957.

————, *Pagan and Christian in an Age of Anxiety*. Cambridge (Eng.), at the University Press, 1965.

Flanders Dunbar, *Emotions and Bodily Changes*. New York, Columbia University Press, 1935; 4th ed., 1954.

John S. Dunne, *A Search for God in Time and Memory*. New York, The Macmillan Company, 1967.

————, *The Way of All the Earth: Experiments in Truth and Religion*. New York, The Macmillan Company, 1972.

Kenneth E. Eble, *A Perfect Education*. New York, Collier Books, 1968.

Arthur (Stanley) Eddington, *The Nature of the Physical World*. Ann Arbor, University of Michigan Press, 1958.

————, *Science and the Unseen World* (Swarthmore Lectures, 1929). New York, The Macmillan Company, 1929.

Loren Eiseley, *The Immense Journey*. New York, Random House, Inc., 1957.

Mircea Eliade, *Cosmos and History: The Myth of the Eternal Return*. New York, Harper & Brothers, 1959.

————, *Myths, Dreams and Mysteries*. New York, Harper & Brothers, 1960.

————, *Shamanism: Archaic Techniques of Ecstasy*. Princeton, New Jersey, Princeton University Press, 1970.

T. S. Eliot, *Four Quartets*. New York, Harcourt, Brace and Company, 1943.

Stephen T. Emlen, "The Celestial Guidance System of a Migrating Bird." *Sky and Telescope*, Vol. 38, No. 1, July 1969, pp. 4-6.

The Encyclopedia of the Lutheran Church, ed. by Julius Bodensieck for the Lutheran World Federation. Minneapolis, Augsburg Publishing House, 1965.

Paul K. Feyerabend, "How to Be a Good Empiricist—A Plea for Tolerance in Matters Epistemological." *Philosophy of Science* (The Delaware Seminar), Vol. 2, 1962-1963, ed. by Bernard H. Baumrin, New York, John Wiley & Sons, 1963, pp. 3-39.

————, "Materialism and the Mind-Body Problem." *Review of Metaphysics*, Vol. 17, 1963, pp. 49-66.

————, "Problems of Microphysics." *Frontiers of Science and Philosophy* (The Pittsburgh Series), ed. by Robert G. Colodny, Pittsburgh, University of Pittsburgh Press, 1967, Chap. 6.

Edward B. Fiske, "Why Priests Marry." *The Christian Herald*, July 1969.

Jerome D. Frank, M.D., *Persuasion and Healing: A Comparative Study of Psychotherapy*. New York, Schocken Books, 1969.

Sigmund Freud, *Beyond the Pleasure Principle.* New York, Liveright Publishing Corporation, 1961.

————, *Civilization and Its Discontents.* New York, W. W. Norton & Company, Inc., 1962.

————, *The Future of an Illusion.* New York, Doubleday & Company, Inc., 1957.

————, *A General Introduction to Psychoanalysis.* New York, Washington Square Press, Inc., 1960.

————, *The Interpretation of Dreams.* New York, Basic Books, Inc., 1955.

————, *Moses and Monotheism.* New York, Vintage Books, 1955.

Paul Friedländer, *Plato: An Introduction,* tr. by Hans Meyerhoff. New York, Harper & Row for the Bollingen Foundation, 1964.

Evelyn Frost, *Christian Healing.* London, A. R. Mowbray & Co. Limited, 1940.

James J. Gill, M.D., "Religion and Psychiatry Today." *Psychiatric Annals,* Vol. 1, No. 2, October 1971, pp. 44 ff.

Amedeo Giorgi, *Psychology as a Human Science: A Phenomenologically Based Approach.* New York, Harper & Row, 1970.

Ronald Goldman, *Readiness for Religion.* New York, Seabury Press, Inc., 1968.

————, *Religious Thinking from Childhood to Adolescence.* New York, Humanities Press, 1964.

Ernest Gordon, *Through the Valley of the Kwai.* New York, Harper & Row, 1962.

Andrew M. Greeley, "Implications for the Sociology of Religion of Occult Behavior in the Youth Culture." *Mental Health Digest,* Vol. 3, No. 6, June, 1971, pp. 40-42.

————, *Priests in the United States: Reflections on a Survey.* Garden City, New York, Doubleday & Company, Inc., 1972.

Ronald and Beatrice Gross, Eds., *Radical School Reform.* New York, Simon and Schuster, 1971.

Adolf Guggenbühl-Craig, *Power in the Helping Professions.* New York, Spring Publications, 1971.

Dag Hammarskjöld, *Markings.* New York, Alfred A. Knopf, 1968.

M. Esther Harding, *Psychic Energy: Its Source and Its Transformation.* New York, Pantheon Books for the Bollingen Foundation, rev., 1963.

————, *The Way of All Women.* New York, G. P. Putnam's Sons for the C. G. Jung Foundation for Analytical Psychology, rev., 1970.

Jane Harrison, *Prolegomena to the Study of Greek Religion.* New York, Meridian Books, Inc., 1960.

James Hastings, Ed., *Encyclopaedia of Religion and Ethics.* New York, Charles Scribner's Sons, n.d.

Samuel I. Hayakawa, *Language in Thought and Action.* New York, Harcourt, Brace and World, 2nd ed., 1964.

G. W. F. Hegel, *The Phenomenology of Mind.* New York, Harper & Row, 1967.

Werner Heisenberg, *Physics and Philosophy: The Revolution in Modern Science.* New York, Harper and Brothers, 1958.

Hermann Hesse, *Demian.* New York, Harper & Row, 1965.

———, *Magister Ludi: The Glass Bead Game.* New York, Bantam Books, 1970.

———, *Narcissus and Goldmund.* New York, Farrar, Straus and Giroux, 1968.

Mary Hesse, *Models and Analogies in Science.* Notre Dame, Indiana, University of Notre Dame Press, 1966.

James Hillman, *Insearch: Psychology and Religion.* New York, Charles Scribner's Sons, 1968.

———, *Suicide and the Soul.* New York, Harper & Row, 1965.

Harald Höffding, *A History of Modern Philosophy,* tr. by B. E. Meyer. London, Macmillan and Co., Limited, 1935.

George C. Homans, *The Nature of Social Science.* New York, Harcourt, Brace & World, Inc., 1967.

Harold Horton, *The Gifts of the Spirit.* London, Assemblies of God Publishing House, 1954.

Raymond Hostie, S. J., *Religion and the Psychology of Jung.* New York, Sheed and Ward, 1957.

Johan Huizinga, *Homo Ludens: A Study of the Play Element in Culture.* Boston, Beacon Press, 1955.

Edmund Husserl, *Phenomenology and the Crisis of Philosophy.* New York, Harper & Row, 1965.

Ronald T. Hyman, *Ways of Teaching.* Philadelphia, J. B. Lippincott Company, 1970.

Ronald T. Hyman, Ed., *Teaching: Vantage Points for Study.* Philadelphia, J. B. Lippincott Company, 1968.

The I Ching, or Book of Changes (The Richard Wilhelm Translation), tr. by Cary F. Baynes. New York, Pantheon Books for the Bollingen Foundation, 1952.

The Interpreter's Bible, ed. by George A. Buttrick. New York, Abingdon-Cokesbury Press, 1952-1956.

Helmuth Jacobsohn, et. al., *Timeless Documents of the Soul.* Evanston, Illinois, Northwestern University Press, 1968.

Aniela Jaffé, *From the Life and Work of C. G. Jung.* New York, Harper & Row, 1971.

William James, *The Varieties of Religious Experience.* New York, Longmans, Green and Co., 1925.

Karl Jaspers and Rudolf Bultmann, *Myth and Christianity: An Inquiry into the Possibility of Religion without Myth.* New York, The Noonday Press, 1958.

Kenneth G. Johnson, *General Semantics: An Outline Survey.* Madison, Extension Division, University of Wisconsin, 1960.

Robert L. Johnson, *Counter Culture and the Vision of God.* Minneapolis, Augsburg Publishing House, 1971.

Journal of Pastoral Counseling (Iona College, New Rochelle, New

York). Issue on spiritual healing, Vol. VI, No. 2, Fall-Winter 1971-1972.

C. G. Jung, *Collected Works.* New York, Pantheon Books for the Bollingen Foundation,

Vol. 5, *Symbols of Transformation.* 1956.

Vol. 7, *Two Essays on Analytical Psychology.* 1953.

Vol. 8, *The Structure and Dynamics of the Psyche.* 1960.

Vol. 9, Part 1, *The Archetypes and the Collective Unconscious.* 1959.

Vol. 9, Part 2, *Aion: Researches into the Phenomenology of the Self.* 1959.

Vol. 10, *Civilization in Transition.* 1964.

Vol. 11, *Psychology and Religion: West and East.* 1958.

Vol. 12, *Psychology and Alchemy.* 1953.

Vol. 14, *Mysterium Coniunctionis: An Inquiry into the Separation and Synthesis of Psychic Opposites in Alchemy.* 1963.

Vol. 16, *The Practice of Psychotherapy.* 1954.

Vol. 17, *The Development of Personality.* 1954.

———, *Collected Works.* Princeton, New Jersey, Princeton University Press for the Bollingen Foundation, Vol. 6, *Psychological Types.* 1971.

———, *Memories, Dreams Reflections,* recorded and ed. by Aniela Jaffé. New York, Pantheon Books, 1963.

———, *Modern Man in Search of a Soul.* New York, Harcourt, Brace and Company, 1933.

Carl G. Jung, Ed., *Man and His Symbols.* Garden City, New York, Doubleday & Company, Inc., 1964.

Erhart Kaestner, *Mount Athos: The Call from Sleep.* London, Faber and Faber, 1961.

Immanuel Kant, *Critique of Pure Reason,* tr. by Norman Kemp Smith. London, Macmillan and Co., Limited, 1929.

Thomas R. Kelly, *A Testament of Devotion.* New York, Harper & Brothers, 1941.

Morton T. Kelsey, "Catholicism in Revolution: A Protestant Report from Notre Dame." *Religion in Life,* Vol. 40, No. 1, Spring 1971, pp. 9-15.

———, *Dreams: The Dark Speech of the Spirit,* Garden City, New York, Doubleday & Company, Inc., 1968.

———, "God, Education and the Unconscious." *Religious Education,* Vol. 65, No. 3, May-June 1970, pp. 227-234.

———, *Healing and Christianity.* New York, Harper & Row, 1973.

———, "The Healing Ministry Within the Church." *Journal of Religion and Health,* Vol. 9, No. 2, April 1970, pp. 105-122.

———, "Is the World View of Jesus Outmoded?" *The Christian Century,* Vol. 86, No. 4, January 22, 1969, pp. 112-115.

———, "Jung as Philosopher and Theologian." *The Well-Tended Tree: Essays into the Spirit of Our Time,* ed. by Hilde Kirsch. New York,

G. P. Putnam's Sons for the C. G. Jung Foundation for Analytical Psychology, 1971, pp. 184-196.

———, "The Place of Affect in Religious Education: Psychodynamics of Affectivity and Emotion." *Lumen Vitae* (Brussels), Vol. 26, No. 1, 1971, pp. 68-80.

———, "Rediscovering the Priesthood through the Unconscious." *Journal of Pastoral Counseling*, Vol. 7, No. 1, Spring-Summer, 1972, pp. 26-36.

———, "Speaking in Tongues in 1971: An Assessment of its Meaning and Value." *Review for Religious*, Vol. 30, No. 2, March 1971, pp. 245-255.

———, *Teenagers in Turmoil and Christ Speaks to the Family.* Privately printed, (1966).

———, *Tongue Speaking: An Experiment in Spiritual Experience.* Garden City, New York, Doubleday & Company, Inc., 1964.

Klaude Kendrick, *The Promise Fulfilled: A History of the Modern Pentecostal Movement.* Springfield, Missouri, Gospel Publishing House, 1961.

Keith W. Kerr, "Terminal Illness Counseling—The Death Experience." *The Marriage and Family Counselors Quarterly*, Vol. 7, No. 2, Winter 1972, pp. 11-38.

Søren Kierkegaard, *Fear and Trembling and The Sickness Unto Death.* Garden City, New York, Doubleday & Company, Inc., 1954.

James Kirsch, *Shakespeare's Royal Self.* New York, G. P. Putnam's Sons for the C. G. Jung Foundation for Analytical Psychology, 1966.

Rivkah Schärf Kluger, *Satan in the Old Testament.* Evanston, Illinois, Northwestern University Press, 1967.

George F. Kneller, *Existentialism and Education.* New York, John Wiley & Sons, Inc., 1967.

Ronald A. Knox, *Enthusiasm: A Chapter in the History of Religion.* Oxford, The Clarendon Press, 1950.

Joseph J. Kockelmans, Ed., *What Is Phenomenology: The Philosophy of Edmund Husserl and Its Interpretation.* Garden City, New York, Doubleday & Company, Inc., 1967.

Herbert R. Kohl, *The Open Classroom.* New York, Vintage Books, 1970.

———, *Thirty-Six Children.* New York, New American Library, 1968.

Joseph V. Kopp, *Teilhard de Chardin: A New Synthesis of Evolution.* Glen Rock, New Jersey, Paulist Press, 1964.

Alfred Korzybski, *Science and Sanity: An Introduction to Non-Aristotelian Systems and General Semantics.* Lakeville, Connecticut, The International Non-Aristotelian Library Publishing Company, 4th ed., 1958.

Jonathan Kozol, *Death at an Early Age: The Destruction of the Hearts and Minds of Negro Children in the Boston Public Schools.* Boston, Houghton Mifflin Co., 1967.

Lawrence S. Kubie, "Blocks to Creativity." *International Science and Technology*, No. 42, June 1965, pp. 74 ff.

Thomas S. Kuhn, *The Structure of Scientific Revolutions.* Chicago, University of Chicago Press, 1962.

Fritz Kunkel, M.D., *Creation Continues: A Psychological Interpretation of the First Gospel.* New York, Charles Scribner's Sons, 1952.

————, *In Search of Maturity: An Inquiry into Psychology, Religion, and Self-Education.* New York, Charles Scribner's Sons, 1943.

Pär Lagerkvist, *The Sybil.* New York, Vintage Books, 1963.

James Michael Lee, *The Purpose of Catholic Schooling.* Dayton, Ohio, National Catholic Education Association Papers, 1968.

————, *The Shape of Religious Instruction.* Dayton, Ohio, Pflaum Press, 1971.

James Michael Lee, Ed., *Catholic Education in the Western World.* Notre Dame, Indiana, University of Notre Dame Press, 1967.

James Michael Lee and L. J. Putz, Eds., *Seminary Education in a Time of Change.* Notre Dame, Indiana, Fides Publishers, Inc., 1965.

James Michael Lee and Patrick C. Rooney, Eds., *Toward a Future for Religious Education.* Dayton, Ohio, Pflaum Press, 1970.

George B. Leonard, *Education and Ecstasy.* New York, Dell Publishing Company, 1968.

C. S. Lewis, *Christian Reflections,* ed. by Walter Hooper. Grand Rapids, Michigan, Wm. B. Eerdmans Company, 1967.

————, *The Lion, the Witch, and the Wardrobe.* New York, The Macmillan Company, 1950.

————, *'Til We Have Faces: A Myth Retold.* New York, Harcourt, Brace & World, Inc., 1957.

Eve Lewis, *Children and Their Religion.* New York, Sheed and Ward, Inc., 1962.

Anne Morrow Lindbergh, *Gift from the Sea.* New York, Pantheon Books, 1955.

Martin Lings, *Shakespeare in the Light of Sacred Art.* New York, Humanities Press, Inc., 1966.

Sara Little, *The Role of the Bible in Contemporary Christian Education.* Richmond, Virginia, John Knox Press, 1961.

Bernard J. F. Lonergan, S. J., *Insight: A Study of Human Understanding.* London, Longmans, Green and Co., 1964.

Konrad Lorenz, *On Aggression.* New York, Harcourt, Brace & World, Inc., 1966.

Arthur O. Lovejoy, *The Revolt Against Dualism.* New York, W. W. Norton & Company, Inc., 1930.

William A. Luijpen, *Existential Phenomenology.* Pittsburgh, Duquesne University Press, 1960.

————, *What Can You Say About God?* *(Except "God").* New York, Paulist Press, 1971.

Harold C. Lyon, *Learning to Feel: Feeling to Learn.* Columbus, Ohio, Charles E. Merrill Publishing Co., 1971.

Violet MacDermot, *The Cult of the Seer in the Ancient Middle East: A Contribution to Current Research on Hallucinations Drawn from Coptic and Other Texts.* Berkeley, University of California Press, 1971.

George MacDonald, *Phantases and Lilith.* London, Victor Gollancz Ltd., 1962.

Douglas Clyde MacIntosh, *The Problem of Religious Knowledge.* New York, Harper and Brothers, 1940.

John Macquarrie, *Twentieth Century Religious Thought: The Frontiers* of *Philosophy and Theology, 1900-1960.* New York, Harper & Row, 1963.

Maria F. Mahoney, *The Meaning in Dreams and Dreaming: The Jungian Viewpoint.* New York, The Citadel Press, 1970.

Norman Malcolm and Georg Henrik von Wright, *Ludwig Wittgenstein: A Memoir.* London, Oxford University Press, 1962.

Arthur March and Ira M. Freeman, *New World of Physics.* New York, Random House, 1962.

Jacques Maritain, *Challenges and Renewals: Selected Readings.* Notre Dame, Indiana, University of Notre Dame Press, 1966.

Bernard Martin, *The Healing Ministry in the Church.* Richmond, Virginia, John Knox Press, 1960.

——, *If God Does Not Die.* Richmond, Virginia, John Knox Press, 1966.

Malachi Martin, "The Scientist as Shaman." *Harper's Magazine,* Vol. 244, No. 1462, March 1972, pp. 54-61.

P. W. Martin, *Experiment in Depth.* London, Routledge & Kegan Paul, 1955.

Abraham H. Maslow, *Toward a Psychology of Being.* Princeton, New Jersey, D. Van Nostrand Co., 1962.

Rollo May, *Love and Will.* New York, W. W. Norton & Company, Inc., 1969.

Ved Mehta, *Fly and the Fly-Bottle: Encounters with British Intellectuals.* Baltimore, Penguin Books, 1965.

——, *The New Theologian.* New York, Harper & Row, 1966.

C. A. Meier, *Ancient Incubation and Modern Psychotherapy.* Evanston, Illinois, Northwestern University Press, 1967.

Karl A. Menninger, *Man Against Himself.* New York, Harcourt, Brace and Company, 1938.

Maurice Merleau-Ponty, "Préface." A. Hesnard, *L'Oeuvre de Freud: et Son Importance pour le Monde Moderne.* Paris, Payot, 1960, pp. 5-10.

Edgar D. Mitchell, "An ESP Test from Apollo 14." *Mental Health Digest,* Vol. 4, No. 1, January 1972, pp. 34-39.

Louis Monden, S. J., *Signs and Wonders: A Study of the Miraculous Element in Religion.* New York, Desclee Co., 1966.

Jacques Monod, *Chance and Necessity.* New York, Alfred A. Knopf, 1971.

Gabriel Moran, F.S.C., *Catechesis of Revelation.* New York, Herder & Herder, 1966.

Antonio Moreno, *Jung, Gods and Modern Man.* Notre Dame, Indiana, University of Notre Dame Press, 1970.

Lewis Mumford, *The Myth of the Machine: The Pentagon of Power.* New York, Harcourt Brace Jovanovich, Inc., 1970.

Isabel Briggs Myers, *Introduction to Type.* Privately printed, (321 Dickinson Avenue, Swarthmore, Pennsylvania 19081), 1970.

——, *Manual: The Myers-Briggs Type Indicator.* Princeton, New Jersey, Educational Testing Service, 1963.

Ernest Nagel and James R. Newman, *Gödel's Proof*. New York, New York University Press, 1958.

John G. Neihardt, *Black Elk Speaks: Being the Life Story of a Holy Man of the Oglala Sioux*. Lincoln, Nebraska, Bison Books, 1961.

Anders Nygren, *Agape and Eros*. Philadelphia, The Westminster Press, 1953.

Elmer O'Brien, S. J., *Varieties of Mystic Experience*. New York, Holt, Rinehart and Winston, 1964.

John A. O'Brien, Ed., *Why Priests Leave*. New York, Hawthorn Books, Inc. 1969.

Edward D. O'Connor, *The Pentecostal Movement in the Catholic Church*. Notre Dame, Indiana, Ave Maria Press, 1971.

Schubert M. Ogden, *Christ Without Myth: A Study Based on the Theology of Rudolf Bultmann*, New York, Harper & Brothers, 1961.

Robert Oppenheimer, "Analogy in Science." *The American Psychologist*, Vol. 11, 1956, pp. 127-135.

Rudolf Otto, *The Idea of the Holy*. New York, Oxford University Press, 1958.

P. D. Ouspensky, *Tertium Organum*. New York, Alfred A. Knopf, Inc., 1922.

Howard Ozmon, *Dialogue in the Philosophy of Education*. Columbus, Ohio, Charles E. Merrill Publishing Company, 1972.

Papers from the Eranos Yearbooks, ed. by Joseph Campbell. New York, Pantheon Books for the Bollingen Foundation,

> Vol. 1, *Spirit and Nature*. 1954; (Friedrich Dessauer, "Galileo and Newton: The Turning Point in Western Thought," pp. 288-321; Erwin Schrödinger, "The Spirit of Science," pp. 322-341; C. G. Jung, "The Spirit of Psychology," pp. 371-444).

> Vol. 2, *The Mysteries*. 1955; (C. G. Jung, "Transformation Symbolism in the Mass," pp. 274-336).

> Vol. 3, *Man and Time*. 1957; (Max Knoll, "Transformations of Science in Our Age," pp. 264-307).

Patrologiae: Cursus Completus (Latinae et Graecae). Parisiis, Apud Garnier Fratres, Editores, et J.-P. Migne, Successores, various dates.

Norman Perrin, *Rediscovering the Teachings of Jesus*. New York, Harper & Row, 1967.

Dorothy Berkley Phillips, et. al, Ed., *The Choice Is Always Ours: An Anthology on the Religious Way*. New York, Harper & Brothers, rev., 1960.

Jean Piaget, *Biology and Knowledge*. Chicago, University of Chicago Press, 1971.

———, *Genetic Epistemology*. New York, Columbia University Press, 1970.

———, *Structuralism*. New York, Basic Books, Inc., 1970.

Josef Pieper, *Enthusiasm and Divine Madness*. New York, Harcourt, Brace and World, 1964.

Diane K. Pike and R. Scott Kennedy, *The Wilderness Revolt: A*

New View of the Life and Death of Jesus Based on Ideas and Notes of the Late Bishop James A. Pike. Garden City, New York, Doubleday & Company, Inc., 1972.

James A. Pike, with Diane Kennedy, *The Other Side: An Account of My Experiences with Psychic Phenomena.* Garden City, New York, Doubleday & Company, Inc., 1968.

The Dialogues of Plato, tr. by B. Jowett, (4 vols.). Oxford, At the Clarendon Press, rev., 1964.

Michael Polanyi, *Personal Knowledge: Towards a Post-Critical Philosophy.* Chicago, University of Chicago Press, 1958.

―――, *The Study of Man.* Chicago, University of Chicago Press, 1959.

Karl R. Popper, *The Logic of Scientific Discovery.* New York, Basic Books, Inc., 1959.

Neil Postman and Charles Weingartner, *Teaching as a Subversive Activity.* New York, Dell Publishing Company (Delacorte), 1966.

A. Poulain, S. J., *The Graces of Interior Prayer: A Treatise on Mystical Theology.* London, Routledge & Kegan Paul Ltd., 1957.

H. H. Price, *Belief: The Gifford Lectures Delivered at the University of Aberdeen in 1960.* New York, Humanities Press, Inc., 1970.

J. R. Pridie, *The Spiritual Gifts.* London, Robert Scott, 1921.

Michel Quoist, *Prayers.* New York, Sheed & Ward, 1963.

Karl Rahner, *The Dynamic Element in the Church.* New York, Herder and Herder, 1964.

―――, *On Heresy.* New York, Herder and Herder, 1964.

―――, *Visions and Prophecies.* New York, Herder and Herder, 1963.

Karl Rahner and J. Ratzinger, *Revelation and Tradition.* New York, Herder and Herder, 1966.

Kevin and Dorothy Ranaghan, *As the Spirit Leads Us.* New York, Paulist-Newman Press, 1971.

―――, *Catholic Pentecostals.* New York, Paulist Press, 1969.

Charles S. Reich, *The Greening of America.* New York, Random House, 1970.

Kurt F. Reinhardt, *The Existentialist Revolt.* New York, Frederick Ungar Publishing Co., 2nd ed., 1960.

Religious Education Association, Merton P. Strommen, Ed., *Research on Religious Development.* New York, Hawthorn Books, 1971.

Mary Renault, *The Last of the Wine.* New York, Pantheon Books, 1958.

―――, *The Mask of Apollo.* New York, Pantheon Books, 1966.

Jean-Francois Revel, *Without Marx or Jesus: The New American Revolution Has Begun,* tr. by Jack Bernard. Garden City, New York, Doubleday & Company, Inc., 1971.

Joseph B. Rhine, *New World of the Mind.* New York, William Sloane Associates, 1953.

Louisa E. Rhine, *ESP in Life and Lab.* New York, The Macmillan Company, 1967.

John A. T. Robinson, *Honest to God.* Philadelphia, The Westminster Press, 1963.

————, *Exploration into God.* Stanford, California, Stanford University Press, 1967.

Carl R. Rogers, *Carl Rogers on Encounter Groups.* New York, Harper & Row, 1970.

————, *Client-Centered Therapy.* Boston, Houghton Mifflin Co., 1951.

————, *Freedom to Learn.* Columbus, Ohio, Charles E. Merrill Publishing Company, 1969.

Sir David Ross, *Aristotle.* London, Methuen & Co. Ltd., 5th ed., 1949.

Theodore Roszak, *The Making of a Counter-Culture.* Garden City, New York, Doubleday & Company, Inc., 1969.

Agnes Sanford, *Behold Your God.* St. Paul, Minnesota, Macalester Park Publishing Company, 1958.

————, *The Healing Light.* St. Paul, Minnesota, Macalester Park Publishing Company, 1947.

————, *The Lost Shepherd.* Plainfield, New Jersey, Logos International, 1971.

————, *Oh, Watchman!* Philadelphia, J. B. Lippincott Company, 1951.

John A. Sanford, "Analytical Psychology: Science or Religion? An Exploration of the Epistemology of Analytical Psychology." *The Well-Tended Tree: Essays into the Spirit of Our Time,* ed. by Hilde Kirsch. New York, G. P. Putnam's Sons for the C. G. Jung Foundation for Analytical Psychology, 1971, pp. 90-105.

————, *Dreams: God's Forgotten Language.* Philadelphia, J. B. Lippincott Company, 1968.

————, *The Kingdom Within: A Study of the Inner Meaning of Jesus' Sayings.* Philadelphia, J. B. Lippincott Company, 1970.

Hans Schaer, *Religion and the Cure of Souls in Jung's Psychology.* London, Routledge & Kegan Paul Ltd., 1951.

George A. Schrader, Ed., *Existential Philosophers: Kierkegaard to Merleau-Ponty.* New York, McGraw-Hill Book Co., 1967.

A Select Library of the Nicene and Post-Nicene Fathers of the Christian Church (1st and 2nd Series). Grand Rapids, Michigan, Wm. B. Eerdmans Publishing Company, various dates.

John L. Sherrill, *They Speak with Other Tongues.* New York, McGraw-Hill Book Company, 1964.

B. F. Skinner, *Beyond Freedom and Dignity.* New York, Alfred A. Knopf, 1971.

————, *Science and Human Behavior.* New York, The Macmillan Company, 1953.

————, *Walden Two.* New York, The Macmillan Company. 1960.

John Skinner, *Prophecy and Religion.* New York, Cambridge University Press, 1922.

James D. Smart, *The Divided Mind of Modern Theology: Karl Barth and Rudolf Bultmann 1908-1933.* Philadelphia, The Westminster Press, 1967.

Norman Kemp Smith, *A Commentary to Kant's 'Critique of Pure Reason.'* New York, Humanities Press, Inc., 2nd ed., 1962.

Frederick Sontag, *The Future of Theology: A Philosophical Basis for Contemporary Protestant Thought.* Philadelphia, Westminster Press, 1969.

————, *How Philosophy Shapes Theology: Problems in the Philosophy of Religion.* New York, Harper & Row, 1972.

William Harris Stahl, *Macrobius: Commentary on the Dream of Scipio.* New York, Columbia University Press, 1952.

Rudolf Steiner, *Knowledge of the Higher Worlds and Its Attainment.* New York, AnthropoSophic Press, (1947).

Kilton Stewart, *Creative Psychology and Dream Education.* New York, Stewart Foundation for Creative Psychology,

Anthony Storr, *Human Aggression.* New York, Atheneum Publishers, 1968.

Merton P. Strommen, et. al, *A Study of Generations: Report of a Two-Year Study of 5000 Lutherans Between the Ages of 15 and 65, Their Beliefs, Values, Attitudes, Behavior.* Minneapolis, Augsburg Publishing House, 1972.

Gerald Sykes, *The Hidden Remnant.* New York, Harper and Brothers, 1962.

Adolphe Tanquerey, *The Spiritual Life.* Westminster, Maryland, Newman Press, 1945.

Charles T. Tart, Ed., *Altered States of Consciousness.* New York, John Wiley & Sons, Inc., 1969.

A. E. Taylor, *The Faith of a Moralist: Gifford Lectures Delivered in the University of St. Andrews, 1926-1928.* London, Macmillan and Co., Limited, 1930.

————, *Plato: The Man and His Work.* London, Methuen and Co., 1929.

Pierre Teilhard de Chardin, *The Appearance of Man.* New York, Harper & Row, 1966.

————, *The Divine Milieu.* New York, Harper & Brothers, 1960.

————, *The Future of Man.* New York, Harper & Row, 1964.

————, *Hymn of the Universe.* New York, Harper & Row, 1965.

————, *The Phenomenon of Man.* New York, Harper & Brothers, 1959.

F. R. Tennant, *Philosophical Theology.* Cambridge (Eng.), The Cambridge University Press, 1956.

Joseph Henry Thayer, *Greek-English Lexicon of the New Testament.* New York, American Book Company, 1956.

Paul Tillich, *The Courage to Be.* New Haven, Connecticut, Yale University Press, 1952.

————, *Systematic Theology* (3 vols.). Chicago, University of Chicago Press, 1951-1963.

————, *Theology of Culture.* New York, Oxford University Press, 1959.

J. R. R. Tolkein, *The Lord of the Rings* (3 vols.). Boston, Houghton Mifflin Company, 1954-1955.

Stephen Toulmin, *The Philosophy of Science: An Introduction.* New York, Harper & Brothers, 1960.

Montague Ullman and Stanley Krippner, *Dream Studies and Telepathy:*

An Experimental Approach. New York, Parapsychology Foundation, Inc., 1970.

Gerardus Van Der Leeuw, *Religion in Essence and Manifestation: A Study in Phenomenology* (2 vols.). Gloucester, Massachusetts, Peter Smith, rev., 1962.

Laurens van der Post, *The Heart of the Hunter.* New York, William Morrow & Company, Inc., 1961.

————, *The Lost World of the Kalahari.* New York, Apollo Editions, 1963.

David Vallaseñor, *Tapestries in Sand: The Spirit of Indian Sandpainting.* Healdsburg, California, Naturegraph Company, 1966.

Marie-Louise von Franz, *The Problem of the Puer Aeternus.* New York, Spring Publications, 1970.

Marie-Louise von Franz and James Hillman, *Lectures on Jung's Typology.* New York, Spring Publications, 1971.

G. E. von Grunebaum and Roger Caillois, Eds., *The Dream and Human Societies.* Berkeley, University of California Press, 1966.

Baron Friedrich von Hügel, *Essays and Addresses on the Philosophy of Religion* (1st and 2nd series). London, J. M. Dent & Sons Limited, 1926.

————, *The Mystical Element of Religion as Studied in Saint Catherine of Genoa and her Friends.* London, J. M. Dent & Sons Limited, 1927.

————, *The Reality of God and Religion & Agnosticism.* London, J. M. Dent & Sons Limited, 1931.

T. W. Wann, Ed., *Behaviorism and Phenomenology: Contrasting Bases for Modern Psychology.* Chicago, University of Chicago Press for William March Rice University, 1964.

Alan (W.) Watts, *Behold the Spirit: A Study in the Necessity of Mystical Religion.* New York, Pantheon Books, 1947.

————, *The Joyous Cosmology.* New York, Pantheon Books, 1962.

The Way of a Pilgrim and the Pilgrim Continues His Way, tr. by R. M. French. London, S.P.C.K., 1954.

Carlo Weber, *The Time of the Fugitive: From Ritual to Self-Discovery.* Garden City, New York, Doubleday & Company, Inc., 1971.

Hugh White, *Demonism Verified and Analyzed.* Ann Arbor, Michigan, University Microfilms, Inc., 1963.

Morton White, Ed., *The Age of Analysis: 20th Century Philosophers.* New York, New American Library, 1955.

Victor White, O.P., *God and the Unconscious.* Cleveland, The World Publishing Company, 1961.

Alfred North Whitehead, *Science and the Modern World.* New York, The Macmillan Company, 1926.

Lancelot Law Whyte, *The Unconscious Before Freud.* New York, Basic Books, Inc., 1960.

Frances G. Wickes, *The Inner World of Childhood.* New York, Appleton Century, rev., 1966.

John Wild, *Plato's Theory of Man.* New York, Octagon Books, 1964.

David Wilkerson, *The Cross and the Switchblade.* New York, Bernard Geis Associates, 1963.

Charles Williams, *Descent into Hell.* Grand Rapids, Michigan, Wm. B. Eerdmans Publishing Co., 1965.

————, *The Descent of the Dove: A Short History of the Holy Spirit in the Church.* New York, Hillary House, 2nd ed., 1950.

————, *Shadows of Ecstasy.* Grand Rapids, Michigan, Wm. B. Eerdmans Publishing Co., 1965.

————, *Witchcraft.* New York, Meridian Books, 1959.

J. Rodman Williams, *The Era of the Spirit.* Plainfield, New Jersey, Logos International, 1971.

Ludwig Wittgenstein, *Tractatus Logico-Philosophicus,* tr. by D. F. Pears and B. F. McGuiness. New York, Humanities Press, Inc., 1961.

Harold G. Wolff, *Stress and Disease* (ed. by Stewart Wolf and Helen Goodell). Springfield, Illinois, Charles C. Thomas, 2nd ed., 1968.

John Woolman, *The Journal and Other Writings.* New York, E. P. Dutton & Co., Inc., 1944.

D. Campbell Wyckoff, *The Gospel and Christian Education.* Philadelphia, The Westminster Press, 1959.

Yearbook of American Churches. New York, National Council of the Churches of Christ in the U.S.A., eds. for 1967, 1969, and 1971.

Marguerite Yourcenar, *The Memoirs of Hadrian.* New York, Farrar, Straus & Company, 1963.

Index

278

279

Troeltsch, Ernst—29, 37, 86

Ullman, Montague—132

Van Buren, Paul—32, 90
Van der Leeuw, George S. (Gerardus)—49
Van der Post, Laurens—132
Vatican II (Second Vatican Council)—33, 149, 215, 260n
Vesalius, Andreas—69
Villaseñor, David—249n
Von Franz, Marie-Louise—229, 231, 251n
Von Grunebaum, G. E.—248n
Von Hügel, Baron Friedrich—10, 27, 37, 49, 177, 188, 201, 256n
Von Wright, Georg Henrik—255n

Watts, Alan—17, 128
Weber, Carlo—247n
Weingartner, Charles—260n
White, Victor—66, 158
Whyte, Lancelot Law—49, 69, 73, 248n
Wickes, Frances—232
Wieman, Henry Nelson—29
Wild, John—248n
Wilkerson, David—18, 36
Williams, Charles—202
Williams, J. Rodman—88
Wittgenstein, Ludwig—91, 122 f., 127, 255n
Wolff, Harold—101 f.
Wundt, Wilhelm—103, 253n

Xenephon—56